A LEADER'S G

Excellence
IN EVERY
Classroom

Creating Support Systems *for* Teacher Success

JOHN R. WINK

Solution Tree | Press
a division of
Solution Tree

555 North Morton Street
Bloomington, IN 47404
800.733.6786 (toll free) / 812.336.7700
FAX: 812.336.7790

email: info@SolutionTree.com
SolutionTree.com

Visit **go.SolutionTree.com/leadership** to download the free reproducibles in this book.

Printed in the United States of America

20 19 18 17   4 5

Library of Congress Control Number: 2016952423

ISBN: 978-1-942496-92-2

Solution Tree
Jeffrey C. Jones, CEO
Edmund M. Ackerman, President

Solution Tree Press
President: Douglas M. Rife
Editorial Director: Tonya Maddox Cupp
Managing Production Editor: Caroline Weiss
Senior Production Editor: Christine Hood
Copy Chief: Sarah Payne-Mills
Senior Editor: Amy Rubenstein
Text and Cover Designer: Laura Cox
Compositor: Rian Anderson
Editorial Assistants: Jessi Finn and Kendra Slayton

To my lovely wife, Carolyn, for being my friend and my inspiration and for always pushing me and encouraging me to chase my dreams. I love you dearly.

To my fantastic children, Hunter, Hannah, Holly, and Haley, for always being my muses. I'm truly blessed to have the honor and privilege of being your father. Thank you for being the outstanding children that you are.

Acknowledgments

John Wink would like to thank countless teachers, staff, and administrators in Tatum Independent School District, Hallsville Independent School District, Gilmer Independent School District, and Longview Independent School District for making a tremendous impact on his life in the field of education. Additionally, he would like to thank every colleague that he has worked with throughout his career, as each person played a valuable role in shaping his thinking for this book. Finally, John would like to thank Bill Ferriter for encouraging him to grow in his craft as a writer, and the great people at Solution Tree Press for being powerful partners in bringing this book to life.

Solution Tree Press would like to thank the following reviewers:

Jenni Aberli
High School English Language Arts
    Specialist
Jefferson County Public Schools
Louisville, Kentucky

Bill Battistone
Assistant Principal
Regina Elementary School
Iowa City, Iowa

Tony Borash
Lead Coach/Science Vertical Team
    Facilitator
Albemarle County Public Schools
Charlottesville, Virginia

Kimberly Dessert
Principal
Kearns Primary School
Granby, Connecticut

Steve Gregoire
Principal
Fossil Ridge Intermediate School
St. George, Utah

Elaine Keeley
Director of Curriculum, Instruction,
    and Staff Development
Merced City School District
Merced, California

Robert Mackey
Superintendent
Unadilla Valley Central School District
New Berlin, New York

Denise McLaughlin
Specialist, Professional Development
Okaloosa County School District
Fort Walton Beach, Florida

Visit **go.SolutionTree.com/leadership** to download the free reproducibles in this book.

Table of Contents

Reproducible pages are in italics.

About the Author xi

Foreword xiii

Introduction 1
Why Are We Here, and What Is Our Mission? 2
What Role Do Teachers Play in Achieving That Mission? 3
How Do We Make *All* Teachers Successful? 4
Overview of the Book 6
Conclusion 8

1 Every Teacher Counts 9
A Teacher's Powerful Influence 10
Instructional Excellence From Day One 13
The Hierarchy of Instructional Excellence 15
The Three-Step Excellence Support System 21
Conclusion 24

2 Leading for Excellence: Learning Resources 27
Starting the First Day on the Job 28
Leveraging Learning Resources 30
Building an Excellence Support System: Learning Resources 32
Conclusion 42
Reflection Tool: Learning Resources *44*

**3 Leading for Excellence: Classroom Routines
and Procedures** 47
Struggling Alone With No Routines 48

Managing Classroom Routines and Procedures 50

Building an Excellence Support System: Classroom Routines and Procedures . . 55

Conclusion 64

Reflection Tool: Classroom Routines and Procedures 66

4 Leading for Excellence: Relationships for Learning 69

Getting to the Heart of Student Behavior 70

Building Relationships for Learning 71

Building an Excellence Support System: Relationships for Learning. 76

Conclusion 83

Reflection Tool: Relationships for Learning 86

5 Leading for Excellence: Student Engagement 89

Engaging Students From Bell to Bell 90

Promoting Student Engagement 93

Building an Excellence Support System: Student Engagement 103

Conclusion 112

Reflection Tool: Student Engagement 114

6 Leading for Excellence: Rigor and Mastery 117

Promoting Students From Average to Excellent 118

Implementing Rigor and Mastery 120

Building an Excellence Support System: Rigor and Mastery 128

Conclusion 142

Reflection Tool: Rigor and Mastery. 145

7 Leading for Excellence: Creative Strategies for Individual Students 147

Accepting It's All in the Details 148

Developing Creative Strategies for Individual Students 151

Building an Excellence Support System: Creative Strategies for

Individual Students 158

Conclusion 168

Reflection Tool: Creative Strategies for Individual Students. 170

8 Leading for Excellence: Teacher Leadership 173

Introducing Shirley Copeland, the Queen of Mathematics 174

Fostering Teacher Leadership. 175

Conclusion 183
Reflection Tool: Teacher Leadership *185*

References and Resources 187

Index 195

About the Author

John R. Wink serves as the superintendent of Blue Ridge Independent School District in Blue Ridge, Texas. From 2014 to 2016, John served as the assistant superintendent of curriculum, instruction, and assessment for the Tatum Independent School District in Tatum, Texas. During his time in Tatum, students and teachers grew tremendously in their performance on standardized testing and in college and career preparation. Prior to that, John served as principal at Gilmer Elementary School (2011–2014), where he led the school through improvement status to academic distinction. As principal of Hallsville Middle School (2002–2008), he led the school from acceptable to exemplary status in four years; and as principal of Hallsville High School (2008–2011), he led the school to become one of the top academic high schools in Texas.

John earned a bachelor of music in vocal performance from Stephen F. Austin State University, a master of education administration from Texas A&M University–Texarkana, and his superintendent's certificate from Texas A&M University–Commerce. Prior to his work as an administrator, John was the choir director at Longview High School in Longview, Texas, from 1996 to 2002, where numerous students earned membership into the Texas All-State Choir. His choirs earned numerous first-division and sweepstakes honors. John and his wife, Carolyn, have four children: Hunter, Hannah, Holly, and Haley.

To learn more about John Wink's work, visit LeadLearning With John Wink (www.leadlearner2012.blogspot.com), www.johnwink.com, or follow @johnwink90 on Twitter.

To book John Wink for professional development, contact pd@SolutionTree.com.

Foreword

by Brian K. Butler

John Wink has written a marvelous book to help education leaders provide the schoolwide, team, and individualized supports teachers need to become truly excellent in their profession. Having been an educator for more than twenty-five years and a school administrator for almost half that time, I have come to realize that supporting teachers' professional learning and development must be varied, intentional, inclusive, collaborative, and nonthreatening. It's not about the principal or administration evaluating and observing individual teachers to a better performance but instead, creating the conditions, culture, and structures for teachers to learn with and from one another.

In a chapter I coauthored in the book *It's About Time* (Mattos & Buffum, 2014) titled "Collaborating in the Core," I wrote, "If our mission is to ensure high levels of learning for all students and adults, adults must be provided with training to perform collectively at high levels" (p. 52). And it is not enough to just provide professional development for teachers; we must provide them with tools for success that continue to build their skills. In his seminal book, *Transforming School Culture*, Anthony Muhammad (2009) writes, "Educators who adopt egalitarian idealism as the center of their educational paradigm must cultivate professionalism as well. In order to achieve an end, a person must have conviction, but that conviction must be buttressed with skill" (p. 41).

If there was ever a book that targeted specific teacher practices and skills, giving precise examples and suggestions on how to improve them, this is it. Wink takes a page directly from the architects of the professional learning community (PLC) process, Richard DuFour, Rebecca DuFour, Robert Eaker, Thomas Many, and Mike Mattos (2016), and transforms the four critical questions into critical questions for teachers to ensure they learn at high levels.

1. What components of highly effective teaching do we expect from teachers to guarantee learning for all students?

2. How will we know when teachers are successful in ensuring learning for all students?

3. How will we respond when a teacher fails to meet the learning needs of all students?

4. How will we embrace teachers who are successful in meeting the learning needs of all students? (p. 52)

These questions provide focus and clarity around the right work to help leaders ensure teacher improvement throughout any school, and particularly schools that embrace the Professional Learning Community at Work™ model.

For school and district leaders who have embarked on PLC transformation, this book will help you along your journey as you embrace the process of learning together. The Professional Learning Community at Work model is "an ongoing process in which educators work collaboratively in recurring cycles of collective inquiry and action research to achieve better results for the students they serve" (DuFour, DuFour, Eaker, & Many, 2010, p. 11).

Collaborative teams play the most vital role in the PLC process. Teams are the fundamental building blocks of a PLC, indicating that the school structure has moved away from teachers working alone in isolated classrooms to working within a culture of collaboration and accountability in which all educators take collective responsibility for all students.

Wink's book is complete with experts and researchers, such as Richard DuFour, Charlotte Danielson, John Hattie, Robert Marzano, and others, who articulate the effects of teaching on student learning. However, the book also offers leaders specific strategies for immediate application of various means of support for teacher improvement, growth, and development.

Wink begins with three fundamental questions that leaders must address if their schools are to become places that guarantee all students can learn and succeed. He asks readers to keep these questions at the forefront of their thinking as they engage in and work through the different sections in the book.

1. Why are we here, and what is our mission?

2. What role do teachers play in achieving that mission?

3. How do we make *all* teachers successful?

Wink then provides a solid framework for teacher improvement by correlating psychologist Abraham Maslow's Hierarchy of Needs to what he calls the *Hierarchy of Instructional Excellence*, which identifies seven skill levels of excellent teachers. For each level, he provides a system of schoolwide, team, and individualized supports leaders can use to promote teacher growth and development. The ultimate goal of this tiered system of support is for *all* teachers to reach their fullest potential.

The following quote by Roland Barth (2001) sums up this comprehensive book for promoting teacher excellence perfectly:

Hand in Hand, We All Learn

Ultimately there are two kinds of schools: learning-enriched schools and learning-impoverished schools. I have yet to see a school where the learning curves . . . of the adults were not steeped upward and those of the students were not. Teachers and students go hand and hand as learners . . . or they don't go at all. (p. 23)

This book will most certainly steep the learning of the teachers in your building and districts upward. The sky's the limit!

Introduction

 There is no system in the world or any school in the country that is better than its teachers. Teachers are the lifeblood of the success of schools.

—Sir Ken Robinson

Student learning is the central purpose of every school in the United States, and, as an education leader, helping schools to ensure that all students are successful at learning—by graduating from their learning experience with a firm foundation for succeeding at college or a future career—has been my primary goal. While most education leaders undoubtedly share that goal, we've had to ask ourselves some tough questions in our search for the best, most effective, and most efficient method for guaranteeing high levels of learning for our students. Not surprisingly, we haven't all arrived at the same answers.

Some might argue that we need better schools to achieve the biggest gains in student learning, while others might propose that what we really need are better teachers. Logic tells us that either one of these improvements could help boost students' learning experiences. Neither on its own, however, is certain to help students achieve learning success. Instead, if we want to do our best to ensure that *all* students achieve the *highest* level of learning excellence, we must make sure that during every year of their education experience they receive excellent instruction delivered by excellent teachers working in excellent schools. That's a big order to fill—one that requires more complex solutions than we can arrive at through a "better schools or better teachers" debate. Do we need better schools and better teachers? Yes. But what we really need are better schools that are deeply committed to helping teachers become truly excellent at their profession.

We won't be able to address that deeply complex task if we continue to get bogged down with the shallow, single-issue questions that so often dominate the discussion about how to best guarantee learning excellence. These examples may sound familiar to you.

- How do we raise test scores?
- How do we recruit better teachers from colleges and universities?
- How do we obtain better walkthrough observation instruments?
- How do we implement better staff development for our teachers?

While these questions are important, they focus on superficial targets, and too often they lead to what I refer to as the silver bullets of bureaucratic habit—misguided decisions, short-term gains, and narrowly focused, well-worn leadership responses. To find solutions that can help leaders move an education system and its students to the highest level of performance, we should explore deeper, more fundamental questions capable of sparking true reflection and transformational change.

This book examines issues, ideas, and research that speak to what may be the three most fundamental questions all education leaders—administrators, teacher leaders, counselors, instructional coaches, principals, superintendents, central office managers, and others—must answer.

1. Why are we here, and what is our mission?
2. What role do teachers play in achieving that mission?
3. How do we make *all* teachers successful?

Leaders who understand the answers to these three questions can use that understanding to create better schools that will, in turn, help make teachers more successful at guaranteeing that all students learn. I've written this book to help leaders in that process. Every chapter offers insights and observations from my own career as an educator, education leader, and leadership coach, along with leading research findings and research-based solutions that leaders can draw on as they form a new and more powerful vision for guiding their schools and the students they serve to the highest levels of education excellence. As a starting point for that work, let's consider more closely those three fundamental questions.

Why Are We Here, and What Is Our Mission?

The mission of a school of excellence should be to guarantee that every student who walks through its doors graduates with a firm foundation for future success at college or in a career. In school, teachers are positioned to have the most direct effect on student learning. However, in their book *Simplifying Response to Intervention*, Austin Buffum, Mike Mattos, and Chris Weber (2012) describe the work of guaranteeing learning for all students as a *collective responsibility,* "a shared belief that the primary responsibility of each member of the organization is to ensure high levels of learning for every child" (p. 9). In such an environment, they add, "thinking is guided by the question, Why are we here?" (Buffum et al., 2012, p. 9).

While teachers have the most direct influence, we shouldn't expect even the best of them to go it alone. Richard DuFour says it best: "There is no way an individual teacher has all the time, all the skills, and all the knowledge necessary to meet the individual needs of every child" (as cited in Buffum et al., 2012, p. 31). The same is true for school leadership. No leader has all the time, knowledge, and experience necessary to meet the needs of every teacher. By working together, everyone in the system is better positioned to excel—and that includes students.

By fostering a culture of collective responsibility for excellence throughout the education system, we strengthen the likelihood that students can and will learn at high levels. As discussed in more detail in chapter 1, a meta-analysis conducted by education researcher and trainer Robert J. Marzano (2003) reveals that even average students can advance to the 96th percentile of their age group when they attend excellent schools with excellent teachers (see A Teacher's Powerful Influence, page 10).

In short, all teachers, leaders, and other members of an education system play a role in guaranteeing that all students succeed at learning. In order to do this, leaders and leadership teams must commit to helping teachers achieve and continuously hone their own professional excellence so that they, in turn, are better able to broaden their focus of responsibility beyond classroom walls. Remember, the question asks, "Why are *we* here?" Everyone in the education system must shoulder the collective responsibility of responding to that question with the answer, "To guarantee learning success for every student."

What Role Do Teachers Play in Achieving That Mission?

Marzano has published several books on the topic of the classroom teacher and the role teachers play in shaping the learning experience. His research about teaching concludes that a "teacher's pedagogical skill in the classroom is causally linked with how well and how much students learn" (Marzano, 2012, p. 3). He further explains that the impact of teaching on learning begins with a teacher's reflective practice, which impacts the teacher's pedagogical skills and then correlates with student achievement. The more frequently teachers reflect on, evaluate, and work to expand and develop their teaching skills, the more improvement they can expect to see in their practice and in the learning success of their students. In other words, excellence as an educator demands a continuous process of professional growth and development. As education researcher John Hattie (2009) notes:

> The art of teaching, and its major successes, relate to "what happens next"—the manner in which the teacher reacts to how the student interprets, accommodates, rejects, and/or reinvents the content and skills, how the student relates and applies the content to other tasks, and how the student reacts in light of success and failure apropos the content and methods that the teacher has taught. (p. 2)

As the demands of teaching evolve, however, the tools we use for evaluating its effectiveness must evolve as well. To address the behaviors and conditions necessary for teachers to succeed, Charlotte Danielson (1996) published *Enhancing Professional Practice: A Framework for Teaching* as a tool to evaluate first-year teachers. The framework became widely accepted throughout the United States, and Danielson's consultant group revised it in 2007, 2009, and again in 2013. The revised framework separates the activities of teaching into twenty-two components categorized into four domains—planning and preparing, classroom environment, instruction, and professional responsibilities—that successful teachers must demonstrate in meeting the Common Core State Standards (CCSS).

Danielson's (2013) explanation for revising the framework to align with the CCSS outlines the massive change in pedagogical skills teachers need to help students successfully master the Common Core and the challenges that change presents:

> Teaching for deep conceptual understanding, for argumentation, and for logical reasoning have not, after all, been high priorities in most school districts or preparation programs. In most classrooms, students don't take an active role in their own learning, nor do they (respectfully) challenge the thinking of their classmates. All of this will represent a major departure, and therefore a major challenge, for many teachers. (p. 3)

These challenges merely add to the responsibility that teachers carry for adapting to evolving education standards and needs. Standards will continue to change and will vary from state to state, but the teacher's ability to guarantee learning is the determining factor in whether students actually master those standards. Teacher effectiveness is the essence of school effectiveness, and when schools have excellent teachers—highly trained individuals committed to their own ongoing learning and professional development—they can expect their students to succeed at learning.

In a 2012 update to his synthesis of findings from more than eight hundred meta-analyses of research on school effectiveness, Hattie (2012) created a list of 150 factors that correlate with student achievement. Of that list, "46 of the top 50 factors, or 92%, can be influenced by schools and the teachers within those schools" (Marzano, 2013, p. 8).

As Hattie's analysis—along with other research findings cited throughout this book—indicates, teachers play a primary role in guaranteeing successful learning for students. Therefore, placing students in classrooms staffed by teachers who are well equipped to excel in their profession is our strongest tool for ensuring that students are prepared to excel as learners. This brings us to the last of the three fundamental questions.

3. How Do We Make *All* Teachers Successful?

There is little doubt that we need excellent teachers in order to produce excellent learners. We can't forget, however, that everyone in the organization shares a collective responsibility for producing these learners. That means we all must invest ourselves in training and equipping teachers for the ongoing, career-long process of becoming and continuing to be excellent educators. As education leaders, we must create the conditions and structures for faculty and staff to organically elicit the best from one another. This support network can be the catalyst that truly changes teacher performance.

The way we present and manage expectations also plays a role in that support network. There is so much for new, struggling, and even advanced teachers to master that without a concise set of expectations accompanied by a responsive system of supports, few teachers will achieve excellence. While we may identify multiple areas of weakness in a teacher's performance, we set up struggling teachers to fail when we demand that they improve all their weaknesses immediately and at the same time. When teachers try to repair everything at once, they typically repair very little, if anything at all. Instead, we can create excellent teachers by providing both the feedback *and* support that can help them peel through the layers of difficulties they are experiencing to uncover and address their greatest area of need first. When teachers have improved their most critical performance issue, we can systematically apply multiple supports from throughout the organization to help teachers address the remaining issues, in the order of their importance. That's how we create a pathway that every teacher can use to progress toward excellence.

We must establish a system in which we can identify where teachers are proficient and where they may need additional support. That system not only must react to performance deficits, it must anticipate them as well. With that system in place, we have a better chance of guaranteeing that the entire organization is engaged in providing teachers with the time and support they need to overcome obstacles and challenges.

The three fundamental questions and their answers are tightly linked.

1. Why are we here, and what is our mission? Our mission is to guarantee learning success for all students.

2. What role do teachers play in achieving that mission? While our education mission involves a collective responsibility that encompasses every member of the organization, our teachers play the most pivotal role in building learner success.

3. How do we make *all* teachers successful? When everyone in the organization is committed to helping teachers achieve ongoing instructional excellence and when education leaders back up that commitment with strong systems for professional training and support, we can eradicate ineffective instruction throughout the school.

As leaders, our most critical task is helping educators identify and address their ongoing professional needs and building an effective network of support to help them in that process. This book offers research-based strategies, examples, methods, and leadership practices for carrying out that work—and to help leaders navigate the complex path toward ensuring education excellence for all.

Overview of the Book

I wrote this book with the specific purpose of defining the characteristics of an excellent teacher and, most importantly, to describe what we, as leaders, can do to help all teachers attain that excellence. Helping every teacher achieve excellence demands a complex, organizationwide effort. No matter what leadership role you occupy, you hold a vital piece of the puzzle. As you read through the examples, approaches, and strategies in the following chapters, I hope they help spark your own unique ideas for leveraging your leadership role to guide and facilitate the process of creating excellence in every teacher.

Chapter 1 lays the groundwork for that process. The chapter begins with an in-depth review of the results of Robert Marzano's research into teacher effectiveness and its impact on learner success. Next, it examines the components of highly effective teaching, the methods leaders use for determining that all educators in their system are ensuring learning success for all, and how we can best identify and leverage the talent of our most successful teachers.

This chapter also introduces the graduated series of steps teachers must take in their professional growth as they advance toward instructional excellence. Modeled on Abraham Maslow's Hierarchy of Needs, the Hierarchy of Instructional Excellence graphically represents the levels of instructional skills teachers must possess and the order in which those skills develop (see figure I.1). Leaders can use the Hierarchy of Instructional Excellence model to help teachers peel back the layers of difficulty they may be experiencing in their work to identify and address necessary improvements in the order of greatest need. The chapter wraps up with a review of the kind of schoolwide, teacher team, and individualized support systems we can create to help teachers in their critical work of continual growth and development.

Each of the remaining chapters (2–8) focuses on an individual level of growth within the Hierarchy of Instructional Excellence, beginning with the first level, learning resources, and concluding with the uppermost level, teacher leadership. These chapters follow a similar structure, opening with a brief story about a teacher who is struggling in the chapter's featured level of growth—a hypothetical scenario that paints a picture of how that struggle plays out in the classroom. The chapters then describe how excellent teachers prepare for, deliver, and reflect on instruction related to that level of growth.

Finally, each chapter provides strategies and supports for helping teachers reach excellence in a specified level of growth in the hierarchy, with systems that progress through a three-step process called the Excellence Support System. This model mirrors response to intervention (RTI), a multitiered approach to student support in which teachers provide Tier 1 instruction for all students, Tier 2 instruction for

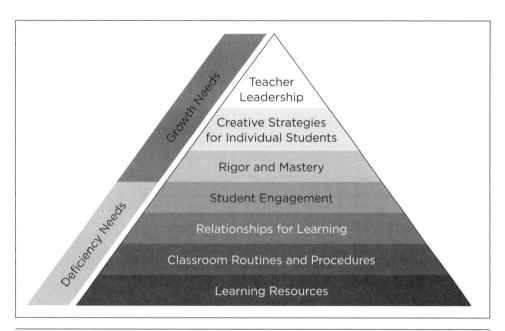

Figure I.1: Hierarchy of Instructional Excellence.

groups of students who need more support, and Tier 3 instruction for individual students who need more support than that provided in Tiers 1 and 2. Similarly, in the Excellence Support System, leaders plan and provide supports for teachers based on the skills they bring to the profession. Support is offered in three steps, depending on the teacher's individual needs.

1. **Schoolwide supports:** Schoolwide supports provide teachers with a systemwide structure of multiple aids and tools for professional learning and development that teachers can access at any time.

2. **Teacher team supports:** When schoolwide supports aren't adequate for addressing a teacher's needs, teacher team supports leverage the power of collaboration. These supports enable teachers to work together in teams to help one another overcome challenges and grow as professionals.

3. **Individualized supports:** This step is reserved for teachers who might need individual intervention. In this step, leaders supply their own guidance and support, targeted to help individual teachers address their unique needs.

The Excellence Support System helps leaders develop excellence throughout the education system—for learners, educators, and themselves. It can be relatively easy for leaders to identify an area or areas of performance in which a teacher needs to grow. Finding the most effective response to that need, however, can be a complex *challenge* task. To support the three steps presented in each chapter, I offer a reflection tool to help leaders review their current approaches to supporting teachers in these levels of growth and discover ways that they can most effectively incorporate the Excellence Support System.

Chapters 2–8 build on one another as they guide leaders up the Hierarchy of Instructional Excellence. However, chapter 8 serves as the ultimate challenge for leaders, as it addresses the highest level of instructional excellence—leadership. All teachers have valuable expertise and ideas to share. In this final chapter, we learn how we can best fulfill our critical role in helping teachers find their worth and grow in their roles as leaders. The structure of this chapter differs slightly from that of the other chapters for one important reason: systemwide supports aren't sufficient for helping teachers excel at the work of advancing to a leadership position. That job is ours alone. As leaders, we are the direct source of support that can best help individual teachers develop and use leadership skills. In this chapter, we examine teacher leadership and why developing leadership skills should be an imperative for *every* teacher. In support of that imperative, the chapter also explains why we must continuously develop leadership capacity in all teachers in every department, school, and district throughout our local system—and how we can accomplish that far-reaching goal. It also highlights how teachers can impact the profession far beyond their ZIP code by becoming global teacher leaders.

Conclusion

Student success is a non-negotiable goal in every school, but only effective schools actually work to supply the tools, systems, and supports necessary to reach that goal. We can best guarantee excellent learning for our students by ensuring that every teacher and leader in the system is committed to providing and supporting excellent instruction. The responsibility for driving school improvement no longer rests on the back of the lone leader telling everyone what to do.

Excellent schools mine for expertise in every person within the organization, and when they find expertise, they empower the expert, whoever it may be, to lead peers toward excellence. Shouldering the collective responsibility for educational excellence helps strengthen everyone in the system, including leaders, teachers, and students. We can use these ideas to encourage and enable our schools and districts to invest their hearts and souls into building a system that guarantees the excellence of every teacher. With that, student success will take care of itself.

CHAPTER 1

Every Teacher Counts

Education is the key to success in life, and teachers make a lasting impact in the lives of their students.

—Solomon Ortiz

Teaching is maybe the noblest of all professions. No other career plays a more powerful role in shaping who we are, how we think, and what we are capable of doing as human beings. Teachers help their students become better thinkers, problem solvers, creators, and dreamers. Teachers also have the ability to help students turn their dreams into a robust reality, to inspire and equip young learners for the hard work of overcoming the many barriers they will confront in life. In short, teachers are the real game changers. If we believe that every student counts, we, as leaders, must believe that every teacher counts as well.

Today, teachers have to overcome some formidable barriers of their own. They are charged with doing more than they've ever done in the history of education, facing more challenging obstacles and higher standards than ever before. Many teachers are successfully adapting to the ever-changing environment of standards-based education and high-stakes testing as they ensure that students achieve. Others, however, are falling through the cracks. With an excellent teacher in the classroom, we know that most students have the best hope of making huge strides in their learning. But when a teacher struggles in his or her craft, we can expect many students to suffer gaps in their learning. Those gaps eventually fall to next year's teacher to fill, diverting time and energy away from the curriculum. One year's failed advancements, in other words, erode the next year's achievements. In the introduction, I defined an excellent school as one whose mission is to guarantee that every student who walks through its doors will graduate with a firm foundation for future success at college or in a career. I also noted that excellent teachers are essential to achieving that mission. Excellent schools guarantee learning excellence in students by promoting and supporting excellence in the ongoing learning of their teachers.

If we agree that the best way to guarantee that all students learn is to guarantee excellent teachers in every classroom, we also must admit that not every school meets that standard. All schools try to hire the best teachers, but what sets the best schools apart is their commitment to providing a strong, effective support system to help teachers advance and excel in their work. An excellent school doesn't leave excellence to chance.

This chapter takes a closer look at the critical role teachers play in ensuring learning for all and the path they must take in their own learning to best fulfill that role. We begin by examining the challenges teachers face during their first five years on the job and the type of mindset we must encourage to promote their excellence from day one. Next, this chapter offers leaders a clear map for constructing the systems necessary to support teachers at *every* stage of professional development. Finally, it outlines the three-step Excellence Support System that offers a framework for providing systemwide, team, and individual supports to help educators succeed so they, in turn, can best help students, colleagues, and leaders throughout the system in achieving the school's mission of learning for all.

A Teacher's Powerful Influence

Marzano's (2003) book *Classroom Management That Works* graphically illustrates the powerful influence of teachers on student success. In his meta-analysis of teacher influence on student achievement, Marzano examines the effect an excellent teacher can have on the life of a student over the course of a specific period of time (Marzano uses the term *effective* rather than *excellent*, but for the purposes of this book and in this context, the terms are interchangeable). His work reveals dramatic differences in learning gains for students based on the quality of their instruction (Marzano, 2003).

As figure 1.1 illustrates, Marzano's analysis reveals that each year, the average student can expect to gain 6 percentile points in learning simply through the daily experiences of a year's maturation. A student under the direction of the most effective teacher, however, could expect to grow approximately 52 percentile points over the period of one year. Under a struggling or less effective teacher, Marzano (2003) finds that the average student could expect to gain only 14 percentile points in learning during that same time period. So, we could assume that an average teacher might fall within those two numbers (14 percentile points and 52 percentile points), which means we could expect him or her to help the average student gain approximately 33 percentile points in one year. While the effects of an average teacher were not included in this study, this illustrates that an average teacher's impact is still much lower than that of an excellent teacher. This study not only confirms that great teaching matters but also quantifies just how *much* it can matter for students.

Marzano's (2003) study also includes research on how both teacher effectiveness and school effectiveness influence student learning, as measured over a two-year period (see figure 1.2). This area of Marzano's analysis again underscores the primary

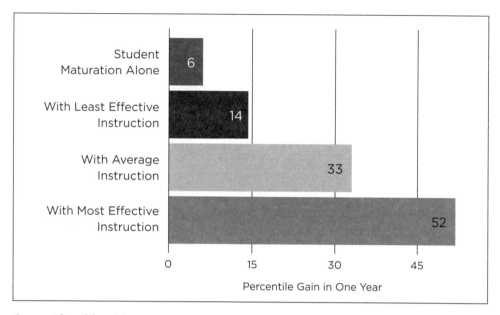

Source: Adapted from Marzano, 2003, p. 2.

Figure 1.1: Teacher effectiveness—impact on student achievement.

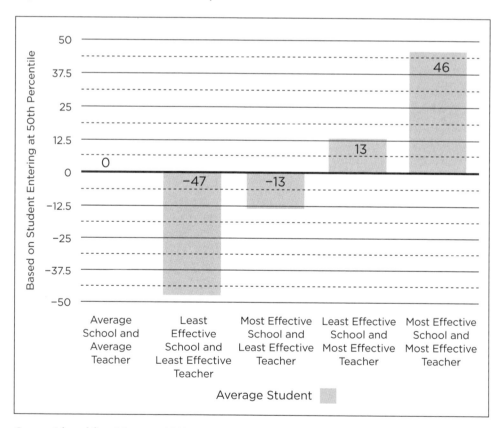

Source: Adapted from Marzano, 2003, p. 3.

Figure 1.2: Teacher impact on student achievement after two years.

role of teacher effectiveness in student learning gains. Marzano's analysis reveals that the average student (50th percentile) who attended an average school and was taught by average teachers for two years could expect to remain at the 50th percentile at the end of that period. In other words, no change would occur. If the same average student attended the least effective school and had the least effective teachers for two consecutive years, he or she dropped to the 3rd percentile (–47 percentile points). Even if that student attended the *most* effective school but had the least effective teachers for two years, he or she still dropped from the 50th percentile to the 37th percentile (–13 percentile points). Surprisingly, the study reveals that when the average student in the study attended the least effective school but had two consecutive years of highly effective teachers, the student grew from the 50th to the 67th percentile—a growth of 13 percentile points (Marzano, 2003). As these results indicate, an effective school can have a positive influence on student achievement, but it can't replace the impact of effective teachers.

The biggest impact on student achievement revealed by this study, however, occurs when a student attends a highly effective school and has two consecutive years of the most effective instruction. In this environment of high expectations and high-quality instruction, the average student grew from the 50th percentile to the 96th percentile—a gain in 46 percentile points! This research proves that when students attend excellent schools with excellent teachers, they can expect to experience tremendous growth in learning (Marzano, 2003). Therefore, the focus for school improvement rests squarely on the school creating the conditions that enable teachers to strive for excellence.

If students are in school for thirteen years, we know that they need thirteen years of excellent instruction in order to achieve their highest learning potential. But it doesn't take thirteen years to trigger dramatic changes in a student's learning success. We've seen that just two years of excellent teaching in an excellent school guarantees learning at high levels, so what can a similarly short period of time under the instruction of struggling teachers or in an ineffective school do to unravel even the most talented student's progress? What about the student who experiences a difficult year due to personal issues, family breakdown, or other at-home upheavals? Any of these challenges, whether at home or school, can create a learning gap that, ultimately, falls on the next teacher to bridge. If that teacher struggles, the student's learning gap continues to widen, which in turn could serve as the tipping point that causes the student to drop out of school altogether.

Highly effective schools don't leave student success to chance. To reduce the possibility that *any* student suffers gaps in learning due to struggling teachers, these schools create and maintain support systems that help all teachers succeed so that they can help guarantee learning for all students. Now, we will take a closer look at what that process involves—for leaders *and* educators.

Instructional Excellence From Day One

In the history of education, very few teachers entered the profession and instantly reached excellence in all aspects of teaching, and even fewer teachers have had excellent results every year in their careers. Almost all teachers struggle in meeting the needs of students at some point in their careers.

Typically, the most difficult years for teachers are the first five years in the profession. Over time, most teachers can expect their classroom experience to help dissipate these initial difficulties. The problem with waiting for experience to improve average or weak instructional performance, however, is that tomorrow's improvements won't help today's students. Many struggling teachers are well aware of which areas of their craft present them with the most difficulties and—in a safe and supportive environment—are open to support from leaders and fellow teachers. Our goal, as leaders, must be to find the best ways of providing that supportive environment and the systems it must offer in time to prevent teachers from failing, rather than intervening after the fact.

What Teachers Have to Say

In *Profile of Teachers in the U.S. 2011* by the National Center for Education Information, C. Emily Feistritzer (2011) cites statistics that point educators toward solutions for preventing failure instead of waiting for experience to remediate it. The study also notes a decided shift in the collective level of experience of U.S. teachers, as shown in figure 1.3 (page 14). In the study, Feistritzer (2011) writes that from 1986 to 2011, the number of teachers with one to five years of experience increased from 8 percent of the teaching force to 26 percent. In that same time period, the number of teachers with six to nine years of experience stayed the same, while the number of teachers with ten to fifteen years of experience dropped from 24 percent to 16 percent, and the percentage of teachers with more than fifteen years of experience dropped from 37 percent to 23 percent (Feistritzer, 2011). In other words, in 2011, the teaching staff of the U.S. school systems was the least experienced it had been since 1986.

Teachers new to the profession know they are inexperienced. The Feistritzer (2011) study of 2,500 teachers reveals that new teachers feel most competent in dealing with content but feel the least prepared to work with students. Time management, classroom management, and classroom discipline are areas in which new teachers feel most insecure (Feistritzer, 2011).

While these statistics are not surprising, we need to pay particular attention to what these teachers indicate about professional development supports and what this information tells us about how to structure meaningful learning opportunities for teachers in our own systems. As the study finds, teachers in all ranges of experience (from one to twenty-five years) rate teaching experience as very valuable in helping to develop their competence (89 percent). But the next variable that teachers rate as

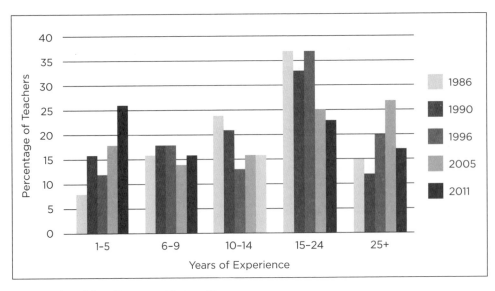

Source: Adapted from Feistritzer, 2011, p. 19.

Figure 1.3: Shift in years of experience for U.S. teachers 1986–2011.

very valuable in developing competence is learning from peers and colleagues (76 percent). The teachers in this study also rated professional development activities (45 percent), studying on one's own (32 percent), and the college of education faculty (22 percent) as valuable (Feistritzer, 2011).

This information tells us that teachers prefer to learn by doing, and they value learning with and from their peers as opposed to learning in isolation or from sit-and-get professional development activities. However, when many school leaders describe professional development for teachers, they don't include the activities that teachers value most. As a result, they fail to intentionally integrate these activities into their plan to help teachers grow.

When teachers in the Feistritzer (2011) study were asked how they would like to improve education, again the results moved away from traditional solutions. They listed greater participation from teachers at the school and district levels as the best way to improve the profession. They prefer these solutions over pay-for-performance initiatives, greater teacher autonomy, or getting rid of tenured teachers or unions. This research indicates that teachers believe strongly in the power of improving the teaching profession as a learning community and that teachers want to help one another improve the profession as a whole.

A New Mindset for Teacher Improvement

As we have seen, the culture and systems within a school are what create excellent teachers. When a school hires a new teacher, systemwide supports should offer more than mere advice on how to navigate day-to-day routines and procedures. Too often, however, that isn't the case. Many districts and schools help teachers get started by providing orientation over one to five preservice days, consisting of multiple presentations. This shotgun approach to orientation can be overwhelming for new teachers. Many systems also assign mentors to new teachers. If the mentorship does little more than show new teachers the ropes for surviving the first year, however, the mentoring process is unlikely to truly provide the guidance necessary to guarantee success for the new teacher and his or her students. To back up our belief in that guarantee, we must develop and promote a new mindset for teacher improvement.

The work of improving the effectiveness of every teacher, right from the start of his or her career, begins with the school leader, and transforming the role of the principal is the first step. Instead of expecting to hire the best teachers and then fire them if they fail to perform, principals should hire the best applicants and create the systemic conditions that guarantee every teacher's success. To accomplish that goal, leaders have to move beyond the faulty assumption that teaming with colleagues automatically translates into academic success. Ensuring that teachers have time to collaborate within the school day is a best practice, but it doesn't necessarily guarantee that every teacher learns from that collaboration.

Instead, leaders should create a system in which all educators have responsibility for guaranteeing every teacher's success. That's how everyone in the system develops and demonstrates a mindset of collective responsibility for student learning. By helping new teachers overcome their struggles, we can help eliminate the gaps in learning that students can experience under the instruction of a struggling teacher. And the development of professional skills must extend beyond a teacher's first years on the job. We want to ensure that teachers continue to grow and develop their skills throughout their careers. The systems we create to support that growth, therefore, must address every stage of a teacher's professional development.

The Hierarchy of Instructional Excellence

Because teaching is a relational business, the characteristics of an excellent teacher mirror human behavior and personal motivation. In 1943, Abraham Maslow, a prominent psychological expert, published a theory he had developed regarding the motivations of human behavior. Maslow separated his findings into seven categories that rank people's needs from lowest to highest in what he called the Hierarchy of Needs (see figure 1.4, page 16). Maslow referred to the first four levels of his Hierarchy of Needs as *deficiency needs*, because if these needs are not fulfilled, a person is left without an essential foundation from which he or she can move on to meet higher needs, which Maslow labeled *growth needs*. Once the person fulfills a lower-level need, a person's desire to satisfy that specific need diminishes; therefore, he or she may pursue fulfilling upper-level needs.

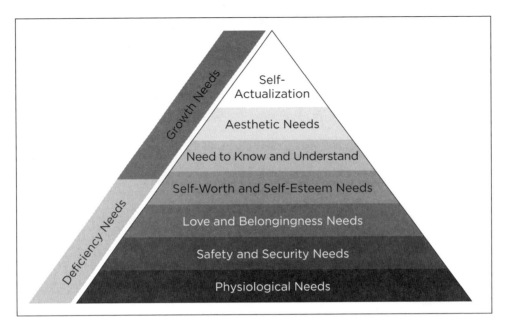

Source: Adapted from Martin & Loomis, 2007, pp. 72–75; Maslow, 1954.

Figure 1.4: Hierarchy of Needs.

As leaders, we can apply this same structure of growth in development and learning to classroom instruction. Excellent teachers know that most students cannot learn if their deficiency needs are not met. Similarly, with Maslow's hierarchy in mind, we must be certain that teachers also work in an environment that ensures their fundamental —or deficiency—needs are met so they are able to develop in higher areas of professional growth.

To help leaders with that process, I have developed a similar model, called the Hierarchy of Instructional Excellence, as outlined in the introduction to this book. See figure 1.5.

In this model, I present those areas of professional growth as levels of progress, each of which rests on the one beneath it. Teachers must develop their professional growth skills in each level before they can move on to develop those skills in the next higher level. In chapters 2–8, we examine specific strategies leaders can leverage to help ensure that all teachers can advance through these levels to become excellent instructors.

The levels in the Hierarchy of Instructional Excellence represent those skills teachers need to master to become truly excellent instructors. Understanding how these levels relate to the levels in Maslow's Hierarchy of Needs can help leaders understand the critical role we play in the professional development of our teachers.

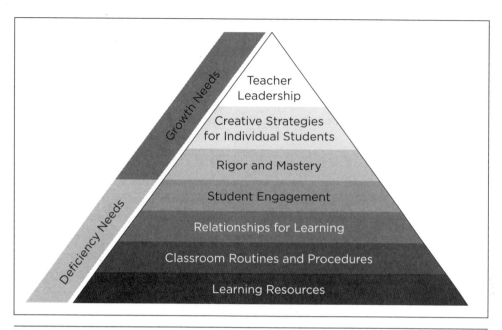

Figure 1.5: Hierarchy of Instructional Excellence.

Level 1: Learning Resources

The first level in Maslow's hierarchy represents physiological needs, such as food, shelter, and water. Until our physiological needs are met, we can't actively work to fulfill any other need. Similarly, in the Hierarchy of Instructional Excellence, access to appropriate learning resources is the most basic need both learners and educators must have met before they can advance in learning their profession. If a teacher does not have the resources necessary to teach or, even worse, lacks the skill for using those resources, that teacher can't learn and grow in his or her craft. Further, if students never develop the skillful use of learning resources, they can't leverage any subsequent learning experience to advance toward their own success. Meeting our teachers' need for access to learning resources, therefore, is our most fundamental responsibility in guaranteeing excellence for both educators and students.

Level 2: Classroom Routines and Procedures

The second level of the Hierarchy of Needs is the need for safety and security. When people feel safe and secure, they don't fear that physical, mental, or emotional harm will come to them. Students who feel their security is threatened are likely to find it difficult to focus on learning. Similarly, teachers must feel safe and secure in school, teaching in an environment free from fear and anxiety, where they can align their classroom management procedures to comprehensive discipline management systems.

The second level of progress in the Hierarchy of Instructional Excellence correlates safety and security needs with classroom routines and procedures. Creating a safe and secure learning environment requires structure, consistency, routines, and procedures that facilitate learning, especially for those students who lack a safe and secure environment at home. Teachers also benefit from their own systems, routines, and procedures that can help them manage their own learning processes as well as those of their students. Leaders must be prepared to offer a consistent discipline management plan, instructional models, team-level supports that align behavioral expectations and responses, and other systems necessary to help teachers fill this need. Only then will teachers be able to structure learning environments that create the conditions for safe and meaningful learning experiences for students.

Level 3: Relationships for Learning

The third level in Maslow's hierarchy addresses our need for a sense of love and belongingness. The desire to be accepted by others is the key motivation driving this need. In the Hierarchy of Instructional Excellence, the third level of progress, relationships for learning, addresses an educator's skill in fulfilling this human need. Meaningful relationships are essential to both our personal and professional development. After all, the failure to belong seems to exacerbate the failure to learn. As such, fulfilling needs at this level is critical for teachers as well as students. In order for teachers to take reasonable risks, they must feel that they belong to and are accepted by the organization. And if we want students to learn, they must feel accepted by the teacher as well as their classmates, and they should feel that their teachers care about them.

In the classroom, fostering strong relationships with and among their students is a critical responsibility for teachers. Achieving excellence in this area demands more than merely basking in the warm fuzzies of a positive teacher-student relationship. Instead, educators also must be skilled at leveraging the relationship in a manner that inspires learners toward a college- and career-ready future. This leverage is most effective when the teacher facilitates strong relationships between students and the class as a whole. Teachers are best able to accomplish this task when they work in an environment that promotes strong relationships among teachers, leaders, and colleagues throughout the system. The responsibility for creating that environment rests on the system's leaders.

Level 4: Student Engagement

The fourth level of Maslow's hierarchy is devoted to the need for self-worth and self-esteem. Once people feel safe and secure and possess a sense of acceptance and belonging, they can begin to develop positive inner feelings about themselves. Deficiencies in self-worth and self-esteem can interfere with the progress of students and teachers alike. Teachers who feel insecure about their abilities might find it difficult to meet students' needs; students who lack self-esteem might choose to avoid learning and look for other ways to establish a sense of pride in their performance.

In the Hierarchy of Instructional Excellence, this level—the last of the four fundamental or deficiency levels of the hierarchy—addresses skills for fostering student engagement. At any age, when we work in a learning environment that excites our interest and challenges our intellect, and in which we are actively involved in driving the progress of the work at hand, we have opportunities to explore our capacity for ideas and innovation and to participate in the learning process.

That kind of engagement moves us out of the role of passive observer, gives us more autonomy and ownership over our work, and, as a result, helps us build improved self-esteem and self-worth. In an article reviewing techniques for improving student engagement, authors and educators Leah Taylor and Jim Parsons (2011) cite previous research that finds that students who were given an opportunity to work on a technology-rich project that dramatically improved their engagement "developed a genuine passion for learning and a solid set of learning and research skills" (p. 16): "[The] findings all indicated improved pupil self-esteem and self-confidence" (Doppelt & Barak, 2002, p. 27, as cited in Taylor & Parsons, 2011). In describing another group of students involved in a technology-based education project, Taylor and Parsons (2011) also note that "students were engaged, staying after school and during lunch hours to work on projects together" (p. 16).

That kind of bell-to-bell focus on learning is a bonus for students and teachers alike. When students are more actively involved in their work, they are less actively involved in acting out with distracting or disruptive behavior. That enables teachers to devote more of their time and attention to student learning and less time to crowd control and enforcement, which results in more successes for everyone. For all these reasons, as leaders, it's important that we fully understand the critical nature of the skills our educators must develop at this level of their professional growth and target specific supports toward their development.

Level 5: Rigor and Mastery

In Maslow's Hierarchy of Needs, the fifth level is the need to know and understand, which represents the first of the three higher levels—growth needs. We spend our lives in a perpetual state of growth, so learning and development within these levels never stops. The same is true for the areas of professional growth represented in the top three levels of the Hierarchy of Instructional Excellence. The fifth level, and the first of the growth levels in that hierarchy, is that of rigor and mastery. It represents the educator's professional growth in the skills necessary to develop students' abilities to engage in rigorous learning and master its content. There's no end point for this level of professional growth.

At this level, teachers are actively engaged in the process of learning better to design more effective learning for students. While students must be engaged in the learning process to feel motivated to tackle learning challenges and master their content, instructional skills in this level go beyond those required to develop student engagement. Teacher teams are among the strongest tools for helping teachers develop these skills. By supporting teachers as they determine what they expect students to learn and how they will know if those students are learning, we can help them use that understanding to develop powerful instruction and rigorous formative assessments. Further, we must provide the productive evaluation, feedback, and guidance that teachers need in order to build their skills in this critical area of professional development.

Level 6: Creative Strategies for Individual Students

Maslow's sixth level encompasses our aesthetic needs, which are needs associated with developing our appreciation for and expression of creativity. People who are focused on growth in their aesthetic needs apply what they have learned in creative ways. In the Hierarchy of Instructional Excellence, this need for developing the appreciation and command of aesthetics correlates to an educator's need to devise creative strategies for engaging *all* students in the process of learning.

In an excellent classroom, instruction requires and promotes creativity and innovation by encouraging individual students to express themselves in meaningful ways through their artistic abilities and creative cognition. At this level in their professional development, teachers draw upon their own creative abilities. They experiment with the nuances of their professional knowledge in order to find new and innovative ways to reach individual students and boost their learning through more personalized experiences. At this level, teachers plan and deliver interventions for struggling students while personalizing meaningful enrichment opportunities for students once they master the content.

This level of growth is where the magic happens, as the term *learning for all* takes on a whole new meaning. To support teachers in this level of professional growth, we must remember that—standards aside—monolithic teaching to the whole will not guarantee learning for all. Our responsibility is to support teachers as they work collectively and individually to build their skills at finding creative strategies for engaging with individual students and helping them achieve their learning potential.

Level 7: Teacher Leadership

In Maslow's hierarchy, self-actualization is the highest order of human need and the pinnacle of human growth. Self-actualized people discover and employ all their mental, physical, emotional, and social faculties and talents in the desire to define and achieve their full potential. Maslow (1943) defines the need for self-actualization, in part, as the need to "become everything that one is capable of becoming" (p. 383). That's a goal few of us will ever meet; like other growth levels in Maslow's hierarchy, this one involves continually building on capabilities that never truly stop expanding.

In fact, Maslow estimated that "less than two percent of [adults] achieve self-actualization" (McLeod, 2014). Still, most of us know the drive to become and achieve our best, and educators are no exception. Self-actualized teachers unleash their potential to positively influence students, colleagues, and peers throughout their school system, whether or not those people are their direct responsibility.

Teachers who have advanced to this level, and who work in an environment that supports their continual development, will eventually find themselves striving to do more, become more, and offer more. At this uppermost level of the Hierarchy of Instructional Excellence, teachers are engaged in leveraging their extensive skills and knowledge in order to guide their colleagues in their professional growth. That's why this level of the hierarchy is labeled *teacher leadership*.

Much of the work teachers engage in at this level of development is about reflection on instructional effectiveness. As leaders, it's our job to give them all the individualized advice, guidance, and concrete support we can offer in these efforts. Systemwide supports aren't effective here, as teachers won't share this goal throughout the system. At this level, teachers possess a mindset of continuous improvement. Our goal as leaders must be to promote that mindset as we unleash the informal leadership capacity these self-actualized teachers bring to their profession and to leverage both their drive and their potential for advancing the school's mission.

The Three-Step Excellence Support System

We know that teachers play a significant role in providing students throughout the school system with the environment, instruction, and strategic guidance they need to achieve learning excellence. We also know the levels of professional growth teachers must advance through in order to continually advance in their own learning as they develop their professional skills and capabilities. In the shared responsibility for guaranteeing learning excellence, leaders also play an important role by building and maintaining structures throughout the school system that support teachers in their professional development efforts.

I refer to structural support systems because there is no possible way that leaders, as individuals, can meet every need of every teacher. Rather than scrambling to support each teacher directly, therefore, we can create a system of multiple supports available at various levels of individual interaction. To make those systems most effective, we also must assign the leadership for those supports to those with the most related expertise (as opposed to title). Educators routinely devise and rely on systems of supports to guarantee students any additional time and assistance they need in order to succeed as learners. We can follow the same approach to guarantee success for every teacher, and the Excellence Support System is my proposal for achieving that goal.

As described in the introduction, the Excellence Support System offers a stepped process for providing support at three levels of engagement: (1) schoolwide supports, (2) teacher team supports, and (3) individualized supports.

Step 1: Schoolwide Supports

Schoolwide supports are in place to ensure that all teachers know and successfully meet the expectations for teaching and learning, no matter what content area they teach. To ensure teacher success in every classroom, schoolwide supports provide resources and professional development to help teachers meet schoolwide expectations. These supports—which might include professional development programs, technology-based learning, and comprehensive plans for behavior, instruction, or intervention—are prevalent throughout the organization, regularly provided, and routinely revised and refined based on staff needs.

Step 2: Teacher Team Supports

Teacher team supports are more specific than schoolwide supports. While schoolwide supports guarantee the implementation of the broad areas of the Hierarchy of Instructional Excellence, team-level supports encourage teachers to actively participate in collaborative teacher teams, common planning time, or RTI teams.

Perhaps one of the most well-known models schools use to help guarantee student learning success is the PLC, in which collaborative teams of teachers work together to assess and improve their own learning and teaching skills with the goal of improving the learning success of their students. Education researchers Richard DuFour, Rebecca DuFour, Robert Eaker, and Thomas Many (2010) describe the PLC as:

> An ongoing process in which educators work collaboratively in recurring cycles of collective inquiry and action research to achieve better results for the students they serve. Professional learning communities operate under the assumption that the key to improved learning for students is continuous, job-embedded learning for educators. (p. 11)

Team-level supports guide struggling teachers and teams toward proficiency with content and knowledge in classroom strategies that support delivery of instruction. Team-level supports only work, however, when we empower teams to personalize schoolwide ideas to meet the needs of all team members.

Step 3: Individualized Supports

Leaders in excellent schools see collaboration as improvement opportunities for teacher teams, and they go a step further to meet the individual needs of specific teachers with individualized plans to achieve excellence. Individualized supports are personalized plans that target the greatest area of need for individual teachers and the most effective types of tools, such as personalized growth plans, intervention plans, or remediation plans, to address that need. Struggling teachers are challenged for a multitude of reasons, but this step enables leaders to identify specific improvement targets and then create concrete and attainable steps to help the teacher improve quickly. We can leverage these supports when systemwide and teacher team steps have proven inadequate for remediating instructional problems. As a result, these supports can save teachers who otherwise would be documented into resignation or termination.

Four Critical Questions for Building an Excellence Support System

Leaders must rely on collaborative teams as an integral part of supporting educator excellence. Teams can be the catalyst for guaranteeing excellence in every classroom, but only when the commitment to that guarantee goes beyond rhetoric. Toward that end, DuFour, DuFour, and Eaker (2008) propose four critical PLC questions for student learning. Leaders whose schools claim the goal of *learning for all* can best pursue excellence by adapting these critical questions to create systems supporting ongoing teacher improvement.

1. **What do we want students to know and be able to do?** *becomes* **What components of highly effective teaching do we expect from teachers to guarantee learning for all students?** Schools of excellence go beyond empty rhetoric to provide teachers and their teams with models of excellent instruction along with access to research findings that help expand understanding of instructional strategies and tools. With every expectation an excellent school sets for its teachers, it also provides an explanation of how to meet those expectations to give teachers tangible targets. Further, these schools celebrate and promote the characteristics of effective teachers to foster a culture of continuous improvement.

2. **How will we know when students have learned it?** *becomes* **How will we know when teachers are successful in ensuring learning for all students?** It's easy to assess teacher proficiency, but it's a whole other issue to determine which components of effective teaching are in place and which components need prescriptive supports. Schools of excellence have systems and tools to identify areas of strength in instructional delivery and areas that need improvement. Common assessments, walkthrough instruments, and formal evaluations are just some of the evaluation tools that schools can use to determine whether teachers are effective and to provide teachers with meaningful feedback that can actually help them improve.

3. **How will we respond when students do not learn it?** *becomes* **How will we respond when a teacher fails to meet the learning needs of all students?** Leaders in schools of excellence not only provide meaningful feedback, but also go beyond it by supporting the prognosis as well as the diagnosis. These schools allocate assets and develop systems to ensure that supports are established to help teachers attain excellence. That's how they demonstrate a belief in the idea *If any teacher fails, we all fail.*

4. **How will we extend learning for students who have learned it?** *becomes* **How will we embrace teachers who are successful in meeting the learning needs of all students?** In excellent schools, excellent teachers are the most revered professionals in the system. Peers, students, and administrators look up to them. Parents request that their children be placed in their classes. In short, they are models for what excellence in every classroom should be. Instead of shifting responsibilities from ineffective teachers to effective teachers, excellent schools find unique ways to use excellent teachers as models and supports for struggling teachers. Excellent schools convert these fantastic teachers into leaders and use their expertise to inspire all teachers and their collaborative teams to engage in continuous improvement.

As I noted at the beginning of this chapter, excellent schools don't leave excellence to chance. Schools of excellence believe in learning for all students *and* all teachers. They back up that belief with concrete systems and structures for guaranteeing that their teachers will continue to grow their professional skills throughout their careers, beginning on day one. By providing, monitoring, and maintaining those systems, we can do our part to ensure that learning excellence isn't a roll of the dice for anyone who works in or attends our schools.

Conclusion

The introduction to this book listed the three most fundamental questions we, as education leaders, must address: (1) Why are we here, and what is our mission? (2) What role do teachers play in achieving that mission? and (3) How do we make *all* teachers successful? In this chapter, we explored a number of ideas that speak to these critical issues. We know that our mission is to guarantee learning excellence for all, and we know that teachers play a crucial role in achieving that mission. Making all teachers successful, however, demands that we, as leaders, help them continually improve in the skills of their profession. When our teachers improve, our schools improve and our students' learning experiences and outcomes improve as well. We expect our teachers to find creative methods for meeting the learning needs of multiple students at multiple levels of learning in order to help them advance. As leaders, we must be able to apply the same level of creativity and focus in helping our teachers continually advance in their craft.

To begin, we should create systemwide supports to orient and advance teachers in their professional roles. We also must provide communities where professionals can comfortably identify where they are in the Hierarchy of Instructional Excellence and develop and implement effective plans for learning with and from each other—a process we begin to explore in the next chapter. Further, we must be prepared to offer individual supports when systemwide and team-level assistance isn't enough to help struggling teachers overcome their difficulties.

To make any of these systems a reality, however, we must abandon a few traditional paradigms. First, a one-size-fits-all approach to professional development doesn't always fit and will only meet the needs of *some* teachers in the building. Second, no leader possesses all the time, talent, and expertise necessary to address the deficits of every teacher. To embrace this responsibility, we must adopt a new philosophy of professional development that recruits multiple resources and leadership from different areas of expertise within the system.

Most important, we must abandon the idea that teachers ever reach a level of development where they can stop learning. The goal of creating an excellent teacher for every classroom only becomes a reality when the education profession and its leaders define teacher excellence not as a condition but as a process of continuous improvement over time. *growth mindset*

CHAPTER 2

Leading for Excellence: Learning Resources

Creating meaningful learning spaces for today's students requires us to remember that the learner is the driver and the tools for learning are the accelerators.

—John Wink

The classroom is a blank canvas. The teacher is the artist, and the resources at his or her disposal are the paintbrushes. The teacher's ability to skillfully create a vibrant learning environment is largely influenced by whether or not he or she has the appropriate resources and the skills to use them. In this chapter, we will explore how excellent teachers develop skillful use of their resources and how we, as leaders, can guide and support teachers to develop these skills.

This chapter offers a quick review of how knowledge of learning resources and their skillful use forms the foundation of the Hierarchy of Instructional Excellence. To help students gain the most benefit from learning resources, teachers must be skillful in the preparation and delivery of resource instruction. After examining the specific skills involved in those efforts, we'll walk through some practices and tools teachers can use to reflect on and continually improve those skills.

Because teachers at every level of their careers can experience challenges in mastering the use of learning resources, excellent leaders must provide specific, structured support to help teachers overcome those challenges. The three-step Excellence Support System offers tools and practices targeted to offer this support on a systemwide, team, and individual basis.

But before we dig into the mechanics of supporting educators as they work to master the use of learning resources, let's take a closer look at one teacher's experience with that challenge. Those of us who have been on the job for some time may have forgotten what it's like to walk into the first classroom we will ever manage. As the following story illustrates, however, our ability to ground ourselves in the basics—our instructional space, texts, tools, and equipment—can play a major role in establishing the confidence we need to take on the sometimes overwhelming responsibilities of teaching. When leaders help strengthen that foundation of resource knowledge, we give teachers and their students a solid base on which to begin building future learning success.

Starting the First Day on the Job

In late July, Emma walked into her new school on the first day at her job as a first-year teacher. Full of excitement, Emma envisioned herself making a heroic difference in the lives of all students at the school. She entered the main office and, as she waited for the principal, read the school's mission statement. She was pleased to note that it boasted a commitment to excellence for all students, lifelong learning, and outstanding preparation of 21st century citizens.

Principal Hughes emerged from his office and warmly greeted Emma. "We're glad you're aboard. Let's get your keys and get you down to your room."

Mr. Hughes gave Emma a basic tour of the building and outlined the school's operations and then ended the tour at Emma's classroom. He opened the classroom door and said, "Here's your room. If you need anything, just let me know."

Emma walked in and found everything stacked up in a corner, the result of summer cleaning. Emma began deconstructing the tangled mass of classroom equipment and learning resources. As she placed textbooks in one pile, consumables in another pile, and student desks into a rough arrangement, Emma thought, "What am I going to do with all this stuff?"

The further she delved into the resources, the more overwhelmed she became. As she fought back the panic of resource overload, Emma's questions mounted.

- What do I use this book for?
- Are all these resources actually useful? Which ones can I get rid of?
- Shouldn't I have some intervention resources in here?
- Will I have enough desks? Where do I get more?
- What other technologies are available besides computers?
- What's the log-in for the teacher and student computers?

The questions raced on until Emma stopped and said to herself, "I need to make a list." She wrote down every question that she had—about the physical aspects of the classroom, the classroom resources she would need to use, and the people and processes she would need to rely on for acquiring supplies or fulfilling her technology needs. At the end of a twelve-hour day, Emma took home her list and prioritized it for Mr. Hughes. After all, he had told her to come to him if she needed anything.

The next day, Emma took her list to Mr. Hughes's office. She was more than a little disappointed when Mr. Hughes could only answer her questions in generalities. He gave her the names of a few teachers she could check with for information about which books to use for instruction. He called the technology department to get answers to Emma's log-in questions. And that was about it. The rest of her questions he only vaguely addressed and left largely unanswered.

Emma left Mr. Hughes's office feeling frustrated. She knew that the start of school was fast approaching, and she wasn't prepared to get her class off to a strong start. On the way back to her room, she saw some teachers talking in her hallway. She introduced herself to the women, who gave their names as Inez and Julie. After greeting her warmly, they asked Emma, "Do you need any help getting your room ready?"

Emma replied, "Well, if you don't mind, I have lots of questions."

For the next hour or so, Inez and Julie helped Emma go through the maze of resources, throwing out antiquated items and offering a basic understanding of others. Their guidance helped Emma check off question after question on her list. As they reached the end of this orientation, Emma thanked them. "I can't tell you how much I appreciate your help. I feel like I have my feet under me now."

Inez smiled. "Well, we're here to help one another. We both know how overwhelming it was when we came here. If you need anything, don't hesitate to let us know."

Emma was relieved. She'd found a true support system that offered much more than empty promises and rhetoric. She had teammates who weren't going to allow her to fail.

So often, teachers take new jobs and immediately are overwhelmed because their new schools don't provide a system to acquaint new teachers with their resources. Excellent schools know that if all teachers have a thorough knowledge of the school's resources, then there is a strong likelihood that teachers will be equipped to skillfully use those resources to help students learn. In the Hierarchy of Instructional Excellence, learning resources are the first and most fundamental level within the areas of growth teachers must progress through as they hone their skills and develop their craft (see figure 2.1, page 30). It's the responsibility of every school's leadership team to ensure that teachers have access to learning resources and the support and guidance necessary to use them skillfully.

This chapter explores processes, strategies, and guidelines education leaders can use to help build and maintain strong systems for supporting teachers' access to and skillful use of learning resources. These resources are key elements of a vibrant learning environment. We shouldn't leave teachers to ferret out available resources. Instead, we need agile systems that orient new teachers in the resources our schools offer and that continually update teachers as resources are added, replaced, or dropped. If teachers fail to understand how to employ learning resources, leaders within the

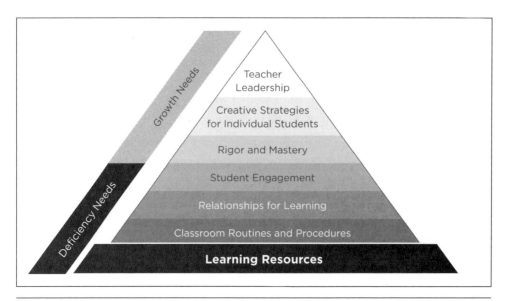

Figure 2.1: Hierarchy of Instructional Excellence—learning resources.

school should be prepared to respond with learning opportunities that diminish those teacher deficits. By making sure teachers are fully grounded in the resources available to them, we lay a strong foundation for learning excellence that extends to every student, faculty, and staff member throughout the school district.

Leveraging Learning Resources

Learning to skillfully use learning resources is a first step in a teacher's professional growth and development. As Danielson (2013) states, "Student learning is enhanced by a teacher's skillful use of resources" (p. 15). As we consider how to best construct a support system for helping teachers master this skill set, we need to remember that learning resources involve much more than just books and technology. Our educators' ability to identify and leverage *every* learning resource available to them is as important as the resources themselves in guaranteeing student learning success. Educators also must be skilled in choosing the best resource for the task at hand from among all those available.

To support our teachers in their use of learning resources, we also must offer them tools and guidance for selecting resources that best align with their students' learning outcomes, as well as evaluating and improving their use of learning resources over time. In other words, our schools must provide systems and structures that support teachers as they prepare to use learning resources, deliver those resources to their students, and reflect on and plan for improvement in their use of learning resources.

Preparation

One of the first resources we need to make available to every educator is access to a system of tools and guidance that prepares them to structure the classroom for learning, outline student codes of conduct, and manage student behavior. Campus discipline management plans, for example, can give teachers a foundation on which to build classroom procedures.

Excellent instruction requires resources adapted to the abilities and learning styles of all students. Because students need access to texts that vary in readability and complexity, for example, teachers should be able to invest time in learning how to successfully employ them. Finally, teachers also must be prepared to scaffold learning for students on level and below level. This task includes deciding which resources best introduce new information to students, which are best for assisting students in guided practice, and which will do the best job of helping students solidify new learning through independent practice. Teachers who are skillful in the use of learning resources can use them to create specific and targeted strategies for assessing learning success, extending the capabilities of learners who master new content with more complexity and remediating those who are struggling to learn.

Delivery

Planning for learning resources is the first step. Delivering those resources to students, however, requires a different set of skills. Primary among those skills is the ability to organize the classroom's physical space. When students enter the classroom, their first impression of the space sets the tone for the learning experiences ahead. A classroom's physical arrangement can influence a student's desire to learn, and it can reflect the teacher's ability to engage students. As teacher and educational journalist Mark Phillips (2014) writes, "The physical structure of a classroom is a critical variable in affecting student morale and learning." Many factors play a role in classroom organization, including the age of the students, what furniture and other physical objects will occupy the space, and where students should be seated in order to arrange the most effective learning environment.

Teachers are responsible for making those choices, but we have to be certain to make every possible resource available to teachers to help them in that process. We also have to offer the guidance necessary to help them identify those resources wherever they may exist. As Danielson (2013) writes:

> Both the physical arrangement of a classroom and the available resources provide opportunities for teachers to advance learning; when these resources are used skillfully, students can engage with the content in a productive manner. At the highest levels of performance, the students themselves contribute to the use or adaptation of the physical environment. (p. 37)

Excellent teachers want students to feel welcomed into their classrooms. They also want students to feel as though the classroom is designed specifically for them. Further, excellent teachers understand that they must sell the learning environment to students as a great resource for their learning experience.

When teachers deliver resources properly, they better prepare students to navigate the learning environment with little direction from the teacher in order to access tasks that help them master learning targets. As Danielson (2013) writes, "There is total alignment between the learning activities and the physical environment" (p. 39). From classroom management tools, textbooks, and technology, therefore, teachers must help students realize the benefits of each resource and know how to effectively use it to master learning independent of the teacher.

Reflection

Teachers who constantly seek improvement reflect on the success of their lessons. For reflection to be useful, however, it must go beyond identifying which lessons were "good" or "bad" to understanding which individual lesson components are effective or ineffective. To gain the most improvement from reflection, therefore, teachers should evaluate themselves daily on their use of available resources to facilitate student learning. Reflection helps teachers evaluate whether students are successfully using resources to drive their learning or if students are missing opportunities for independent learning. As leaders, we must be sure that we are providing all teachers with the tools and guidance necessary to gain the most value from the time they spend in reflecting on and assessing their use of learning resources.

Figure 2.2 offers a reflection tool that we can use to guide teachers as they engage in this process. This reflection tool allows teachers to analyze their resource use by category so they can narrow their focus for improvement.

With reflection, teachers can make adjustments to help the class better engage or direct their support to struggling students. Excellent teachers understand that mastering the tools at their disposal is the foundation for guaranteeing learning for every student. The more we, as leaders, understand about the teachers' knowledge of resources and how they share that knowledge with students, the better able we will be to help teachers make the most dramatic improvements in their instructional outcomes.

Building an Excellence Support System: Learning Resources

The skillful use of learning resources does not come easily for all teachers. The Excellence Support System is a leadership tool that not only provides professional development for all teachers but also creates a pathway for responding to teacher deficits with efficiency and immediacy.

Step 1 of this model identifies every new and existing resource in the school and offers every teacher a series of professional development tools and practices they can use to improve their understanding and use of available resources. When teachers need more help than these systemwide supports provide, teacher team supports

Resource	Reflection
Classroom Environment	How well do students respond to the physical layout of the room?
	Which students seem apprehensive about the classroom environment?
	Does the physical layout of the room impede learning or appropriate behavior?
	Do students communicate their concerns about the room or their assigned seats?
	What changes are necessary to improve the layout of the room?
Textbooks and Resources	How do students respond to the textbooks or instructional resources?
	Which students need additional clarification or expectations pertaining to these resources?
	Which students struggle with these resources because of their reading level?
	Which students reject these resources and avoid using them?
	How will I adjust my use of these resources to better engage students?
	Which resources do I need to study more?
Presentation Technology	What percentage of students responds positively to my use of presentation technology?
	What software or hardware am I still struggling with in my delivery?
	Do students engage more with visual graphics, text, or video?
	What technology do I need to study more?
Student Technology	How well do students embrace instructional technology?
	Which students lack understanding of the software or hardware?
	Which students substitute my work with off-task technology use?
	Which technology do students need to practice or study more?
	Which technology do I need to practice or study more?

Figure 2.2: Reflection tool for skillful use of learning resources.

Visit **go.SolutionTree.com/leadership** *for a free reproducible version of this figure.*

identify and leverage expertise in the teacher team to provide struggling teachers opportunities for ongoing learning and collaboration. When a teacher fails to develop the skillful use of resources even after leveraging step 1 and step 2 supports, we can move on to step 3, individualized supports, by creating an individualized plan for addressing the issues specific to that teacher.

Step 1: Schoolwide Supports

At the schoolwide level, support systems must identify every resource we expect teachers to use with fidelity. Beyond providing those resources, excellent leaders also must create implementation plans and procedures to help teachers acquaint themselves with unfamiliar resources and tools. The following sections describe just some of the tools we can include in our arsenal of schoolwide supports.

Resource Wikis

When teachers leave their schools, their knowledge of resources (among other things) leaves with them; therefore, we should proactively plan to create a schoolwide database of information and ideas about learning resources that the next teacher can access in order to become familiar with those resources. To make this information widely available and easy to use, leaders and their school systems are moving away from paper documentation and creating wikis, such as Google Sheets, to provide electronic versions of resource records and guidance. These wikis serve as digital warehouses of explanations, instant professional development tools, and resource overviews.

Figure 2.3 is an example of how Gilmer Elementary School (Gilmer, Texas) used Google Sheets during the 2013–2014 school year to provide teachers with an explanation of virtually every resource that teachers were expected to use to promote learning. From explaining how to navigate the school's staff blog to outlining how teachers should teach the discipline management plan, the school's wiki served as a living record of *CHAMPS* (topic-related ideas for conversation, help, activity, movement, participation, and success) and other information that teachers could access at any time and from any location.

Because they are living documents, resource wikis continue to grow in value as they develop over time. When teachers are unable to locate existing guidance or answers in the wiki, they and their teams can develop those answers and then add them to the wiki records. This way, questions and answers are useful not only for wiki users but also for other teachers who might need guidance in the future.

Flipped Video Training

To make better use of students' class time, many teachers have adopted the use of *flipped videos*, video-recorded teacher lectures that "flip" the typical arrangement

Topic	Link	Date Added
CHAMPS for Recess	http://youtu.be/Mp8B4EafXxs	July 2013
CHAMPS for the Cafeteria	http://youtu.be/QygxtoB4R9Q	July 2013
CHAMPS for the Hallway	http://youtu.be/xZyeaki_EXA	July 2013
GES Principal's Page Blog	www.gesprincipalpage.blogspot.com	Aug 2013
GES Staff Blog	www.gesstaffblog.blogspot.com	Aug 2013
How to Navigate the Blog	http://youtu.be/I7S6AKlLJog	Aug 2013
Print Request Website	www.gilmerisd.org/Employee /PrintRequest.html	July 2013
Curriculum Site and Resources	www.gilmerisd.org /TeacherResources.asp	July 2013

Figure 2.3: Resource wiki.

of lecture during class time and practice at home. Students can watch these video lectures outside of class when and as often as they like so they can do the work associated with the lectures during class with the support of their teacher and study groups. Some schools are using the same kind of recorded training videos to replace written or verbal explanations of how teachers use learning resources. Those explanations can be cumbersome, vague, or confusing due to ambiguous language or a failure to specifically address fundamental aspects of unfamiliar procedures. Flipped videos actually show teachers how to use resources so they have a detailed visual example of what those resources involve, how they work, and how teachers use them. These videos are effective and efficient methods for training teachers about digital resources with the aid of screen-recording tools and video apps, such as the following.

- **Screencast-O-Matic (https://screencast-o-matic.com):** Fast app for creating and sharing screen recordings

- **Explain Everything Interactive Whiteboard (www.explaineverything .com):** Digital whiteboard for tablets that enables interactive collaboration among teachers, students, and leaders around the world

- **iMovie (www.apple.com/ios/imovies):** Video editing software that enables users to create and edit short video segments from clips, photos, and other digital content

- **YouTube (www.youtube.com):** Perhaps the world's largest video-sharing platform

Flipping instruction is not a new concept. In fact, many teachers in schools everywhere are using it to accelerate learning by giving students constant access to everything that teachers want them to learn. By using the flipped format to offer professional development information and guidance on resources, processes, and procedures to our teachers, we also are modeling its use for educators within our system. At the same time, we are creating a culture that encourages teachers who master specific resources to make their expertise available to other teachers by providing a simple and powerful resource that all educators can use as part of the school's system of supports.

Technology Training on the Fly

Digital tools have exploded in classrooms throughout the world, and excellent schools harness the potential of digital resources by building professional development into their schedules. Some schools have worked diligently to provide an organized plan of frequent professional development about technology through the use of media specialists, librarians, technology staff, and teachers. Schools can offer these frequent and short trainings throughout the year that prove helpful for teachers who want to learn how to integrate technology into their curriculum.

Digital badging is one example of the tools districts are employing to incentivize educators to further their learning about technology. *Digital badges* are electronic certification symbols teachers earn online when they demonstrate that they have developed new skills that contribute to their professional growth and development. These badges serve to recognize and record the teachers' learning accomplishments as well as motivate teachers to continually learn new skills so they can accumulate more digital badges and demonstrate ongoing growth.

A great example of digital badging is the system created by Laura Fleming (www .twitter.com/NMHS_lms), library media tech at New Milford High School in New Jersey. She describes how her school uses the digital badging system, Worlds of Learning (http://worlds-of-learning.com), to:

> provide professional learning with a pinch of gamification. For some time now, we have been hearing about digital badges and how they can be used to guide, motivate, document and validate formal and informal learning. In recent years, Digital Badges have evolved from what were originally static images, to a tool used for capturing and communicating knowledge. (Fleming, n.d.)

Digital badging is a flexible tool for supporting professional growth in that it is personalized to the needs of individual teachers, while also providing a systemwide support for all teachers.

Another technology training strategy schools are using is a short, face-to-face, weekly training model. Teachers and teams gather for Techie Tuesdays and Web Wednesdays to delve deeper into tools and topics that support educators as they learn and become more proficient with technologies. These thirty-minute trainings are led by principals, teacher leaders, and technology specialists and leave teachers better prepared to integrate technology into the classroom.

Technology can accelerate learning only when teachers develop the skills to successfully integrate the tools into their instruction. These are just some of the many ideas we can employ to boost teacher skills in using technology resources so they, in turn, can help their students improve their own technology skills.

Ongoing Professional Development

Most new learning resources have taken a great deal of time, research, and experimentation in order to become useful for enhancing learning. When we merely purchase these new resources and distribute them to teachers without an accompanying plan for how to use them to promote ongoing professional development, we are wasting the district's money and our teachers' and students' time. To prevent this, we must provide teachers extensive initial training of any new resource and follow up with an ongoing professional development plan that guarantees multiple opportunities for continuous learning for staff. Following are the kinds of questions we should consider prior to rolling out any new resource.

- What initial training will teachers require in order to successfully use this new resource, and who will provide it?

- What follow-up training will teachers require? How often will they require that training, and who will provide it?

- When we hire new teachers, what training plan will we offer for this resource, and who will provide it?

- How will we know if our training for this resource is effective and meets the needs of our teachers?

In short, learning resources play a critical role in nearly every aspect of the learning experience, and schoolwide supports for mastering those resources are essential to ensure every teacher's success. Until all teachers are comfortable in their knowledge of those resources and their skills in using them, they will struggle in their efforts to advance in any other area of professional growth. Just as we expect our teachers to guarantee student learning, we must commit to creating a support system to aid ongoing training in the use of learning resources for all teachers throughout our districts. Robust, systemwide supports for guiding teachers' growth in the use of learning resources, therefore, are an essential first step in building the kind of excellent teachers that contribute to excellent schools.

Systemwide supports on their own, however, aren't adequate for addressing all professional development needs for every teacher and every stage of *any* teacher's skill growth. That's why an effective Excellence Support System also offers team-level supports as a second step in the support process.

Step 2: Teacher Team Supports

When a school offers a systemwide support structure for learning resources, it's the responsibility of the teacher teams within that school to ensure that all educators know how to use those resources effectively. Whether they refer to themselves as collaborative teams or with another organizational name, teacher teams accomplish that goal by "building shared knowledge regarding best practices and strategies for implementing those practices" (DuFour et al., 2010, p. 133). As new teachers join the team, returning members have an obligation to demonstrate how best to use available resources to support learning. The focus of teacher team training, however, must remain on the end goal of supporting learning rather than the memorization of rote processes. Furthermore, teachers must commit to learning new resources for the explicit purpose of reaching their ultimate goal, guaranteeing learning for all students. "Teams that focus on results are more effective than those that center their work on activities and tasks" (Katzenbach & Smith, 1993, as cited in DuFour et al., 2010, p. 192).

Team Experts

The best way to ensure that a teacher team maintains its focus on learning is to arrange for individual members to become experts in the use of one or two resources for instruction, and then to train other members in that use. Instead of every team member trying to master technology in isolation, for example, a team technology expert could show other members how to integrate technology tools into instruction, or a team member who is proficient in using assessment resources could lead peers in understanding how to develop rigorous assessments. This kind of team training can be more effective than relying on individuals to self-train in every facet of learning resources.

To divide and share the load of team training and guarantee that all team experts are covering the same basic training elements, we can look for guidelines in the four critical questions of PLCs that I first outlined on pages 23–24 in chapter 1 (DuFour et al., 2010). See how you can adapt these questions to apply to teacher learning and improvement. As figure 2.4 illustrates, teams can use these questions to identify those resources teachers should use in the course of answering the questions. Then the team can determine which team member is best prepared to guide peers in becoming experts with those resources.

Specifics From Experience

As educators, authors, and collaborative teamwork specialists William Ferriter, Parry Graham, and Matt Wight (2013) note in *Making Teamwork Meaningful*, it's important that team training offers specific ideas and practices: "Often, the greatest mistake that school leaders make when designing professional development is tackling broad topics instead of focusing on *specific* skills and knowledge" (p. 85). The PLC is perhaps the best source for providing teachers specific skills and knowledge

Learning Components	Learning Resources	Resource Leader
Question 1: What do we want students to know and be able to do? (List curriculum documents and resources.)		
Question 2: How will we know when students have learned it? (List assessment resources to gauge learning.)		
Question 3: How will we respond when students do not learn it? (List classroom intervention resources.)		
Question 4: How will we extend learning for students who have learned it? (List extension resources.)		
Instructional technology: Which digital resources can we use to enhance learning?		

Source: DuFour et al., 2008, p. 182.

Figure 2.4: Team norms for learning resources.

Visit **go.SolutionTree.com/leadership** *for a free reproducible version of this figure.*

about resources, and that's because teacher experts within teams typically have had adequate time to work out the kinks with a new resource. Often, initial professional development training doesn't offer that kind of seasoned approach. Collaborative teams can also offer ongoing training refreshers and updates as resources evolve over time. Teacher teams in search of excellence can use well-crafted team training programs to help members continuously learn about the resources that impact their craft. And, by working together, team members can collectively ensure consistent implementation in every classroom.

Teacher teams are the greatest resource a school can use to improve overall teacher quality, and they play an especially critical role in supporting struggling teachers. By supporting and serving one another, team members have the potential to strengthen the collective efficacy of the entire team by remaining focused on improving student learning and improving each teacher's effectiveness. With a thorough understanding of how to work and learn together, teacher teams can develop every teacher's expertise in their knowledge of resources and how to leverage those resources to optimize student learning.

Step 3: Individualized Supports

When a teacher continues to struggle to master the use of learning resources, even after making use of systemwide and teacher team supports, we must be prepared to offer that teacher individualized training and support. Selecting the right person to provide that support is a matter of identifying an individual within the system who is skilled in both the use of learning resources and in guiding colleagues through the learning experience.

Teacher Coach or Mentor

Often, a mentor or buddy of the struggling teacher can be the best person to explain a routine, process, or procedure. Learning resources that demand higher-level skill sets, however, may require explanation by a more experienced leader. A digital resource, for example, might best be taught by the person within your school who is most experienced with technology, while a math coach could be the best person to help a new teacher navigate a math resource or curriculum.

Whoever we select to coach the teacher through his or her challenges must take time to develop a positive working relationship with the teacher-learner. As Marzano and Simms (2013) write:

> A coach and teacher must establish a set of shared understandings and conditions that will drive the rest of their interaction. These shared understandings might include an agreement about what constitutes good teaching, a system to measure the teacher's progress, an evaluation of the teacher's current level of performance, and the establishment of growth goals for the teacher. (p. 19)

The goal of the coach or mentor is simple: to improve the teacher's skillful use of the resource. The following three steps offer a solid process that coaches and mentors can help teachers work through in order to improve their use of learning resources.

1. Identify key components of the resource that must be mastered first.

2. Clarify alignment between the resource and learning goals in the classroom.

3. Design a plan to empower students to take ownership of the resource.

When struggling teachers can address these three issues, they are positioned to improve both their students' learning experience and their own confidence in their effective use of learning resources.

Problem Simplification Plan

A problem simplification plan can ensure that coaches are using the most effective methods to help struggling teachers address issues of professional growth. The idea behind these plans is that simplification is a powerful tool for making complex problems easier to address. Using a problem simplification plan, mentors and coaches can help teachers by isolating the problem, simplifying the cause of the difficulty, evaluating the effectiveness of prior training, brainstorming possible solutions, and, finally, creating a plan of action. Figure 2.5 shows a problem simplification plan that coaches and teachers can use to collaboratively scaffold their work to better overcome difficulties with specific resources.

Problem Simplification Plan: Learning Resources
1. The teacher is struggling with the following resource.
2. What are the norms for using this resource to improve instruction, and what training has the teacher received to better understand the resource?
3. Identify the best intervention to help the teacher develop a better understanding of the resource. ☐ Plan for the resource with _____. ☐ Observation of _____ using the resource in instruction. ☐ Co-teach with _____ using the resource. ☐ Have _____ model using the resource with the teacher's class. ☐ Other: _____ Notes:

Figure 2.5: Problem simplification plan—learning resources.   continued →

4.	Set a date when the resource should be successfully integrated into instruction.
5.	How will we know if the resource has been successfully integrated into instruction?

Visit **go.SolutionTree.com/leadership** *for a free reproducible version of this figure.*

The problem simplification plan helps underscore the importance of the relationship between coach and learner in the success of individualized supports. The manner in which the coach builds trust, conveys understanding, and shows commitment to the teacher's overall success throughout the process plays a pivotal role in the teacher's improvement. That's why we must work closely with coaches to ensure they have the necessary skills to capitalize on the relationship we've asked them to undertake with teachers.

Conclusion

Just as Maslow's (1943) Hierarchy of Needs tells us that the first and most basic need people have is the need for their physiological requirements for survival—food, water, and shelter—when it comes to survival in the classroom, the most basic need teachers have is to become proficient in the use of learning resources available to them. As Danielson (2013) suggests, some of these resources are "provided by the school as 'official' materials; others are secured by teachers through their own initiative" (p. 15). Excellent teachers know that resources are the necessary tools for learning, but their knowledge and skillful use of those tools are also necessary for success. Learning resources are the foundation of a teacher's ability to guarantee student learning. Without grounding in these fundamental elements of instruction, teachers will have difficulty developing skills in any successive area of professional growth, such as organizing routines and procedures, building relationships with students, or promoting student learning.

Education leaders have an obligation to provide resources to support student learning, but we are equally obligated to develop specific, structured responses to teachers who face their own challenges. Nowhere is this obligation more critical than in our support for training teachers in the most effective use of learning resources. As described in this chapter, teachers draw on multiple skills in their effective use of learning resources. They must be prepared to introduce resources to students in a way that makes the students feel safe and comfortable in their surroundings and confident in their ability to use the resources at hand to pursue learning on their own, independent of teacher guidance. Teachers also have to be adept at reflecting on their use of learning resources so they can evolve and adapt that use to continue growing in their professional skills. It is our role as leaders to offer our teachers well-structured and consistent support in these efforts.

Excellent leaders don't want new teachers to feel helpless and abandoned as they first enter their classrooms and begin the sometimes overwhelming task of learning the ropes. Nor do we want experienced teachers who are struggling to gain mastery over a new resource to feel as though they are being left behind. With the advancement of technology and the globalization of knowledge, we can expect our schools to have unending opportunities to identify and incorporate new tools for enhancing our students' learning success.

This chapter concludes with a reflection tool (pages 44–45) that leaders at any level in the school system can use to evaluate their understanding of the challenges teachers face when identifying and making the most effective use of learning resources, the strength of their supports for that professional development, and potential avenues for strengthening those supports. Consider the following questions and your responses to them as you explore possibilities for improving those systems based on information and ideas in this chapter.

Reflection Tool: Learning Resources

Definition of Excellence for Learning Resources

What is our school's definition of teacher excellence in the area of using learning resources?

Schoolwide Supports

1. Before we select a resource for teachers, how do we create a professional learning plan to ensure that all develop skillful use of the resource?

2. For all resources that we expect teachers to use with fidelity, what face-to-face professional learning do we require of our teachers?

3. To provide ongoing professional development for learning resources, what web-based or flipped instruction resources do we provide teachers that they can access anytime?

4. What types of technology training on the fly do our teachers need to be more proficient and current with the latest trends in technology integration?

5. For all learning resources, how do we ensure fidelity of use through ongoing professional development?

6. How effective is our system of schoolwide supports at meeting our teachers' needs with learning resources?

A Leader's Guide to Excellence in Every Classroom © 2017 Solution Tree Press • SolutionTree.com
Visit **go.SolutionTree.com/leadership** to download this free reproducible.

Teacher Team Supports

1. Have our teams identified resource leaders to lead the team in learning more about each resource?

2. How well do members of each team lead their colleagues in developing skillful use of the resource?

3. How well do our collaborative meetings focus on using the resources to support learning?

4. When a teacher experiences difficulty with a particular resource, what steps does he or she take to seek out help from teammates?

Individualized Supports

1. Before we help a teacher experiencing difficulty with a resource, what steps do we take to evaluate the systemwide supports and teacher team supports and their effectiveness at helping the teacher? *(If schoolwide or teacher team supports are not in place, they are addressed as needed.)*

2. What evidence do we collect to confirm that the teacher has difficulty with the resource?

3. Before we help the teacher, what steps do we take to isolate the teacher's area of greatest difficulty in using the resource?

4. When we prescribe a personalized plan of supports, how well do we prescribe interventions from a wide variety of options, including observing, coaching, collaborating with another teacher or the teacher team, and using outside resources?

5. Once we prescribe a plan of supports, what steps do we take to set a goal that defines the desired improvement needed, a date by which that improvement will be made, and a date by which we will follow up to ensure that improvement has been made?

A Leader's Guide to Excellence in Every Classroom © 2017 Solution Tree Press • SolutionTree.com
Visit **go.SolutionTree.com/leadership** to download this free reproducible.

CHAPTER 3

Leading for Excellence: Classroom Routines and Procedures

Students do not learn when they are disciplined. They learn when the classroom is organized for learning and success.

—Harry Wong

Students rarely learn at high levels in a poorly managed classroom. At the same time, they can't maximize their learning in a classroom where the teacher micromanages them. The effective use of classroom routines and procedures can help educators avoid both of these problematic conditions for learning. Effective classroom management offers students a safe and secure learning environment where they know what to expect and what is expected of them.

What defines a well-managed classroom? According to Danielson (2013), "Hallmarks of a well-managed classroom are that instructional groups are used effectively, noninstructional tasks are completed efficiently, and transitions between activities and management of materials and supplies are skillfully done in order to maintain momentum and maximize instructional time" (p. 31). Organized classroom management results in smooth routines, little to no loss of instructional time, and high levels of student involvement and ownership of procedures. Ultimately, well-designed routines and procedures enable all students to know exactly what to do, how to do it, and when to do it, every time. In essence, highly effective routines and procedures work like a well-oiled machine.

This chapter explores the workings of that machine as we review the critical role of well-established routines and procedures in excellent instruction, the skills teachers must develop to establish and maintain the most effective routines and procedures for their classrooms, and the tools, practices, and systems we can offer to support teachers' growth in this fundamental area of their craft.

The skillful use of routines and procedures represents the second most fundamental level of the Hierarchy of Instructional Excellence, and in this chapter, we examine how excellent teachers demonstrate a command of this critical area of their professional growth. The chapter outlines the skill set involved in classroom management and the strategies, tools, and techniques excellent instructors use to implement routines and procedures that create the most fertile environment for student learning.

From preparation to delivery to reflection, these practices and research-based approaches offer leaders a solid footing from which to evaluate and assist teachers as they work to continually improve their use of classroom routines and procedures to promote learning. Most important, this chapter offers a concise overview of tactics and practices we can use to fulfill our responsibilities to help struggling teachers transform dysfunctional classrooms into well-managed classrooms and convert good classroom management into powerful, student-directed learning.

Before we begin examining the challenges, skills, and supports involved in promoting the successful use of classroom routines and procedures, let's review another story from the classroom front lines. In this story, persistence and support helps stop a classroom's slide into dysfunction when a leader supports a struggling teacher confronting weaknesses in his existing routines and procedures by developing a successful professional learning plan for improving these skills.

Struggling Alone With No Routines

Marco's first six weeks at his new school were challenging to say the least. He knew his curriculum well. He studied the instructional best practices that would yield the most from his students. Lesson plans were packed with activities that engaged even the most difficult students, but there was a problem. No matter how hard he worked, students didn't respond as he had planned. No matter how many hours he put into his lessons, the learning environment continued to suffer due to problems with student behavior.

Marco was embarrassed. He wanted to impress his colleagues and didn't want to reveal his flaws. What he was doing wasn't working, and he knew it. He didn't want the principal to know he couldn't manage his class, so he allowed his pride and ego to prevent him from asking for help. He was determined to fix this problem all by himself—that is, until his principal, Ms. Johnson, came to visit.

Ms. Johnson made regular pop-in visits to Marco's class, but the length of her observations was typically short enough that Marco could fake his way to an acceptable walkthrough. Upon Ms. Johnson's arrival, the students' behavior immediately changed. Behavior was appropriate and ritually compliant for the principal, and

Ms. Johnson could sense it. She knew that something wasn't right, so she scheduled herself to conduct an observation that lasted the entire period.

The next day, Ms. Johnson entered the classroom before the students did. She greeted Marco and said, "I know you are working hard, and I like what you're doing." Marco's "Thank you, Ms. Johnson" reply was positive, but his tone revealed a hint of skepticism.

Ms. Johnson continued, "I'd like to watch your entire lesson today because I'd like to help you make your instruction even better." She ended with this final statement: "All I ask is that you do everything the same way that you normally do it. If I can watch your class in its normal routine, I am confident that together we can make your instruction even better."

Marco quickly responded, "That sounds good to me."

The students slowly entered the classroom and quickly engaged one another in nonacademic activities, and it took an excessive amount of time for Marco to corral them. Once Marco had their attention, he began his lesson. Not even one minute into the lesson, students were blurting out unrelated information, which halted the pace of the lesson. Marco redirected immediately and politely, but the interruptions continued. After fifteen painful minutes of repeated distractions during his stalled instruction, Marco released the students into small-group work.

Before Marco had even completed giving directions, students left their seats for group work and wasted even more time talking, asking questions about the directions, or arguing about the task at hand. In place of monitoring students and giving specific feedback to help students learn, Marco jumped into reaction mode by clarifying the task for confused students, correcting off-task students, and giving endless threats of future consequences for poor behavior. Ms. Johnson patiently watched as Marco struggled to maintain control of his class, which was beginning to look more like a train wreck.

After fifteen minutes of group work that yielded little more than lost time and incomplete tasks, Marco directed students back to their seats for independent work. The task was simple, and most students could have handled it with little teacher support. But once again, students failed to respond. The final results of the lesson were off-task conversations, students moving about the room to avoid work, and others failing to engage in the task. Ms. Johnson stood up from her seat and approached Marco with a smile. "Come see me during your planning period." Marco feared the worst.

When Marco entered Ms. Johnson's office later that afternoon, Ms. Johnson warmly greeted him and thanked him for coming. Caught off guard by her politeness, Marco thanked her and had a seat at the conference table. Ms. Johnson sat in the chair next to him and asked, "Well, how do you think you did?"

Marco softly replied, "Not so good."

Ms. Johnson quickly responded, "Not so fast. There are some good things in place. First of all, you know your content, which is great. You have a thorough understanding of your curriculum, and you have excellent ideas for instructional activities when students move to group work. These elements are important, but the main thing preventing you from making it happen is classroom management."

Marco shrugged. "I just don't know how to get their attention."

Ms. Johnson continued, "What you are lacking is routines and procedures for learning. Without these specific protocols for behavior and learning, students create their own routines and procedures that best suit their personal needs. If you are willing to learn from me as well as your colleagues, I am confident that we can remedy this situation. And if we can make a strong plan, I truly believe your classroom instruction will take off. So, what do you think, Marco?"

Marco perked up. "Well, I never thought of it that way, and I haven't really been focusing on procedures. I learned in college that procedures are important, but I have been more focused on planning for instruction rather than planning for the needs of my students. You're absolutely right. I can correct this problem."

Ms. Johnson smiled. "I know you can do it."

For the next three weeks, Marco worked with Ms. Johnson, observed his colleagues, and reflected about his routines and procedures. Based on his observations, Marco made structural changes to his own expectations for student behaviors and then clearly explained to his students the new procedures and routines to support those changes. After three weeks of focused work, Marco's students' behavior improved drastically, and student learning increased exponentially.

How many times have we, as leaders, seen this scenario play out? It happens all too often; a promising teacher struggles to maintain order in the classroom, limiting the success of both the teacher's instruction and the students' learning. If we want to retain teachers like Marco, we owe it to them to clearly define and model what effective classroom routines and procedures of excellence look like and sound like. Those models will only offer examples, of course, because there is no one best set of classroom procedures. In fact, creating, establishing, and maintaining effective routines and procedures is an individualized process that involves a skill set most educators take years to develop on their own. That's why we must create a support system that offers ongoing training and personalized supports to help teachers reach excellence in this area.

Managing Classroom Routines and Procedures

Classroom management is a multifaceted task for teachers. Learning the minutiae of setting expectations, monitoring them, and providing feedback, redirection, and praise is a time-consuming process that can take years. Unfortunately, we can't allow teachers to slowly work their way through that learning process. Students deserve a teacher every year who possesses excellent classroom management skills. Failure to implement strong classroom routines and procedures will most certainly take the focus off learning and put it squarely on maintaining order. Danielson (2013) writes, "A smoothly functioning classroom is a prerequisite to good instruction and high levels of student engagement" (p. 31).

This failure also can hamper a teacher's ability to build other types of instructional skills. David Berliner (1988) writes about the importance of competency in classroom management:

> Classroom management also represents a significant aspect of the teacher's pedagogical knowledge and is often found as a component of taxonomies and descriptions of core knowledge for educators (e.g., Council for Exceptional Children, 1998). Some researchers have suggested, moreover, that novice teachers may need to reach a minimum level of competency in management skills before they are able to develop in other areas of instruction. (as cited in Emmer & Stough, 2001, p. 103)

As a result of their fundamental role in the development of teachers' professional skills, classroom routines and procedures occupy the second level in the Hierarchy of Instructional Excellence (see figure 3.1).

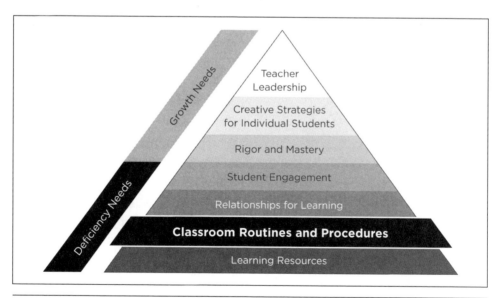

Figure 3.1: Hierarchy of Instructional Excellence—classroom routines and procedures.

Just as Maslow's Hierarchy of Needs tells us that we must have basic physiological needs met before we can focus on securing our second-level needs of safety and security, when teachers are confident in their knowledge and use of the basic resources available to them, they can turn their attention to organizing the way their classrooms must function in order to maximize the learning outcomes those resources make possible. As Marzano (2003) writes, "Research and theory, then, support the intuitive notion that well-articulated rules and procedures that are negotiated with students are a critical aspect of classroom management, affecting not only the behavior of students but also their academic achievement" (p. 17).

Now, let's examine the skills educators can use to create and implement an effective set of classroom routines and procedures.

Preparation

The first step to excellent classroom management is planning around the active nature of students. This step begins with setting goals for student behavior that will prepare them to succeed in the current year's class and beyond. From there, teachers should decide the most common situations students will encounter in the classroom and design procedures and routines that yield automaticity and adherence.

Classes are composed of students of different races, genders, economic challenges, and cultures, and they enter the room with their own norms for what appropriate behavior looks and sounds like. Students also have differing propensities for how they solve their own problems with learning or with a classmate; therefore, teachers must take all these factors into consideration when preparing a classroom management system.

An important element of a classroom management plan's success involves its power for steering students away from misbehavior. Randy Sprick (2009), creator of CHAMPS, claims that most behavior infractions happen not because of choice but because of not knowing what the expectations for behavior and learning look like and, more importantly, sound like. As described in chapter 2, *CHAMPS* is an acronym that represents all the behavioral expectations students must know to behave appropriately. Teachers can ask themselves the following CHAMPS questions as they form their plan for establishing these expectations.

- **Conversation:** What level of student conversation is necessary to carry out each activity successfully without impeding the learning of others?

- **Help:** When students have difficulty learning or have a problem with another student, whom should they contact for help, and how can students access help without disrupting the learning of others?

- **Activity:** What is the learning activity or transition activity, and what does it look like and sound like when students complete it expediently?

- **Movement:** What physical movement, if any, is permissible during the activity?

- **Participation:** How will students demonstrate that they are participating in these behaviors and processes?

- **Success:** Teachers need not ask probing questions about success. When students engage in appropriate conversation, solicit help when needed, complete the activity correctly, and move as directed, they demonstrate the successful behaviors that can contribute to successful learning.

By encouraging our teachers to carefully consider and formulate answers for questions such as those in the previous list, we are prompting them to solidify behavior goals for their students. Rather than having a vague notion of classroom order, exercises such as these enable teachers to create concrete descriptions of every behavioral expectation for students, as well as a plan for gauging and responding to students' participation in those behaviors. In order for these expectations to align with learning outcomes, excellent teachers plan for the following criteria.

Routine Behaviors	Learning Procedures
Entering the room	Whole-group instruction
Leaving the room	Small-group instruction
Transitioning in the room	Independent work
Requesting permission to use the restroom	Technology usage
Accessing classroom resources independently	Partner work
Responding to visitors as they enter the room	Testing

Beyond planning expectations for routine behaviors, excellent teachers also plan lessons for teaching the procedures to students and giving them an opportunity to practice the procedures. As part of this planning, teachers prepare to anticipate student misbehaviors and intercept them and respond to students who fail to meet behavioral expectations by developing and practicing how they will give feedback to correct mistakes. Finally, teachers must prepare and practice how they will respond positively when students meet expectations. The best teachers know that the behaviors that are celebrated are accelerated.

Delivery

Once teachers have their plans in place, it's time to deliver. The best teachers welcome students into the room and immediately engage them in classroom routines. Whether they post routines on the board or describe them verbally, teachers should be very explicit in delivering routines and procedures to the class as a whole and referring to them regularly after that. Excellent teachers invest a lot of time in teaching procedures and routines, and often, they allow students to help create them.

In summarizing Marzano's (2003) recommendations for establishing rules and procedures, the Association for Supervision and Curriculum Development (ASCD) lists involving students as a second step of the process, noting that "effective management includes getting input, feedback, and suggestions from the students" (p. 2). Student involvement in developing procedures helps students gain ownership in and commit to the routines that guide their behavior.

To further encourage student ownership over classroom routines and procedures, and to maximize instructional time, teachers also can empower students to "take initiative in the management of instructional groups and transitions, and/or the handling of materials and supplies" (Danielson, 2013, p. 33). By engaging them in this process, excellent teachers encourage students to go beyond merely understanding expectations by following them automatically with little or no direction. In essence, the most effective form of classroom management gives birth to student leadership, because its goal is not student adherence but student ownership.

Throughout the year, effective teachers take time to teach, practice, and provide feedback on routines and procedures that fall out of automaticity. They understand that it is human nature for students to reject rules that promote order and organization, but they also know that the teacher's first job is not to teach content but to teach and reinforce life skills that help students become productive and engaged members of society.

When excellent teachers notice that they are responding to the same behaviors repeatedly, they recognize that students are acting out of compliance, not commitment. In this case, teachers should stop the lesson and lead students in a conversation about the significance of expectations, how they support the learning goals of the class, and how failing to meet those expectations undermines those goals. Teaching, praising, and reinforcing expectations with consistency is ultimately what makes highly effective teachers most successful in delivering classroom routines and procedures —and in building learning excellence.

Reflection

The best teachers reflect on their students' performance at the end of every lesson and consider elements of the lesson in which student behavior was at its best and where it needs improvement. When student behavior is excellent, teachers can determine which factors created the conditions for this behavior and find ways to incorporate student leadership as a way to ensure that it remains excellent. Teachers also can determine how to replicate these conditions in areas where student behavior is lacking. Excellent teachers reflect on their own efficacy by analyzing how their leadership results in good behavior or in behavior that still needs improvement.

In *The Framework for Teaching Evaluation Instrument*, Danielson (2013) states that a teacher at the highest level, the distinguished level, "makes a thoughtful and accurate assessment of a lesson's effectiveness and the extent to which it achieved its instructional outcomes" (p. 62). If a teacher at this level experiences difficulty with a given group of students, he or she can consider different groupings or consult with a fellow teacher to find a new strategy to better engage the group. ~~Excellent teachers take full responsibility for student behavior, especially when it is failing.~~

Once reflection is complete, excellent teachers can use the information to inform planning and delivering routines and procedures. For positive behaviors, the teacher can develop a plan to release responsibility and leadership over to students. For behaviors that need improvement, he or she can reteach expectations with an emphasis on revamping monitoring for adherence as well as providing both positive and constructive feedback. ~~Reflection is critical but is often overlooked~~ because some might believe it takes too much time. Instead, great teachers view reflection in this way: if you didn't use a mirror to get ready for work, would you look more or less professional when you arrived at your job?

Building an Excellence Support System: Classroom Routines and Procedures

Most schools in the United States develop a student code of conduct. It is important to communicate to teachers, students, and parents how students must behave in order to learn. However, we know that a student code of conduct doesn't guarantee great student behavior in any school. ~~Our ability to collaborate with teachers regarding the most effective way to use a code of conduct to keep the focus on learning plays a major role in guaranteeing great student behavior.~~ Student behaviors offer challenges for all teachers, but those challenges are especially great for those who struggle with classroom management.

In schools of excellence, ~~leaders provide systemwide supports that guarantee every teacher access to ongoing professional development to help them~~ improve in all ~~areas of growth, including classroom routines and procedures.~~ As a second step, ~~teacher teams establish schoolwide norms for behavioral expectations~~ and responses to behavior to offer students a consistent approach to routines and procedures from classroom to classroom. A school's discipline is as strong as its weakest teacher, so as a third step, ~~leaders are prepared to provide teachers who are struggling with an individualized plan for improvement.~~

Step 1: Schoolwide Supports

One of the most critical components for maintaining learning excellence, student behavior, starts with the principal's commitment to providing schoolwide expectations for student behavior that teachers can build on as they prepare and deliver routines and procedures in the classroom. Most principals develop a student code of conduct and a teacher handbook, and these documents generally tell teachers "how we do things around here."

Excellent schools, however, don't leave interpretation of these documents to chance. ~~These schools~~ provide teachers with structure, guidance, and time to align individual expectations and responses for behavior to the schoolwide expectations and responses. Then the success or failure of student behavior lies solely in the consistency of every teacher's ability to set expectations, monitor them, and respond to student behavior without negatively impacting learning.

Collaborative Framework

Principals committed to excellence invest time on the front end of the process of communicating and clarifying schoolwide student conduct rules by soliciting input on rules and procedures from school staff. These principals also work with teachers to develop schoolwide responses to behavior. Once principals and teachers collaboratively develop these procedures and responses, school leaders should spend time at the beginning of the year training staff in those procedures, clarifying how teachers should respond to minor infractions in a consistent manner, and then defining which major infractions warrant immediate referral to the office. The critical part of this communication should be in giving staff members time to discuss procedures with one another, ask questions, and offer ideas for improving cumbersome or ineffective procedures.

Creating the most effective form of systemwide supports for routines and procedures demands the active collaboration of educators throughout the system. To facilitate that collective dialogue, principals and other school leaders must ensure that all teachers answer the following four questions regarding student expectations for appropriate behavior. As noted previously, these questions are based on the four critical questions of a PLC (DuFour et al., 2008, p. 182) and then adapted to reflect student behavior.

1. **What do we want students to know and be able to do?** *becomes* **What are the appropriate learning behaviors that we expect all students to exhibit?** School leaders' main focus for ensuring consistency in behavior expectations is to answer this question. What learning behaviors must staff consistently expect from students, and how will school personnel work interdependently to ensure that students develop and consistently exhibit these behaviors in class every day?

2. **How will we know when students have learned it?** *becomes* **How do we know when students are successfully demonstrating those behaviors?** What do these appropriate behaviors look and sound like? Leaders must be certain that any systemwide supports for establishing and maintaining routines and procedures specifically address metrics for assessing how well students are demonstrating expected behaviors.

3. **How will we respond when students do not learn it?** *becomes* **How will we effectively respond when students fail to demonstrate appropriate behavior?** Establishing routines and procedures requires more than having teachers post their rules on the wall and explaining them at the beginning of the year. Leaders must create systems that guide

and support teachers in aligning their communication of expectations as well as their response when they intercept students who exhibit negative or counterproductive behaviors.

4. **How will we extend learning for students who have learned it?** *becomes* **How will we reinforce and praise students who successfully demonstrate appropriate behavior?** Leaders should view positive behavior supports as the critical component in defining as well as refining schoolwide expectations for student behavior. Whenever excellent schools want to see a specific behavior improve, they complement corrective responses to inappropriate behavior with positive behavior supports that motivate students. By providing positive responses to appropriate behavior, all students see a meaningful incentive for choosing that behavior.

If teachers and school leaders can focus their discussion on these four questions, they can avoid getting lost in meaningless conversations about who is to blame when student behavior becomes an issue.

Systemwide Supports

Principals also must take time at regular intervals throughout the year to ensure that expectations and responses remain consistent, and these four questions also provide a framework for that step in the process. By providing the staff with data that highlight disciplinary successes and problems, principals and other leaders can guide collaborative discussions around the four questions for monitoring behavior. Most important, leaders must provide teachers time to provide input and feedback on overall campus effectiveness and work together to make adjustments accordingly.

Schoolwide supports for positive student behavior offer teachers a model for recognizing and rewarding appropriate learning behaviors in their classrooms. Examples of schoolwide incentives can include, for example, privileges, assemblies, and special events that reward students for meeting campus goals for individual behavior. These incentives provide teachers with tangible goals that they can tether to their own personal classroom systems, which, again, contribute to consistency in classroom expectations, management, and response for students.

To ensure that consistency continues throughout the school year, leaders must guide teachers in identifying problematic behaviors and developing a plan to respond in a unified fashion to that behavior. As part of their systemwide support for routines and procedures, therefore, leaders can ask teachers to review the following four questions to identify and refine their responses to behavior issues through the use of both positive reinforcements and corrective responses.

1. What is the top behavioral infraction?

2. What are the reasons for the high frequency of the infraction?

3. What is our plan to respond to this inappropriate behavior?

4. What is our plan to reinforce appropriate behavior?

Finally, leaders must work to achieve alignment in teacher commitment to school-wide expectations and the systemic responses to behavior. When teacher commitment is established before students begin the school year, schools stand a greater chance of beginning the year with consistency. Once consistency is established, principals save precious time that would otherwise be devoted to responding to excessive behavioral infractions. With a system that monitors and adjusts to behavior, instructional time is saved and, in many cases, increased.

The essence of a schoolwide excellence system for routines and procedures is to continuously develop consistency from classroom to classroom, while at the same time creating automaticity in the campus response to student behavior. A leader's role is to continuously advocate for students by creating a learning environment that is safe and secure. The best learning environment for students is one that is stable, consistent, and—most important—predictable. When principals create a culture that results in this kind of learning environment, schools can move one step closer to learning for all.

Step 2: Teacher Team Supports

Schoolwide rules are critical for student success, but they are best supported when grade-level or department-level teams personalize their adherence to and enforcement of rules and procedures. It is essential for teams to take time throughout the year to review and refine how schoolwide expectations should look and sound within their teams. The best teams take time to create norms for how they will work together, as well as norms for what they expect from students inside and outside of the classroom. Additionally, teacher teams that build excellence establish norms for their collective response to students who violate a classroom or school rule.

Team Responses to Student Behavior

For positive behavior supports, teams work together to create team-specific positive behavior supports and incentives that motivate students to make smart choices in their behavior and learning. High-performing teams ensure that every member responds the same way when students commit minor infractions, regardless of which teacher is responding or which student is exhibiting the behavior. In other words, high-performing teams take ownership for the success of all students, and behavior is a big part of that success.

Creating norms for behavioral responses is important for two reasons. First, new teachers or teachers who struggle with classroom management benefit from the expertise of others, as team norms for behavioral responses show commitment to schoolwide rules. Second, students rarely interact with just one teacher, especially at the secondary level; instead, they typically encounter several teachers. If they know that all teachers are on the same page with disciplinary expectations and behavioral responses, students are more inclined to respond positively, regardless of which teacher is addressing them.

Figure 3.2 illustrates how teams might establish norms for behavioral expectations, corrective responses, and positive reinforcements. Leaders must encourage teacher teams to be specific in designing and using these models, because specific expectations help more students succeed and guide teachers to respond more appropriately.

What do we expect from all students?	What does that look like and sound like?	How do we respond when students fail to meet our expectations?	How do we respond when students meet our expectations?
All students follow expectations for hallway behavior.			
All students enter the class prepared to learn.			
All students are engaged in learning tasks.			
All students respect the teacher and classmates.			
All students seek help from a teacher when they experience difficulty.			

Figure 3.2: Team norms for student behavior.

Visit **go.SolutionTree.com/leadership** *for a free reproducible version of this figure.*

The best teams unite students around team goals for behavior. They understand that most students have a "What's in it for me?" mentality, especially if they are apathetic to school rules. To address this issue, teacher teams can set goals for behavior, such as competitions among classrooms for the best behavior or a team reward, such as a kickball tournament or popcorn party, that the entire team can earn and enjoy together.

Room for Flexibility

Even as teacher teams align their expectations for classroom behavior with schoolwide expectations, they also must ensure that their efforts do not take away flexibility or autonomy from individual teachers. Table 3.1 illustrates some of the routine behaviors and learning procedures that students would experience in most classrooms. When teachers can create commonalities in these procedures, students stand a greater chance of following them. Those commonalities, however, don't have to represent exact duplications of procedures. Teacher teams must support their members in aligning common procedures and, at the same time, promote each teacher's individual teaching style, student population, and coursework.

Table 3.1: Universal Routines and Procedures for Every Classroom

Routine Behaviors	Learning Procedures
Entering the room	Whole-group instruction
Leaving the room	Small-group instruction
Transitioning in the room	Independent work
Requesting permission to use the restroom	Technology usage
Accessing classroom resources independently	Partner work
Responding when visitors enter the room	Testing

To guide teacher teams in aligning their basic expectations for these common routines and procedures while allowing for flexibility, leaders should ask teams to turn, once again, to an adaptation of the four critical PLC questions (DuFour et al., 2010). For individual teachers and classrooms, these questions allow for customization.

1. What do we expect all students to do in following each of these routines and procedures?

2. How will we know if they are exhibiting the behaviors correctly and independently?

3. How will we respond when students are not meeting expectations without negatively impacting the learning of all students?

4. How will we reinforce and empower students who are meeting our expectations?

When teachers can agree on their basic expectations and responses to behavior, they level the playing field for all students. Having this conversation is critical for teachers who share students as well as teachers in secondary schools. Students have to adjust to a new teacher and their procedures each time they change classes, and when teachers can lessen that adjustment, they have more time to invest in teaching students as opposed to responding to student behavior. Finally, aligning expectations from class to class helps struggling teachers develop their skill set in effectively providing classroom routines and procedures.

Step 3: Individualized Supports

If schoolwide rules are in place and teacher teams have developed norms for student behavior and teacher responses, we can expect most teachers to be able to use those supports to reach excellence when it comes to classroom management. Traditional leaders often lean on evaluation tools as the first response to poor classroom management. But simply pointing out a teacher's shortcomings doesn't represent true support for the teacher's improvement. This style of leadership typically results in compliance first and conceptual understanding second. Instead, to create and implement a successful individualized support plan, leaders must follow the identification of specific problems within a teacher's approach to routines and procedures with some specific, individualized guidance and support.

Problem Simplification Plan

In an excellent school, leaders look to interventions first. They understand that in most cases, teachers are giving their best but need more personalized support in how to deliver expectations and hold students accountable. Before giving personalized support, school leaders must isolate the precipitating factor that causes classroom management problems. Figure 3.3 (page 62) illustrates a series of questions leaders can use to help teachers identify these issues. The answers to these questions can help leaders and teachers isolate classroom management problems and then develop a personalized plan for addressing them.

Excellence Plan

After the struggling teacher isolates the problem, the teacher and school leader can work together to set a goal to solve the problem and then develop a plan to reach the goal quickly. Working together is important in maximizing the success of this individualized support process. The leader has the expertise necessary for solving the problem, but the struggling teacher knows how he or she can best use that expertise to improve student performance. To make growth a positive and sustaining reality, the plan should focus on both the planning and delivery of expectations for routines and procedures. The chart in figure 3.4 (pages 63–64) can help teachers and leaders create a plan for improvement.

Problem Simplification Plan: Classroom Routines and Procedures
1. What is the predominant problem affecting classroom routines and procedures?
2. When are these problems most prevalent? Circle all that apply: Beginning of class   Small group Middle of class   Partner work End of class   Independent work Whole group Notes:
3. Which students repeatedly demonstrate inappropriate behaviors?
4. Define your current expectations for the top behavior issue.
5. Define your responses when students meet your expectations.
6. Define your responses when students fail to meet your expectations.

Figure 3.3: Problem simplification plan—classroom routines and procedures.

Visit **go.SolutionTree.com/leadership** *for a free reproducible version of this figure.*

Excellence Plan for Classroom Routines and Procedures
1. What is the goal for improving classroom routines and procedures? (Identify the top two problems for improvement.)
2. How will we know if the goal has been attained? (Indicate independent student behaviors that indicate that the goal has been reached.)

3. Which actions should the teacher take to be better prepared for addressing the target behaviors?
 	
☐ Observing these teachers _____
 	
☐ Planning for behavior with _____
 	
☐ Meeting with team about norms
 	
☐ Using outside resources
 	
    Book study: _____
 	
    Twitter chat: _____
 	
    Blog: _____
 	
    Other: _____

4. What routines or procedures will the teacher develop to address this area of need?
5. What actions will the teacher employ to better deliver expectations and responses for behavior? (Describe all that apply.) ☐ Setting expectations ☐ Modeling expectations ☐ Using positive responses ☐ Using corrective responses

Figure 3.4: Excellence plan for classroom routines and procedures.   continued →

6. What data will we use to gauge improvement?

☐ Reduced interruptions

☐ Number of students completing tasks

☐ Reduced number of teacher corrections

☐ Increased number of positive responses

☐ Performance on common assessments

☐ End of grading period grades

☐ Walkthrough data

☐ Mentor or coach observation feedback

☐ Other: _____

Visit **go.SolutionTree.com/leadership** *for a free reproducible version of this figure.*

Struggling with student behavior is an embarrassing issue for teachers because controlling students is considered by many to be the easiest expectation for a teacher to meet. While the supports outlined here can help any teacher achieve real improvement in his or her approach to classroom management, leaders, teachers, and coaches must acknowledge that mastering routines and procedures requires a great deal of experience. Teachers can best gain the experience necessary for this mastery by working with experts who have ideas and successful experiences to share. While helping struggling teachers overcome problems with establishing and maintaining effective routines and procedures can be a long and demanding process, it is essential to establishing an environment conducive to student learning and success.

Conclusion

This chapter reviewed the essential role of consistent, effective routines and procedures for ensuring the instructional excellence of teachers and the learning excellence of students. Just as Maslow (1943) considered safety and security to be the second most fundamental human need, teachers must provide students with a safe and secure environment if they want them to participate fully in learning. Routines and procedures are the key to providing that safe and predictable learning environment. Ineffective classroom management can diminish every other aspect of the classroom experience. A teacher's ability to plan for and deliver expectations for student behaviors and learning routines, therefore, determines whether that teacher's progress in other areas of professional growth will rest on a foundation that is as solid as a rock or as instable as sand.

Leaders most effectively fulfill their responsibility for promoting teacher effectiveness in routines and procedures by clarifying expectations and then creating a system of supports that guarantees a systemwide and consistent response structure. Teacher teams must develop plans that support this consistency, while allowing for the flexibility necessary to address individual teaching styles, student groups, and the nature of the class subject or course topic. That flexibility enables teachers to personalize and align routines and procedures within that structure and leverage their strengths to meet the needs of all students. Excellent schools serve as a support system for routines and procedures in a way that helps teachers find their own successful method for creating the conditions that promote learning for all students.

Routines and procedures aren't meant to limit or stifle students' independence. Instead, they are meant to give students a strong and reasonable framework for their learning processes, the freedom of self-direction, the ability to spend more time focused on learning, and the opportunity to play an active role in their learning experience. In effect, students empowered by a strong command of classroom management routines become yet another resource for driving learning success. As student and educational blogger Adora Svitak (2012) observes, "By empowering students, you can engage them further in learning, provide a more democratic learning experience and, of course, find the most powerful resource in your classroom: us." As leaders, it's our job to make sure that teachers have the support and guidance necessary to make the empowerment possible.

Education leaders can use the following reflection tool (pages 66–67) to gauge their own understanding of the challenges teachers must overcome in developing skills for designing and implementing effective classroom routines and procedures, the strength of their current supports for that professional development, and potential avenues for strengthening those supports.

Reflection Tool: Classroom Routines and Procedures

Definition of Excellence for Classroom Routines and Procedures

What is our school's definition of teacher excellence in the area of classroom routines and procedures?

Schoolwide Supports

1. How well do we clearly define our expectations for schoolwide behaviors?

2. How well do we communicate the expectations to all teachers, students, and parents?

3. What is our systemwide professional learning plan for both experienced and new teachers?

4. What positive behavior supports do we use to promote appropriate behavior?

5. How effective is our system at responding to and correcting inappropriate behavior in a consistent manner?

6. What data do we collect to identify the most problematic inappropriate behaviors, and how frequently do we gather and respond to those data?

A Leader's Guide to Excellence in Every Classroom © 2017 Solution Tree Press • SolutionTree.com
Visit **go.SolutionTree.com/leadership** to download this free reproducible.

Teacher Team Supports

1. How do our teacher teams work to define and align their expectations for routine behaviors and learning procedures across their classrooms?

2. How consistent across teams is the definition of *student success* in classroom routines and procedures (in effect, when students exhibit these behaviors correctly and independently)?

3. How well do teams align their responses to students who fail to exhibit appropriate behaviors?

4. How well do our teams align their reinforcement of appropriate behaviors?

5. When teams experience difficulty with behaviors or inconsistency in their expectations or reinforcement of behaviors, what steps do they take to work together to address the issue quickly?

Individualized Supports

1. Before we help a teacher with difficulty in routines and procedures, what steps do we take to evaluate the systemwide supports and teacher team supports and their effectiveness at helping him or her? *(If schoolwide or teacher team supports are not in place, they are addressed as needed.)*

2. What data do we collect that confirm that the teacher has difficulty with routines and procedures?

3. Before we help the teacher, what steps do we take to isolate the teacher's area of greatest difficulty in classroom routines and procedures?

4. When we prescribe a personalized plan of supports, how well do we prescribe interventions from a wide variety of options, including observing, coaching, planning with another teacher, collaborating with the teacher team, and using outside resources?

5. Once we prescribe a plan of supports, what steps do we take to set a goal that defines the desired improvement, a date by which that improvement will be made, and a date by which we will follow up to ensure that improvement has been made?

A Leader's Guide to Excellence in Every Classroom © 2017 Solution Tree Press • SolutionTree.com

Visit **go.SolutionTree.com/leadership** to download this free reproducible.

CHAPTER 4

Leading for Excellence: Relationships for Learning

In the end it is going to be the basis of the relationship that allows the student to be vulnerable enough 2 engage in learning.

—Ben Johnson

A strong command of available resources for learning and an effectively managed system of classroom routines and procedures provide teachers and students with a sound structure for learning. In order to develop a culture that promotes active and engaged learning experiences, however, teachers must develop meaningful relationships with students. Without those kinds of relationships, students can feel disconnected from learning experiences.

This chapter explores the role of teacher-student relationships in promoting learning excellence; techniques, approaches, and tools teachers use to establish and maintain meaningful relationships with their students; and the many ways we can support teachers as they pursue this goal.

Maslow (1943) placed love and belongingness as the third level within his Hierarchy of Needs. When educators and staff throughout the school system establish strong working relationships with students, they demonstrate that they care for those students and consider them to be integral to the school community. As Mark Boynton and Christine Boynton (2005) write in *The Educator's Guide to Preventing and Solving Discipline Problems*, the role of student relationships has been the subject of much research: "And according to Zehm and Kottler (1993), students will never trust us or open themselves up to hear what we have to say unless they sense that we value and respect them" (p. 7). To inspire students to learn at high levels, we must be certain that teachers and other staff throughout the school system understand the critical nature of student relationships and are well prepared to develop and strengthen those relationships over time. This chapter will examine how teachers can form and manage those relationships to improve classroom discipline and learning outcomes.

Leaders, in turn, also must be certain that we are providing well-developed and integrated systems to support teachers *and* their students in developing meaningful relationships and using the strength of those relationships to overcome and avoid barriers to the learning process. This chapter also offers ideas for systemwide, teacher team, and individualized supports that leaders can institute in order to promote the highest levels of learning for all students.

We begin with the story of one teacher's experience to understand why his students fail to respond to him and his class content. The story also reveals the power of support, as a leader's guidance helps this teacher depersonalize his students' negative behavior so he can calmly consider concrete, positive measures to remediate his problems in classroom discipline by strengthening his student relationships.

Getting to the Heart of Student Behavior

Jack had a great first week of school. He developed a great understanding of his resources and put them to good use. He established his classroom routines and procedures, and the students responded as expected. All in all, he felt like he and his class were off to a great start.

As the second week began, however, Jack sensed a change in the classroom. Jack set expectations, but a few students failed to follow them. He responded to misbehavior exactly as his classroom management plan directed, but the problems continued to surface. Not only were more students ignoring him, some began verbally expressing their dislike for him and his class. Indignant to their blatant disrespect, Jack completed referral after referral and sent students to the office. He was certain his automatic response to their behavior would eventually teach them to respect him.

By the third week of school, Jack's classroom was spiraling out of control, and he complained to his neighboring teacher, Mr. Soto. "I can't teach this class. They are completely out of control, and they have no respect for me or their learning. They ignore my expectations, and when I threaten to send them to the office, they tell me to go ahead and send them. They obviously have no fear of getting in trouble."

Mr. Soto paused for a minute and pondered Jack's situation. "So, are you saying that every student is a discipline problem?"

Jack replied, "Well, no, but there are too many to count."

Mr. Soto asked, "Have these problems been occurring every day since school started?"

Jack pondered. "No, actually, the first week was great. They all did what I asked them to do, but then they slowly started to ignore me. Now no one's paying attention to me."

"Okay, so what do you know about the students?" questioned Mr. Soto.

Jack replied, confused, "What do you mean?"

"What do you know about your students besides their names and their faults?"

Jack had no response.

"Well, that sounds like where you need to begin," Mr. Soto responded. "If you don't know anything about your students, you can't build relationships with them. And without relationships, there's little chance that they will want to know anything about you or your content. If you want your students to learn more about the content you're teaching, you have to learn as much as you can about them. Does this make any sense?"

Jack nodded. "I think I get it. They don't behave because they don't know me or trust me."

Mr. Soto smiled. "Right! But you can fix this problem, and I'll be glad to help you every step of the way."

Jack isn't the only new or struggling teacher to treat relationships with students as an afterthought. After all, it's easy to overlook the many ways that student relationships shape learning experiences and outcomes. That's why an experienced outsider's questions and observations, such as those of Mr. Soto, can be so important in helping struggling teachers understand just how critical student relationships are to the entire classroom experience. When educators connect with their students on a human level, they are strengthening their students' connection to the entire learning process.

As we see in this story, however, sometimes educators allow their focus on instruction and classroom procedures to overshadow the *people* they are teaching and the utterly human need those people have for feeling valuable and recognized. That's why it's essential that all of us within the school system actively recognize the importance of relationships with learners and that we work together to find the most effective methods for acknowledging and supporting our teachers in building those relationships.

Building Relationships for Learning

Many teachers consider building relationships with students as a very important part of learning, but excellent teachers make building student relationships their first priority. It doesn't matter how well versed teachers are in their class content if they don't know their audience—students. As Danielson (2013) notes, "Teachers must know not only their content and its related pedagogy but also the students to whom they wish to teach that content" (p. 9).

Relationships for learning occupy the third level of the Hierarchy of Instructional Excellence, shown in figure 4.1, because teachers need to learn how to develop strong relationships with students before they can move on to build skills in promoting student engagement, rigor and mastery, and other higher levels of professional growth and development. Further, weak relationships with students can actually erode a teacher's effectiveness in preserving excellent classroom routines and procedures. Marzano (2003) views relationships as the glue that holds classroom routines and procedures together. "Without the foundation of a good [student] relationship, students commonly resist rules and procedures along with the consequent disciplinary actions" (Marzano, 2003, p. 41).

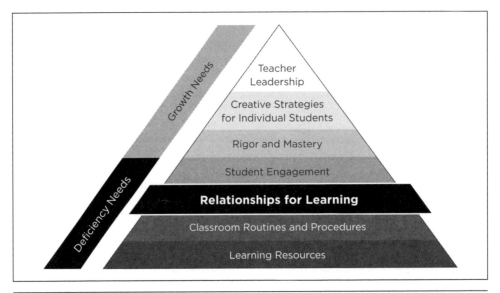

Figure 4.1: Hierarchy of Instructional Excellence—relationships for learning.

Preparation

The best time for teachers to begin getting to know their students is the minute they know which students are assigned to their class. The greatest teachers understand the nature of student learning, and before students even enter the classroom, they make plans to begin the task of establishing the optimal relationship with each student.

Marzano (2003) references the work of Theo Wubbels and Jack Levy when discussing the importance of building the optimal teacher-student relationship. Wubbels and Levy (1993) and Wubbels, Brekelmans, van Tartwijk, and Admiraal (1999) identify two dimensions that define the relationship between teacher and student. One dimension is dominance versus submission; the other is cooperation versus opposition. To ensure a teacher finds the perfect balance, Danielson (2013) claims that the excellent teacher "systematically acquires knowledge from several sources about individual students' varied approaches to learning, knowledge, and skills, special needs, and interests and cultural heritages" (p. 11). This information serves as the starting point for deciding how to personally connect to the student's heart before engaging his or her brain.

Discovering the right balance of dominance and cooperation can mostly be found by examining the students' background. In that process, excellent teachers analyze prior academic performance, consult with last year's teachers, and review documents in cumulative folders. Using the information they gather as starting points for building relationships, teachers can select the best instructional methods, routines, and procedures to provide high levels of cooperation. In other words, the teacher skillfully combines relationship building with classroom routines and procedures and learning resources to make students feel comfortable and welcome in their learning space.

Teachers must be attentive to students' academic needs as well as show concern for their individual needs. The most effective teachers, therefore, use their students' information to set attainable goals. While it's true that setting challenging goals is an attribute of dominance, excellent teachers understand that they must avoid the opposite of dominance—submission. To find the right level of dominance, teachers can leverage the organization of classroom routines and procedures to guide students in a structured manner to comfortably engage and interact with one another in the learning environment.

Figure 4.2 illustrates how the balance between dominance and cooperation yields the optimal teacher-student relationship. Marzano (2003) writes, "It is the right combination of moderate to high dominance . . . . and moderate to high cooperation . . . . that provides the optimal teacher-student relationship for learning" (p. 43).

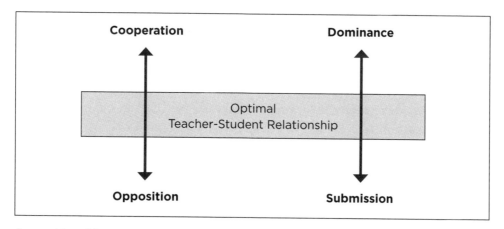

Source: Adapted from Marzano, 2003, p. 43.

Figure 4.2: Finding the optimal teacher-student relationship.

Knowing students and planning to make them feel welcomed and appreciated is the first step in building relationships. But balancing dominance and cooperation alone won't set the stage for learning. It also takes the perfect balance of culture and structure to make a classroom exceptional.

Delivery

If preparing for relationships is about planning to know our students, then building relationships is the execution of that plan. Excellent teachers create unique and innovative ways to build relationships with students as soon as they enter the classroom, and they form strong lines of communication to maintain those relationships. The most powerful tools a teacher has to form a meaningful relationship with each student are communication, consistency, and compassion.

Communication is composed of three elements: (1) words, (2) tone, and (3) nonverbal cues. Of these three elements, words may have the least impact on effective communication. When all these components are combined effectively, students receive messages that are clear and coherent and help move them forward.

It is important to note that teachers must choose words carefully in order to clearly and concisely express their meaning. But even if the words are clear, if the tone conveys extreme dominance or submissiveness, students may shut down or tune out. If negative facial expressions or other nonverbal cues signal submissiveness or indifference, students might ignore the teacher.

Excellent teachers communicate with a positive tone and open, nonverbal cues. A timid volume or shy posture sends the message that the teacher cannot back up his or her expectations if students choose to challenge them. At the same time, demonstrations of frustration and sarcasm can get in the way of the message teachers are trying to convey. As Nina Sears (n.d.) writes, if teachers resort to sarcastic jokes or cutting comments when disciplining students, "everyone is uncomfortable. Educators can create an environment where students feel comfortable learning and the teacher maintains order without using such language, simply by being mindful of the choice of words used."

In short, it's not what you say; it's how you say it. A teacher's posture, eye contact with students, positive tone, and well-conveyed level of interest in the content he or she is teaching can either stimulate or stifle students' desire to reciprocate a relationship for learning with the teacher. When students engage in off-task behavior, the way educators communicate with them about the behavior can encourage—or discourage—students from re-engaging in the learning task. Demeaning students in front of their peers is never a good way to guide them back to desired behaviors. Instead, effective teachers remind students of the learning goals and focus on the desired behaviors rather than on the student who is failing to exhibit them.

Another factor that shapes relationships between teachers and students is the consistency teachers demonstrate in their interactions with students. Students find it very hard to connect with teachers who are unpredictable in their routines or how they communicate. Students distance themselves from a teacher who is overly demanding one day and extremely cooperative the next. To ensure consistency, "an essential skill of teaching is that of managing relationships with students and ensuring that relationships among students are positive and supportive" (Danielson, 2013, p. 25).

Further, when teachers consistently model positive communication and respect, they can encourage their students to emulate those same behaviors with the teacher and one another. Students are usually more willing to take reasonable risks in their learning efforts when they expect to be treated with openness and respect by their teachers and peers. Finally, the teacher's responsibility for consistency extends to his or her messages and actions designed to shape both student behavior *and* learning. If the teacher is inconsistent in redirecting off-task behavior, for example, students might reciprocate by being inconsistent in choosing on-task behavior.

3. *Compassion* is the third component excellent teachers display as they build relationships with students. By understanding students' backgrounds and histories and communicating with them in a consistently respectful, supportive way about issues beyond course content, teachers demonstrate a genuine interest in students' personal lives. When students are experiencing difficulty or setbacks in any area of life, excellent teachers show real empathy by listening and offering support. By showing compassion for students, teachers send the message that they aren't there just to drive learning but to offer students guidance in the difficult processes of their social and emotional development.

Because it forges a strong personal connection with students, a teacher's compassion can have significant leverage on learning. Especially when working with students who suffer from negative or traumatic events in their personal lives, compassion can be a teacher's strongest tool for convincing those students to stay committed to learning. These students "don't need another adult to tell them what is wrong with them. . . . [They need] an adult who treats them with simple sustained kindness, an adult who can empathize with the challenges they face" (Wolpow, Johnson, Hertel, & Kincaid, 2009, p. 72). A compassionate student-teacher bond can convince students to work and learn even when they don't want to. They may not always want to engage in a given task, but they always want to please a teacher who cares for them as people first and as students second.

Building relationships is the biggest investment a teacher can make in a student's learning, and in a classroom of excellence, successfully building relationships is not the goal but the constant. Teachers initiate relationships at the beginning of the year and continue to build on them through daily interactions focused on moving students forward. When teachers are able to reach the optimal teacher-student relationship, they are positioning students to accelerate their learning and achieve success.

The key to building relationships is to work on them every day. Teachers develop a compassionate relationship with their students one day at a time, one interaction at a time, and one word at a time. Just as we can't keep any relationship strong through neglect, we can never take for granted that student-teacher relationships will survive and thrive without careful attention and focused effort.

Reflection

Every teacher reflects on his or her performance, but the excellent teacher goes deeper by reflecting on his or her relationship with students. These teachers analyze their interactions and outcomes with students to determine when they may have been too submissive or overly demanding, or where they have been lacking in discipline for specific students. This reflection enables teachers to gauge the quality of their relationships with students as well as relationships among students.

Beyond assessing their effectiveness, excellent teachers can use reflection to determine how they will respond to students who fail to meet expectations for learning. By pinpointing causal factors for student resistance, teachers can determine if they need to be more or less dominant, more or less cooperative, or a combination of the two. From there, teachers make a plan to adapt to the needs of students without lowering their expectations for learning.

Lastly, excellent teachers build strong relationships with students by building strong relationships with families. As part of their reflection, therefore, teachers should assess how effective they have been in forging those relationships, how their understanding of students' family dynamics is informing their approach to working with students, and where they may need to become more familiar with student family backgrounds. This kind of reflection can produce a variety of ideas for improving learning relationships. Knowing that parents and guardians have the greatest influence on their children, excellent teachers take time to call families with good news or email them with important information about their child's future or prior learning. By being proactive with family communication and relationship building, teachers can build even stronger ties with students.

Building an Excellence Support System: Relationships for Learning

In the opening pages of this book, I stated that every school's mission must be to guarantee learning for all. For educators and other school personnel to succeed in achieving that mission, they must be equipped with the tools and skills necessary to build meaningful relationships with every student. These relationships are about much more than making students feel welcome in the school. They also must inspire students to learn at high levels in every classroom with every teacher.

As with other levels of professional growth and development in the Hierarchy of Instructional Excellence, leaders can build an Excellence Support System to help teachers build strong relationships for learning with students. Schoolwide systems are the first step, offering broad plans, processes, and other tools that guide teachers in building relationships with students. Teacher teams offer the next step by collectively offering plans, insights, and guidance that can help struggling teachers find ways to connect with their students on a more meaningful level. Finally, if teachers need additional help, leaders can offer individualized advice and assistance to build strong relationships with individual students or the class as a whole.

Step 1: Schoolwide Supports

There are many ways that schools can support teachers in building relationships with students. The most comprehensive of these is to provide staff with a campus behavior management plan that incorporates positive behavior supports and student leadership strategies, which teachers can use to reinforce appropriate behavior. Capitalizing on good behavior helps teachers build stronger relationships with students. From campus incentives to privileges for those who excel in behavior and learning, the plan supplies all teachers with a common system for recognizing, praising, and reinforcing student efforts. These structures and supports help teachers build relationships with students and, therefore, have the potential to fuel exponential growth in learning success. The following sections outline some of the specific methods leaders can use to support teachers as they build powerful relationships with students.

Counselor Leadership

Counselors are often underused for school leadership purposes, and when it comes to building relationships with students, counselors often offer an untapped resource for expertise and leadership potential. Schools of excellence capitalize on counselors' knowledge and skills by having them design systems and provide professional development on positive behavior supports that incorporate a relationship-building component. Behavior programs, such as CHAMPS, Love and Logic (www .loveandlogic.com), and Conscious Discipline (https://consciousdiscipline.com), include strategies for building relationships with students, and counselors can be a powerful resource for showing staff members ways to effectively integrate these programs into their classrooms.

Student History Files

Schools of excellence guarantee that teachers have as much information as possible about their students so they can make a plan to establish the strongest relationship possible. All schools have a system for archiving and transitioning required information about students from grade to grade, but schools of excellence ensure that all teachers access this information when they are assigned new students. These systems guide teachers to discover if their students have a history of failure, lack of parental support, persistent behavior issues, medical issues, or any other problems that could potentially inhibit the motivation to learn. To gain the most from student history reviews, schools also must establish a system for students' former and current teachers to collaborate in order to create a plan to ensure that all teachers start school on the right foot with each student.

Transition Sheets

So much work goes into helping students succeed, but how much of that work actually helps students transition successfully to the next year? If schools fail to make sure that teachers pass along critical information about student behavior management and other issues they have observed and addressed in previous work with students, then next year's teachers start the year off with a blank slate. That means they must waste time experimenting with strategies and tactics in order to find what does or doesn't work to help individual students succeed. Schools of excellence don't just create student supports; they curate them and pass them on through the systematic use of transition sheets.

To create transition sheets, teachers record important information about individual students that the next teacher needs to know, including behavior and instructional strategies they have tried, the success of those strategies, student strengths, and more. Teachers also use the transition sheets to record difficulties students have experienced, but always in conjunction with the student's abilities.

In addition to providing quantifiable performance data, transition sheets give teachers a springboard for advancing student success throughout the coming year, rather than running the risk of repeating approaches and techniques that have failed in the past. Having this information can help teachers understand students as individuals and share strategies to help improve their learning experiences and outcomes as they move through the following year.

Relationship-Building Plan

Schools of excellence don't leave anything to chance when it comes to relationships, so they provide staff professional development. Following professional development, they create a plan to take action based on their newfound knowledge. Knowing that not everybody is skilled at the art of building relationships with students, campus leadership teams should design schoolwide plans for all staff. It's the little things that make the biggest impact. Here is a short list of strategies that schools of excellence encourage teachers to use in order to build meaningful relationships with students.

- Stand outside your door to personally greet every student as he or she comes to class each day.

- Send a personalized postcard to each student two to three times per year.

- Make a positive phone call to students' families in the first three to six weeks of school.

- Send a student to the office with a positive referral for exhibiting excellent behavior.

- Provide students with a cool-off place in the classroom or hallway if they are frustrated or angry.

- Establish a nonverbal communication system for students to communicate to the teacher without fear of being noticed or embarrassed.

- In collaboration with colleagues, determine how to address difficult students without escalating behavior.

Schools of excellence don't require teachers to build relationships in the same way. They do, however, provide teachers with a variety of tools within a unified system that offers a shared pathway toward stronger, more meaningful learning relationships. With schoolwide systems in place, teachers can determine how to use professional development and information about students to create a plan of action to form the optimal teacher-student relationship with every student.

Step 2: Teacher Team Supports

Through teacher teams, leaders give teachers opportunities to collaborate in a multitude of ways to build relationships with students. To build powerful relationships with challenging students, for example, teachers can collaborate with a preventive mindset. In such a collaboration, teachers in two consecutive grade levels might sit down and discuss specific tactics for students with difficulties from the previous year, which actions were most effective in improving their behavior, and whether those actions should continue in the following year. They can discuss how they used interventions and strategies to strengthen relationships with students and their families so students' current teachers can continue those same interventions.

When teachers collaborate in teacher teams, they can answer the following questions.

- What strengths does the student have?

- What difficulties did he or she have last year?

- What kind of teacher communication helps this student move forward, and what kind of communication shuts him or her down?

- What are the most critical areas in which you must provide consistency to help the student engage in the learning environment?

- What does the student need from you to help him or her build positive relationships with other students in the classroom?

- What personal, non-school-related characteristics about the student can you use to begin to build a positive relationship?

In essence, teacher team collaboration can help ensure that teachers are one step ahead of students who had difficulty during the previous year and leverage effective strategies from that year to help students improve in the coming year.

Collaboration Among Teachers Who Share Content, Not Students

From an instructional standpoint, teacher teams can enable teachers who share content instead of students to come together and decide how to use instructional activities to build relationships with students, especially those who are reluctant to participate in the learning process. For students who finish learning tasks early, teachers can collaborate on the best use of student tasks requiring varying degrees of ability. They also can collaborate about how they can help withdrawn students connect with classmates. These teachers also can share valuable ideas about how they communicate with students about their current levels of mastery and how they encourage them to be aware of and improve their performance.

Questions to help teachers who share content might include the following.

- In what ways can we generate excitement about the learning we present to students?

- In what ways can we engage reluctant students when they appear apprehensive about the learning task?

- How can we challenge students to work hard in learning our content?

- What does consistency look like? What actions should we take to be consistent in our expectations as well as in holding students accountable for meeting them?

- When students are struggling behaviorally, socially, emotionally, or academically, how can we respond with compassion and empathy?

When teachers who share content collaborate on connecting with students first, the content takes care of itself. The mindset of *students first* helps teachers—especially those with poor relationship-building skills—develop a useful plan to intercept potential problems in advance.

Communication With Families

Finally, teacher teams can collaborate about unique ways to communicate with students' families and the community. Some interdisciplinary teams that share students might commit to attending students' sporting events. Many teacher teams promote positive student relationships by arranging to conduct home visits with the *divide and conquer approach*. In this approach, teachers conduct home visits with students in their homeroom class and then communicate information to all other teachers who have these students in their classes. Teacher teams may also commit to tried-and-true methods of communication, such as phone calls, emails, and take-home papers.

Teacher teams also are unleashing the power of social media and technology to build strong relationships with students and their families. By using blogs, class Facebook and Twitter accounts, Remind101, Google Classroom, and Google Docs, teachers are making their classrooms more transparent to families. Teachers may write their lesson plans on blogs and post them for virtually anyone to see at any time of day, or they may choose to limit access by using a password or controlling the sharing features so that only parents and students can see the lessons. They also can post pictures and videos to show families the products of student learning.

Some teachers might even flip their instruction for students and their families. As I described in chapter 2 (see Flipped Video Training, page 34), *flipped instruction* is a teaching strategy in which teachers post lectures online for students to watch before they come to class, where they then can practice the work associated with the lecture with the support of the teacher and student groups. While flipped videos are powerful tools for helping students learn, they also can facilitate strong relationships with families. By sharing in their children's learning experiences, families not only know what is going on in the classroom, but they also have a resource to help their children successfully learn the concept.

Questions to guide teachers in connecting with families include the following.

- How do we initially communicate with every student's family, and what communication tools can we use to engage in this communication on a regular basis?

- What kind of information do we communicate to every family at the beginning of the year, as well as throughout the year?

- How frequently and in what ways do we communicate the following information to families?

  - Overall academic performance

  - When a student fails a given task

  - Overall behavior

  - When a student commits a minor infraction

  - Upcoming events

- How do we communicate to families instructions for accessing our lesson plans and other academic information?

- What is our plan to use flipped instruction to help enlist family members to help their children learn at home?

- Which social media or digital communication tools will we use to convey what our classes are learning?

These family-centric strategies are in keeping with the overall goal of teacher team supports. If teams can help their members align in building strong relationships with students, they can move their schools one step closer to excellence. Students and their families benefit from open and transparent relationships with teachers. At the same time, when teachers develop a common plan for how they will build relationships with students and families, they actually strengthen their instruction. A National

Education Association (2011) policy brief supports this idea in its statement, "Parent, family, and community involvement in education correlates with higher academic performance and school improvement." The reason for this correlation is simple. Just as students learn best in an environment in which they feel valued, families can be more willing to assist in the education process when they know that educators value their children *and* their support in helping those children learn.

Step 3: Individualized Supports

When schoolwide and team-level supports aren't enough support for an individual teacher's professional development, those teachers should seek help and feel comfortable doing so. Using the questions from the teacher team supports (page 79), principals, counselors, and teacher leaders can work with struggling teachers to isolate issues preventing them from forming optimal learning relationships with their students and then determine the best path for improvement.

Counseling, Observation, and Feedback

There are several ways that teachers who struggle in building relationships with students can seek individualized support, depending on whether the inability to build relationships is due to inadequate preparation or a lack of skills necessary for getting to know students. Teachers can work with school counselors in a one-on-one setting to address these problems. In this work, the counselor can help the teacher understand the student's background information or help the teacher develop relationship-building skills with all students. By possessing a working knowledge of the psychological aspects of students and their learning environment, counselors have a wealth of information that can help struggling teachers develop meaningful relationships with their students.

If a teacher is struggling with a particular group of students, and he or she knows that a fellow teacher does not experience difficulty with this group, the teacher can meet with his or her peer to gain more effective strategies for relationship building. The struggling teacher can go a step further and observe his or her peer working with these students. By watching a successful colleague in action, the teacher can learn new ways to communicate and create a challenging and consistent environment in which students interact positively. If the teacher is struggling with one specific student, he or she can collaborate with, observe, or even co-teach with a peer. These strategies can provide great ideas for connecting with students.

Finally, observing the teacher interacting with students is excellent practice for supporting struggling teachers. Principals, counselors, and fellow teachers can watch the teacher work with students, and through a feedback protocol, they can help the teacher pinpoint specific issues that prevent the teacher from forming effective teacher-student relationships. Feedback can help the teacher in realizing what he or she is doing right as well as missed opportunities. The purpose of such observation is diagnostic in nature, and it is formative, not evaluative. The goal is to get a baseline, determine next steps for progress, and monitor growth regularly.

Problem Simplification Plan

Finally, as in previous chapters, leaders can use a problem simplification plan to help teachers identify and address their problems in forming effective learning relationships. The following problem simplification plan (figure 4.3, page 84) outlines strategies leaders can use to help an individual teacher overcome those struggles. This plan can help isolate a teacher's greatest area of need in relationship building and develop an action plan to address it.

Building relationships with students can be difficult, especially if the teacher has a hard time understanding how to connect with students of different races, cultures, socioeconomic statuses, and languages. We leaders can help teachers overcome these obstacles. If we don't provide that support, and the teacher has to overcome these obstacles in isolation, the process will take much longer. While experience is a great teacher, we can't leave student learning to languish while a struggling teacher gains that experience. When we respond effectively and in a systematic process to a teacher's deficits, we eliminate the drain on next year's teachers as they attempt to remediate last year's instructional gaps.

Conclusion

Building relationships with students is easier for some teachers than others. Finding the most effective ways to relate to, empathize with, and effectively challenge students requires a powerful skill set that some teachers don't easily acquire. If we want to guarantee learning for all students, school leaders must equip their teachers with a powerful system of resources, skill-building tools, and supports for connecting effectively with their students.

To ensure that teachers have the skills to build optimal relationships, we must provide a schoolwide system of supports that continuously and routinely trains teachers in the art of building relationships with students. Schools of excellence also must help teacher teams develop norms and protocols that guide teachers in getting to know their students better each day so those relationships can be leveraged to support learning.

Finally, we can't allow teachers who struggle with individual students or groups of students to write them off. Instead, we must build a system of supports that offers struggling teachers an individualized approach to counseling, observation, feedback, and advice from counselors and peers who can provide new and successful strategies for connecting with students. Although teachers play a central role in every school's achievement of its mission to guarantee excellence for all, teachers don't always have the answers to every problem they confront. Leaders, therefore, and the schools we lead, must provide those answers. That's how we can create the conditions in which

Problem Simplification Plan: Relationships for Learning
1. The teacher is struggling with establishing the following relationships.   ☐ Entire class: _____   ☐ Boys: _____   ☐ Girls: _____   ☐ Specific group: _____   ☐ Individual students: _____   Notes:
2. Describe the strengths and areas for growth in each of the following elements of relationship building with the targeted group or groups identified.   Communication: _____   Consistency: _____   Compassion: _____   Families: _____   Notes:
3. List the best intervention to help the teacher develop a better understanding of the targeted group and how to build solid relationships.   ☐ Research targeted students with _____.   ☐ Observe _____ interacting with students.   ☐ Co-teach with _____.   ☐ Observe as _____ models relationship building with the struggling teacher's class.   ☐ Model family communication plan after _____.   ☐ Other: _____   Notes:
4. Set a target date for when the teacher will be successfully establishing relationships with targeted students.
5. How will we know if relationships have been successfully established with targeted students?

Figure 4.3: Problem simplification plan—relationships for learning.

Visit **go.SolutionTree.com/leadership** *for a free reproducible version of this figure.*

teachers feel comfortable asking for help so that they receive the help they need to support student learning.

Leaders can use the following reflection tool (pages 86–87) to help assess the current approach to supporting learning relationships in our schools and to help identify ways in which we can improve that approach as we advance our own skills in guaranteeing learning excellence.

Reflection Tool: Relationships for Learning

Definition of Excellence for Relationships for Learning

What is our school's definition of teacher excellence in the area of relationships for learning?

Schoolwide Supports

1. How well do we clearly define our expectations for building the optimal relationship with all students?

2. How well do we leverage principal or counselor leadership to make relationships for learning a priority in our professional learning plan?

3. What is our system for teachers to review student histories or transcript files to learn more about their students prior to the beginning of the year?

4. What is our system for creating transition sheets on which teachers can pass along important information and strategies to help next year's teachers start off the year by building great relationships for learning with all students?

5. What is our campuswide plan for building relationships with all students, and how do we ensure that all teachers are consistent in committing to our plan?

page 1 of 2

Teacher Team Supports

1. What work have our teacher teams done to learn about their students and their backgrounds prior to the beginning of the school year?

2. How well do our teams plan to create content and lessons that entice even the most apprehensive students to learn?

3. How do our teacher teams that share students communicate with families in a manner that is positive, informative, and proactive?

4. When the team experiences difficulties with a particular student, what steps are taken to evaluate the relationship the teachers have with that student prior to providing academic or behavior responses?

Individualized Supports

1. Before we help a teacher with difficulty in relationships for learning, what steps do we take to evaluate the systemwide supports and teacher team supports and their effectiveness at helping the teacher? *(If schoolwide or teacher team supports are not in place, they are addressed as needed.)*

2. What data do we collect that confirms the teacher has difficulty with relationships for learning?

3. Before we help the teacher, what steps do we take to isolate the teacher's area of greatest difficulty in relationships for learning?

4. When we prescribe a personalized plan of supports, how well do we prescribe interventions from a wide variety of options, including meeting with the counselor, observing, coaching, collaborating with another teacher or the teacher team, and using outside resources to help the teacher?

5. Once we prescribe a plan of supports, what steps do we take to set a goal that defines the desired improvement needed, a date by which that improvement will be made, and a date by which we will follow up to ensure that improvement has been made?

A Leader's Guide to Excellence in Every Classroom © 2017 Solution Tree Press • SolutionTree.com
Visit **go.SolutionTree.com/leadership** to download this free reproducible.

CHAPTER 5

Leading for Excellence: Student Engagement

Student engagement is the product of motivation and active learning. It is a product rather than a sum because it will not occur if either element is missing.

—Elizabeth F. Barkley

Aside from the quality and effectiveness of teachers, the greatest factor impacting student learning is student engagement. Engaged students are actively involved in the learning process and motivated to make that process successful. "Engaged students do more than attend or perform academically; they also put forth effort, persist, self-regulate their behavior toward goals, challenge themselves to exceed, and enjoy challenges and learning" (Klem & Connell, 2004b, as cited in Christenson, Reschly, & Wylie, 2012, p. v). While a number of individual and family dynamics can influence a student's ability and willingness to engage in learning, the teacher's ability to make learning relevant and to transfer the responsibility for learning to students also plays a critical role in that process. The very best teachers do everything in their power to keep all students engaged in the learning process from bell to bell.

The need for self-worth and self-esteem occupy the fourth level of Maslow's (1943) Hierarchy of Needs, and for educators to promote their own feelings of self-worth and self-esteem, as well as their students' pride in their own academic success, they must develop skills in building student engagement in learning. Engagement is a strong predictor of successful learning, and the reason is simple: "Students who are engaged in school are more likely to earn higher grades and higher test scores, and have lower dropout rates" (Klem & Connell, 2009a, p. 2).

While learning to skillfully use resources, manage classroom routines and procedures, and develop meaningful relationships with students all provide a solid foundation on which teachers can grow professionally, a failure to engage students is a failure to maximize student learning. A failure to engage students, therefore, can stall any teacher's efforts toward becoming truly excellent in his or her craft. That's why skills for student engagement represent the final deficiency level in the Hierarchy of Instructional Excellence.

Of course, as leaders, we are responsible for helping teachers advance in that development. Fulfilling that responsibility demands that we offer supports for engagement building that address educator needs in several ways: through ongoing, schoolwide professional development; targeted strategies created by teacher teams; and individualized supports that include processes, observation, and customized feedback to meet individual educator needs. The Excellence Support System I outline later in this chapter describes specific approaches and strategies for providing that support to lead teachers toward improved skills in student engagement.

First, however, I think it's important that we fully understand how easy it can be for teachers to overlook the need for student engagement, as well as their own weaknesses in developing it. Disengaged students aren't necessarily problem students, although in some classes, disengagement can result in disruptive or unruly behavior. As the following story illustrates, however, compliant learning isn't the same as *excellent* learning—the kind that results from student engagement.

Engaging Students From Bell to Bell

Dante was the coolest teacher in school. *Funny*, *witty*, and *everyone's favorite teacher* were just a few ways students described this awesome algebra instructor. When students got their schedules, they celebrated when they saw that they were assigned to Dante's class—and why wouldn't they? From the moment they walked into his classroom, Dante's students had a great time. They could work at their own pace. They could ask Dante questions about anything, and he'd stop what he was doing to listen.

There was just one problem. Dante's cool factor didn't necessarily result in all students growing in their learning. Dante's classes regularly performed lower than the rest of the school in virtually every way on common and standardized assessments. His only saving grace was that parent satisfaction was very high, and that was simply because Dante took a personal interest in all his students and gave them all a strong sense of belonging.

As the school year began, the new principal, Mrs. Grace, made her rounds in her first week on her new campus. She heard great things about Dante as the teacher that students loved, but she also knew that his students' performance was far below the campus average. To get a better picture of his instruction, she stopped by his class to see what he did to make students love school. As she walked into Dante's classroom, Mrs. Grace observed students visiting with one another while they waited for Dante to finish a conversation with a student. She noted that the students weren't misbehaving, but they were really just killing time rather than engaging in any form of learning.

Dante completed his conversation about five minutes into the period and then began his lesson on solving for an unknown variable (solving for *x*). He started off the lesson with a joke that got a great student response and then delivered a twenty-five-minute lecture to students about how to solve for *x*. The students sat politely and passively throughout the lecture, while Dante solved problem after problem and occasionally asked the students a question to make sure they were paying attention. After the lecture ended, Dante gave the students the last fifteen minutes of class to solve ten problems on their own. During this time, students worked on problems and nonchalantly chatted with one another about off-task topics, while Dante milled around the room checking in on their work and answering their questions about the lesson or any other topic on their minds.

As students finished their problems, they continued their conversations with one another and Dante as they waited for class to end. When the bell rang, the students high-fived Dante and happily exited the room to head to their next class. Mrs. Grace left the room too, and as she walked out, she felt certain she understood the primary reason that Dante's students consistently performed below the school average. They simply weren't engaged.

Later that day, Mrs. Grace invited Dante to her office to discuss her observations. After she welcomed him into the room, Mrs. Grace said, "I really like how comfortable you make your students feel in your classroom. You have fantastic rapport with every single student."

Dante humbly replied, "Thank you. I have a great group of kids this year."

Mrs. Grace went on. "Yes, they are great, but I want to ask you a question. Do you think you are getting the most out of your students, and what I mean by that is, do you think they are truly engaged in your lesson?"

Caught off guard, Dante responded, "Well, they seem engaged to me. They listen, they don't cause problems, and they do exactly what I ask them to do."

Mrs. Grace agreed, "You're absolutely right. They do everything you ask of them because it's evident that they respect you very much. But how much of your class time is spent with the students being completely immersed in learning your content?"

Unsure of how to answer her question, Dante replied, "What do you mean? They are learning because they are paying close attention and following along as I present, and when I'm done, they do the work I assign them."

Mrs. Grace continued, "Yes, they are following along and doing your work, but I want you to think about their learning with these questions. Are they actively engaged in relevant learning tasks throughout the period? Do they take an interest in exploring their own learning activities? Do they ask questions or suggest ideas that indicate that they understand how the content you're teaching relates to their other learning topics, their own interests, or their lives outside school? In other words, we all learn more by doing than by listening. In class, your students were not learning in the first five minutes while you were having an important conversation with a student. During your twenty-five-minute lecture, they were passively listening to you while you presented your lesson. The only time that your students were actively learning was when you released them to work independently on problems for the last ten to fifteen minutes of class. And when they finished the problems, they stopped thinking about the lesson completely and engaged in off-topic conversations with one another. In other words, out of a fifty-minute period, your students were actively engaged for only about ten to fifteen minutes. I know your students really like you, but I don't see them engaged at their optimum level, and that means they aren't learning at optimum levels either."

Dante asked defensively, "What are you trying to say, that I'm not a good teacher?"

Mrs. Grace replied, "Actually, I'm saying that your students aren't productive *learners* in your classroom." Dante looked confused as Mrs. Grace continued. "Let me ask you a question. Do you believe that your students are learning to their full potential by listening to you teach?"

Dante answered, "Well, now that you put it that way, I guess not. But what do you expect me to do? I've been teaching this way for ten years."

Mrs. Grace smiled and said, "Well, first of all, I don't want you to be discouraged. You have a special gift in connecting with your students, and we need that to continue. What I want you to begin thinking about is how you can build that same level of connection between your students and your content. To support you in that effort, I want to work with you to find ways for you to get the most out of your students from the moment they walk in the room. I think you can capitalize on your relationships with students to keep them actively engaged and enthusiastic about learning your content through every facet of your lesson, from bell to bell, both in working with you and with each other. But most importantly, I want to help you ensure that your students have just as much responsibility for their learning as you do. If you can do that, I am confident that your students will grow by leaps and bounds."

Dante smiled. "And I'm assuming that you have a plan to help me do this?"

Mrs. Grace said, "You and I will work together and come up with a plan to ensure that you get the most out of your students this year."

Dante replied, "I'm ready. Now where do I begin?"

❖   ❖   ❖   ❖

As this story illustrates, some educators still believe that a highly functioning class is one in which students behave politely, listen to the teacher's lecture, and follow instructions. In order to help every student learn at higher levels, however, every teacher's focus on teaching from bell to bell must make the shift to *learning* from bell to bell. That kind of learning takes place when students are engaged in the learning process, when they understand why the learning matters to them, when they feel challenged to meet attainable goals, and when they feel that they have some owner-ship, control, and responsibility for the learning process.

To accomplish that kind of engaged learning, excellent teachers demonstrate a solid command of the skills necessary to create classroom environments and learning processes that inspire student confidence, promote student ownership in the learning process, fill their learning time with active and interactive learning experiences, and encourage them to persist in the face of challenges. That's a big challenge for teachers and for those of us responsible for making sure they're prepared to meet it. When it comes to creating a system to support educators in building effective student-engagement skills, as education researchers Nancy Frey and Douglas Fisher (2009) write, "Principals are key to making this happen" (p. 18).

I'm a big believer in the idea that what gets measured gets done. The Excellence Support System outlined in this chapter includes a focus on classroom time manage-ment. How does a class's use of time reflect its level of student engagement? While a leader's observation of a class may produce few data-point metrics that can accurately assess student interest levels, motivation, and belief in the relevance of coursework, we certainly can gauge what portion of class time is filled with students actively pur-suing learning versus time spent waiting for directions, sitting in silent compliance, or engaging in distractions.

In addition to using time as the measure for active engagement, leaders also can use observation to determine if students are actively engaged. Observation can tell us whether the students and teacher seem interested in the coursework and whether students seem motivated to actively pursue learning even when faced with challenges. We can observe levels of student interactivity and the responsibility students take for the learning process. When we search for and evaluate these behaviors through obser-vation, we have some relatively clear and effective methods for assessing educators' professional skills for promoting student engagement. As the chapter also explains, those same metrics and observations offer a structure on which we can build a strong system of supports for guiding teachers in the acquisition and ongoing development of these essential skills.

Promoting Student Engagement

Student engagement can be a difficult topic to pin down. Even its definition varies from source to source. Multiple sources, for example, cite education researcher Phillip Schlechty's (1994) definition, which describes engaged students as attracted to their work, persistent in that work in spite of challenges, and noticeably delighted in accomplishing their work (Geocaris, 1996; Levy & Campbell, 2008). The Schlechty Center on Engagement (n.d.) expands on this definition, adding that engaged stu-dents "learn at high levels and have a profound grasp of what they learn; retain what they learn; can transfer what they learn to new contexts"; view classroom activity as "personally meaningful," and have a focus on "getting it right" (p. 5).

The National Research Council Institute of Medicine of the National Academies (2003) writes, "Engagement in schoolwork involves both behaviors (e.g., persistence, effort, attention) and emotions (e.g., enthusiasm, interest, pride in success . . .)" (p. 31). We even have some idea of how children define student engagement. When Edutopia blogger Heather Wolpert-Gawron (2015) asked two hundred eighth graders how they defined student engagement, their responses highlighted classroom interaction, movement, and variety; the use of technology; the relevance of course material; strong relationships between the teacher and students and among students; and the level of respect and responsibility the teacher extended to the class.

These definitions tend to reference observable qualities, rather than quantifiable data, and my own definition of student engagement includes the same type of observable information. When I walk into a classroom in which students are actively involved in learning tasks throughout class time, collaborating excitedly to solve problems, and—perhaps most importantly—doing more work than the teacher, I know that I am observing a group of engaged students. Engaged students actively pursue learning rather than passively wait for the bell to signal that they can leave class. They ask questions, initiate and stay focused on learning tasks, offer ideas, and work throughout the class period without excess prodding by the teacher. As a result of this active engagement, students can take more ownership of the learning process and more pride in their learning success, and those qualities, in turn, foster student confidence, resilience, and self-esteem.

While many of these characteristics are largely observable, high levels of student engagement produce measurable differences in learning success. As education researchers Adena M. Klem and James P. Connell (2004a) write:

> An abundance of research indicates that higher levels of engagement in school are linked with positive outcomes such as improved academic performance. In fact, student engagement has been found to be one of the most robust predictors of student achievement and behavior in school. (pp. 1–2)

As figure 5.1 illustrates, skills for building student engagement occupy the fourth area of professional growth and development in the Hierarchy of Instructional Excellence. Those skills bring teachers powerful benefits in the work of promoting learning excellence, including more actively engaged, interactive learners; increased student ownership over learning processes; more productive use of class time; and higher levels of academic achievement and student self-esteem. Excellent teachers build on their strong command of learning resources, well-established routines and procedures, and meaningful learning relationships to structure lessons and classroom activities that promote high levels of student engagement. When teachers fail to foster that engagement, they can't achieve the highest levels of excellence in their professional growth *or* in their students' learning success.

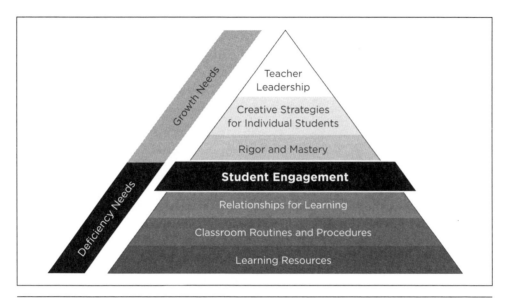

Figure 5.1: Hierarchy of Instructional Excellence—student engagement.

Klem and Connell (2004a) outline three sets of psychological variables that connect a student's learning experiences to his or her level of engagement: (1) the student's belief in his or her own competence and the sense of personal control it provides; (2) the student's values and goals, based in part on "the work's intrinsic interest to the student and/or its importance to achieving goals important to the student" (p. 4); and (3) the student's feelings of social connection to the school, in effect, the student feeling that he or she is respected, that his or her opinions are valued, and that others at the school care for him or her.

Classroom conditions that affect these variables can be demonstrated in multiple ways. Klem and Connell's (2004b) variables offer a framework for organizing these conditions into three major categories that form critical components for promoting student engagement. Teachers committed to maximizing student engagement can consider these three components when preparing for and delivering instruction.

1. **Relevance:** Is the learning related to the students' strengths, affinities, and interests?

2. **Responsibility:** Does the learning process gradually transition the responsibility for learning from the control of the teacher to that of the students?

3. **Optimized time:** Are students actively, interactively, and productively pursuing learning throughout the majority of class time?

As figure 5.2 (page 96) illustrates, when educators prepare for and deliver lessons using a model that incorporates all three of these components, the result is an optimized environment for nurturing student engagement.

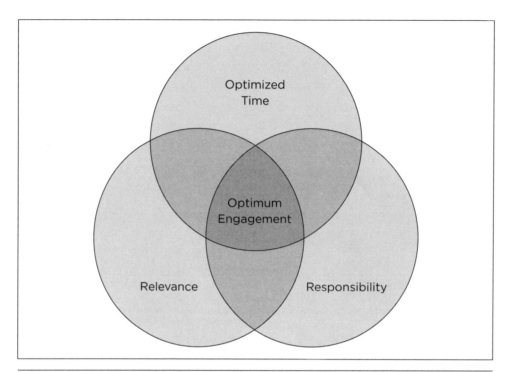

Figure 5.2: Student engagement in learning.

The following sections examine some of the specific skills teachers draw on when preparing for and delivering lessons that encompass each of these three components of student engagement and techniques they can adapt to improve their skills in building student engagement over time.

Preparation

Before a teacher can begin the process of preparing a lesson on any concept, he or she should know two pieces of information: (1) the lesson's goals and student learning target and (2) the relevance of those goals to the students' existing abilities, interests, and personal goals for learning. Knowing this information helps the teacher devise a plan that finds the best ways to connect all students to the learning target while still offering lessons that challenge students. According to Klem and Connell (2004a), challenging but achievable work is among the aspects of schooling "that have been found to best engage students in their learning," while at the same time "promoting perceptions of competence and control over achievement outcomes" (p. 6).

Here, the teacher's relationships with students can play a formative role. By familiarizing themselves with student histories and transition sheets, and through discussions with students, teachers can form and adjust plans to ensure that students are adequately prepared to take on the lesson's challenges. One way to think about preparing for engagement is to create a strong culture for learning: "In classrooms with robust cultures for learning, all students receive the message that although the work is challenging, they are capable of achieving it if they are prepared to work hard" (Danielson, 2013, p. 28). Teachers should consider students' personal interests and how lesson delivery and activities can leverage those interests to motivate student learning.

While addressing students' interests and a culture of learning are important to engagement, teachers can't maximize student learning by simply dumping the responsibility for that learning on students. Fisher and Frey's (2008) gradual release of responsibility model offers educators a framework for delivering lessons in a way that gradually prepares students to assume responsibility for learning tasks and transitions them smoothly through that process. Through eight years of research, Frey and Fisher (2009) determined that "this instruction framework leads to significant improvement in student engagement and achievement" (p. 20).

The gradual release of responsibility model establishes that, every time students and teachers meet, class time involves the following four components (Frey & Fisher, 2009).

1. **Focus lesson:** This ten- to fifteen-minute lesson establishes (or reestablishes) the purpose of the lesson and models how the teacher thinks about the content, or what questions and issues represent the teacher's or other expert's thinking in regard to that content. This modeling gives "students access to academic language and academic thinking as well as information about expert problem solving and understanding," access that helps prepare students to engage in complex content (Frey & Fisher, 2009, p. 20).

2. **Guided learning:** Teachers can help prompt students' own thinking about the content using strategic questions or prompts, either directed toward the whole class or to small groups. By encouraging students to go beyond the information they learned in the focus lesson to begin to explore their own questions and ideas, teachers are better able to scaffold learning to meet individual learner needs, even as they begin to shift the focus for content exploration to students.

3. **Collaborative learning:** Frey and Fisher (2009) note that "to really learn, students must be engaged in productive group tasks that require interaction" (p. 20). Their participation in these groups, the language that they use to describe task elements, and their contributions to those tasks are just some of the ways students indicate their level of comfort with the content and control over the learning experience. Collaborative learning, therefore, is effective when students are interactively engaged in discussing and pursuing the task at hand and when they are accountable for their individual contributions to that task.

4.   **Independent learning:** This is the portion of class time in which
students apply their learning by creating, for example, quick written
summaries of daily lessons or ideas for future goals or plans for tasks
associated with the lessons. Frey and Fisher (2009) recommend that
teachers accommodate this independent practice time *before* they assign
students the related homework.

Adapted from Fisher and Frey's (2008) book *Better Learning Through Structured
Teaching*, figure 5.3 illustrates how the responsibility for learning initially begins with
the teacher and slowly progresses from guided learning to collaborative learning and,
finally, to independent learning.

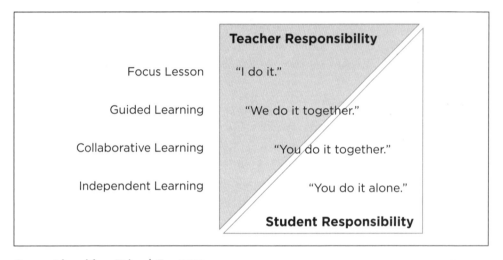

Source: Adapted from Fisher & Frey, 2008.

Figure 5.3: Gradual release of responsibility.

Beyond guiding students to assume responsibility for their own learning processes,
teachers can also build student engagement by demonstrating their own interest
and engagement as they deliver learning content and guide learning experiences. As
Heather Wolpert-Gawron's (2015) students note:

> Instead of talking like a robot, teachers should speak to us like
> they're really passionate about teaching. . . . If a teacher acts like
> this is the last thing they want to be doing, the kids will respond
> with the same negative energy. If you act like you want to be there,
> then we will too.

In essence, teachers build student engagement by delivering lesson content in a way
that actively and enthusiastically involves students in the learning process. By gradually transitioning responsibility for those processes to the students, teachers not only
help promote their learners' cognitive investment in learning the content but also can
boost students' perceptions of that content's relevance to their own interests. Further,

they demonstrate trust in the students' competence and control in the learning process. By structuring class time within a framework of introductions to content and its associated models of thinking, guided interactive activities, collaborative group work, and independent study, teachers can be certain that they are filling the majority of class time with productive learning activities.

The lesson-planning template in figure 5.4 (pages 100–101) is a collaborative tool to help teachers plan and deliver content by keeping the focus on relevance, responsibility, and optimized time. By using Google Sheets, teachers and leaders can view, edit, and use the comment feature to have asynchronous dialogue about a teacher's plans for student engagement. Leaders can use the lesson-planning template as a walkthrough instrument to give teachers targeted feedback on how well their plans align with their instructional delivery and identify where they successfully promote engagement, miss opportunities for engagement, or actually add to disengagement in the classroom.

When teachers leverage student interests, cultural affinities, and existing competencies, they can creatively design engaging lessons that intentionally advance learning targets through various components of engagement: student-directed learning, productive group collaboration, active independent study, and other classroom activities. When the preparation for engagement is detailed and aligned to the nature and needs of students, teachers can expect to see an increase in the ownership of and pride in the learning process. By planning lessons designed to accomplish learning goals and align with student abilities and interests, teachers are well positioned to connect students with their learning and to inspire them to *want* to know more about the content.

Delivery

While planning is essential for preparing relevant learning experiences that keep students involved in the learning process, teachers can't guarantee bell-to-bell engagement if their students spend large portions of class time as passive recipients of information. Students won't retain knowledge unless the instruction inspires them to apply that knowledge in relevant ways. "The acquisition and retention of facts are important but are by no means enough for excellent education" (Deci, Vallerand, Pelletier, & Ryan, 1991, p. 326). Encouraging students to become actively involved in their learning processes through, for example, asking and answering questions in class, engaging in conversations that explore lesson topics, collaborating in interactive group work, and undertaking self-directed independent learning projects involves transitioning responsibility for learning from teacher to student. When students feel more responsible for designing and guiding their learning processes, we can expect their level of commitment to that learning, their confidence in their learning abilities, and their pride in successful learning to rise.

| | Essential Skills | | | | | | | | |
Component	Number of Minutes	What to Document	Monday	Tuesday	Wednesday	Thursday	Friday	Students Will	Teacher Will
Warm-Up		Question or task for students to complete						Prepare for learning, retrieve required materials, and submit homework.	Submit attendance, ensure homework is turned in, and manage student needs.
Focus Lesson		Concept to cover						Follow along with lesson and take notes, ask questions, and initiate further discussion with teacher.	Teach concept, answering and encouraging questions, discussing student ideas, and ensuring that all students are following along.
Guided Learning		Intervention groups and tasks						Work in groups or pairs independently or with the teacher in intervention. Ask questions about the concept or others ways to understand it.	Set expectations for working and learning. Encourage students to explore ideas and information. Work directly with struggling students.

Collaborative Learning	Collaborative learning activities			Work on tasks tied to the focus lesson in groups. Contribute new ideas or opinions to help peers. Ask questions of peers if they do not understand the concept.	Monitor groups to ensure they are working and learning together. Gather observation data on student interaction and performance. Provide students with additional support.
Independent Learning	Activities for students			Work independently on a task tied to the focus lesson or their greatest area of need. Ask questions of the teacher as needed to clarify concepts and maximize learning.	Monitor students to ensure they are working and learning. Pull out students for additional support. Offer students extension activities when they successfully pass the task.
Wrap-Up or Exit Ticket	Homework expectations or questions to ask to gauge learning			Ask questions about homework or the day's lesson.	Communicate progress for the day's lesson and set expectations for homework and tomorrow's lesson.

Figure 5.4: Student engagement lesson-planning template.

Visit **go.SolutionTree.com/leadership** *to download a free reproducible version of this figure.*

Beyond guiding students to assume responsibility for their own learning processes, teachers can also build student engagement by demonstrating their own interest and engagement as they deliver learning content and guide learning experiences. As Heather Wolpert-Gawron's (2015) students note:

> Instead of talking like a robot, teachers should speak to us like they're really passionate about teaching. . . . If a teacher acts like this is the last thing they want to be doing, the kids will respond with the same negative energy. If you act like you want to be there, then we will too.

In essence, teachers build student engagement by delivering lesson content in a way that actively and enthusiastically involves students in the learning process. By gradually transitioning responsibility for those processes to the students, teachers not only help promote their learners' cognitive investment in learning the content, they also can boost students' perceptions of that content's relevance to their own interests. Further, they demonstrate trust in the students' competence and control in the learning process. By structuring class time within a framework of introductions to content and its associated models of thinking, guided interactive activities, collaborative group work, and independent study, teachers can be certain that they are filling the majority of class time with productive learning activities.

Reflection

Great teachers always reflect on their effectiveness for meeting students' needs. As noted previously, while many indicators of student engagement are more observable than quantifiable, great teachers can help evaluate how effectively they are promoting student engagement by assessing how much class time is consumed with students actively involved in interactive, collaborative, and independent learning projects. In the three-component model for student engagement in figure 5.2 (page 96), I refer to this component as *optimized time*. Excellent teachers understand that time is a constant, but how they use it to engage their students is the variable. Teachers can gauge the effectiveness of their instruction, in part, by determining how effectively they optimize their class time for student engagement.

Optimizing class time involves more than just using up the minutes on the clock. Instead, teachers have to fill those minutes with conditions that encourage students to choose to be actively engaged in learning. That's a task that grows more difficult as students grow older: "By the time many students hit middle school, disengagement has become a learned behavior" (Himmele & Himmele, 2011, p. 8).

In reflecting on how successfully they have encouraged student engagement, teachers should consider how effective their learning tasks have been at connecting student interests to lesson content and the associated learning activities. How much of class time is occupied by group activities? How often are students engaged in collaborative exercises? How much time does the class spend using tools and technologies that interest students and connect with their personal goals for learning? Do focus lessons or other introductory materials seem adequate to help students grasp the lessons' goals and introduce them to the cognitive issues and questions surrounding the task at hand? If not, is it an issue of the amount of time spent in delivering that material, or is it the quality of the material itself? By answering these and similar questions, teachers can determine how they can revamp focus lessons and learner activities in order to better engage students from bell to bell.

Building an Excellence Support System: Student Engagement

Both teachers and learners must juggle multiple demands and goals in the classroom, and so every minute of class time is precious. When it comes to supporting our teachers in their efforts to improve student engagement, therefore, time can be an effective metric for assessing how well teachers are doing. It's not the only metric, of course, and I'm not advocating clocking teachers like contestants in a game show, but in addition to observing students' classroom interactions and activities and noting their progress toward learning outcomes, we can use our observations of how teachers divide and devote their class time to determine how to best advise, guide, and support them.

We can use that support to help teachers ensure that their instruction is relevant, that they thoughtfully transition the responsibility for learning to their students, and that they devote an optimal portion of class time to learning activities that challenge and engage students in the learning process.

The following sections outline an Excellence Support System that answers those needs by offering tools, practices, and procedures that provide schoolwide supports, teacher team supports, and supports uniquely created to leverage individual teachers' strengths and address areas in need of improvement.

Step 1: Schoolwide Supports

Leaders are unwise to adopt an approach to student engagement that stresses only one way to achieve it. Every school teaches a wide variety of content; employs teachers who bring their own personalities, capabilities, and teaching styles; and serves a student body made up of equally unique individuals. Finding the strongest means for promoting student engagement within that kaleidoscope demands creativity, ingenuity, and flexibility. At the same time, schools have a responsibility to establish a general framework for defining and assessing student engagement and an obligation to help all teachers become highly effective at that aspect of their craft. The first step in addressing that obligation is to establish a system of schoolwide supports.

We can begin building these schoolwide supports on a philosophy about instructional delivery. A core belief of this philosophy is that all students should be engaged with their academic goals from the moment they enter the classroom until the moment they leave it. On that foundation, schools can systemically incorporate lesson plans and instructional delivery models, such as Madeline Hunter's Elements of Lesson Design (Wilson, n.d.), the 5E Model of Instruction (Round Rock Independent School District, n.d.), or the Frey and Fisher (2009) gradual release of responsibility model. By adopting these models and plans throughout the system, schools give teachers choices for meeting learning goals *and* optimizing student engagement.

Next, rather than just collecting and assessing teachers' lesson plans, schools can better ensure that teachers create and deliver engaging lessons by offering ongoing professional development opportunities that help them build their student-engagement skills. These professional development strategies can provide ideas to engage students, but even more importantly, they can guide teachers in the most effective ways to integrate those strategies into the overall instructional delivery model.

As a third element of schoolwide supports, we can leverage the experience and examples of our most effective teachers through the use of instructional coaching. Most schools have teachers who offer excellent models for promoting student-engagement. Those teachers are a tremendous resource, and our schoolwide systems can take advantage of their talent by encouraging them to share ideas in all-faculty presentations, through video observation, and by offering their rooms for peer observation. The following sections examine in more detail each of these components of schoolwide support systems for building student engagement.

Instructional Delivery Model

All leaders have an obligation to offer teachers a clear and complete description of their expectations for student engagement, but excellent leaders provide teachers with a model to meet those expectations. A great way to help all teachers meet expectations for student engagement is to adopt an instructional delivery model that outlines instructional planning and instructional delivery components that the school deems essential. That process involves three components.

First, school leaders can work with high-performing teachers to identify high-leverage instructional strategies that help all students learn and develop a plan to replicate those strategies throughout the school. Second, school leaders can adopt "learning from bell to bell" as a schoolwide expectation and then accompany that expectation with, as noted earlier, examples of lesson-planning templates built around that instructional delivery model. Additionally, they can provide examples of time management tools and professional development to help enhance the skills excellent teachers use to maximize time in their instructional delivery. Within this schoolwide structure, we should incorporate adequate flexibility so proficient, high-performing teachers can exercise their own initiative and creativity in determining how to best optimize instructional time.

Finally, school leaders can consistently identify exemplars of excellent student engagement in learning, both within and outside their own systems, and share their discoveries with the campus through school blogs, tweets, videos, or emails to the staff. School leaders typically encounter more examples of excellent instruction than do individual teachers, so they can improve their faculty's efforts by sharing these great strategies with the rest of the staff.

Effective Professional Development Programs

Professional development is a mainstay in schools around the world, and it should be because all teachers must continue learning if they want to be able to address the ever-changing needs of students. At the same time, schoolwide programs for professional development can be little more than time wasters if they fail to address teachers' actual existing capabilities and needs for improvement.

Figure 5.5 shows a reflection tool that leaders can use to heighten their awareness of those existing issues as they prepare to create a schoolwide system that guarantees high levels of engagement in every classroom. This tool enables leaders to articulate their vision of what they expect of teachers in creating high levels of student engagement; to identify effective engagement practices that are evident in excellent teachers' classrooms; and to determine how they can design professional development around those successful practices.

Component	Plan
Instructional Delivery	What components do we expect all teachers to incorporate into their instruction in order to maximize student engagement?
Engagement Audit	Which of these components are we currently using effectively, and how can we incorporate these strategies into our professional development plan?
Professional Development	What is our plan to train teachers about the components of effective student engagement and an instructional delivery model?
Instructional Coaching	What is our area of focus, and how frequently will we coach teachers in this component?
Instructional Planning	How will our lesson plans incorporate engagement strategies to help teachers plan more time-efficient lessons?

Figure 5.5: Reflection tool for schoolwide systems to support student engagement.

Visit **go.SolutionTree.com/leadership** *for a free reproducible version of this figure.*

Professional development is effective only when it includes follow-up training and when teachers walk away with a plan to integrate new learning into their classrooms. To help integrate new learning into classroom practice, leaders can include templates and other plans for incorporating student-engagement strategies into lesson-planning documents as well as their instruction as part of these professional development processes.

Instructional Coaching

Beyond establishing school norms and expectations, leaders also have an obligation to provide teachers with both schoolwide and individual coaching systems that can improve their student-engagement skills. All educators can benefit from a relationship with an instructional coach, and many districts invest money in creating specific positions for coaches. That's not the only way to go, however; leaders—principals, teacher leaders, counselors, and so on—also can shoulder the responsibility for guiding teachers in this area of their professional development.

We succeed best at those efforts when we remember that an effective coach is not a superior but rather a peer, partner, and confidant. Coaches help teachers grow in many ways, for example, by planning instruction, conducting assessments and interventions, and sometimes even by co-teaching lessons. But the coach's primary tool for improving teacher skills is observation and feedback. Frey and Fisher (2009) describe a three-part model for effective feedback for helping teachers develop and continually improve skills in student engagement. Based on the work of John Hattie and Helen Timperley (2007), the model involves the following three forms of feedback.

1. **Feed up,** in which the coach and teacher agree on the learning goals they will pursue through the coaching process. These goals may be related to a need for increased relevance in lesson plans and content, increased student responsibility for learning processes, or increased time devoted to active learning. Unless teachers have a clear and concise understanding of the need for improvement in their instructional practice, the coaching process will be less effective and teachers may continue to struggle.

2. **Feed back**, in which a coach shares his or her observations of the teacher's strengths and weaknesses in promoting student engagement based on class observation and data supplied by student reports, student assessments, and the observations of peers and colleagues.

3. **Feed forward**, in which the teacher and coach agree on a plan for instructional improvement based on feed-up and feed-back data. As Frey and Fisher (2009) note, "This process is much less evaluative and more collaborative than the feedback process" (p. 22). In this phase of coaching, teachers have an opportunity to find their own creative solutions to growing their engagement skills. Frey and Fisher (2009) go on to write, "Principals should encourage teachers to try things out, to experiment, and to think deeply about what works and what doesn't work" (p. 22).

In designing both schoolwide and individual coaching programs, we should bear in mind that instructional coaching only works when the goal is growth, not proficiency. Our priority has to be helping teachers attain that growth.

Step 2: Teacher Team Supports

Collaborative teams need opportunities to have meaningful discussions about how to create an engaging environment for learners. One of the best strategies for aligning student engagement from class to class is to develop activities and lessons as a team. While the way teachers deliver the lessons may differ from class to class, teacher teams enable members to converse about the nuances and steps within specific activities. That way, the teams effectively share strategies for engaging at high levels with the same relevant work. Three strategies that teams can use to help one another with student engagement are (1) instructional planning, (2) instructional rounds, and (3) modeling. The following sections review each of these strategies in more detail.

Instructional Planning

Collaborative planning is a high-leverage strategy to promote student learning, but it can't be the only strategy teams use. We also can encourage teams to discuss how they engage students through focus lessons, guided instruction, collaborative learning, and independent work, and how effectively the time they spend in each of these components is engaging learners. The ultimate goal of collaborative planning is to promote active learning at high levels, and the best learning opportunities come from failure, not success. Through honest conversations, teachers can identify and discuss areas where their instructional practice is falling short in promoting student engagement and ask their peers for suggestions. Often, one teacher's difficulty with student engagement is shared with one or more teachers, and collective problem solving for one teacher's challenges can translate into powerful solutions for all teachers. By engaging in conversations about difficulties, teams can move from working together to learning together.

Instructional Rounds

One of the most powerful professional development activities is watching other teachers in action with students. Collaborative teams can use *instructional rounds* to visit one or more classrooms to observe specific instructional components as a method to learn with and from one another. For example, if teachers want to strengthen the level of engagement during their opening minutes of class time, they can schedule their collaborative time to watch five different teachers as they begin the first five minutes of class. Or, to explore ways for improving small-group instruction, collaborative teams can work with the principal to schedule dates to observe teachers when their small groups are in action. By observing strong and struggling delivery models, collaborative teams can glean powerful strategies for improving student engagement from high-performing classes and discover missed opportunities in struggling classes. If scheduling time during the school day for teacher teams to conduct instructional rounds proves difficult, we can make videos of lessons during the day so the team can review the videos later during collaborative time.

When using instructional rounds, teacher teams should agree to focus on one component of instructional delivery and then center their collective learning around that component. They can then use their observation data to help create strategies the entire team can use for optimizing student engagement during this segment of their class time or lesson.

Modeling

As noted earlier, modeling is a best practice to help students understand new content through the eyes of the teacher. Similarly, principals can encourage collaborative teams to use modeling as a strategy for helping teams to find effective strategies for dealing with difficulties in a particular engagement component.

If a team, for example, has one teacher who is effective in guided instruction, the team should use its collaborative time to have this teacher model how he or she conducts a guided instruction lesson for the team. We should be certain that our teams use modeling processes that include interactive discussions in which the modeling teacher and other team members discuss issues, ideas, questions, challenges, and opportunities associated with the modeled skill. By presenting the structure as well as the mental processes within that structure, an excellent teacher can model for teammates how to make guided instruction and other instructional skills efficient and effective at promoting student engagement.

When modeling, it's important that we encourage teachers and colleagues throughout the system to understand that any and all of us can improve our approach to instructional practices. After all, keeping students engaged in learning is difficult for almost every teacher, including the very best teachers in the school. Leaders aren't exempt from the need for ongoing improvement in engagement, either. We can work to improve our own approach to engaging members of our teacher teams in the critical work of finding solutions that can help every teacher improve student engagement in their classrooms and throughout the school.

Step 3: Individualized Supports

Sometimes, teachers who have difficulties hooking students into learning need more support than school structures or collaborative teams can provide. For teachers who need help in student-engagement skills that goes beyond the schoolwide and teacher team supports, we can create individualized plans for improvement that are prescriptive in nature and specific in the diagnosis. The three-part feed-up, feed-back, and feed-forward model (page 106) offers an excellent framework for creating and implementing that plan.

I recommend that, before prescribing supports, the focus teacher and school leader determine and agree on the teacher's strengths and weaknesses in planning for engagement. Does the teacher have a coherent plan that flows from the beginning of instruction to the end of the class period? If not, the first step is to help that teacher develop an organized lesson plan that addresses how transitions should look, how the teacher will communicate lesson goals with students, and how the teacher will monitor student engagement and respond to disengaged students. Having a plan of action is good, but having a clear picture of how that plan will unfold is even better. The following sections outline some of the typical problems that cause teachers to continue to struggle with student engagement, and some specific ideas leaders can use to help them overcome those struggles.

Communication for Engagement

Communication problems between students and teachers—and among students themselves—can impair student engagement. The teacher may need to focus on improving his or her style of communicating information or the tone. In that case, we can help that teacher develop a plan of video observation, practice, and self-monitoring to learn to avoid the use of sarcasm or ridicule, or to develop a more enthusiastic tone when communicating with the class. If student-to-student communication disengages students from learning, the teacher and leader should work together to set expectations and responses for off-task student communication that inhibits learning. Communication must enhance learning, not inhibit it, and the leader must help the teacher learn how to leverage student communication for learning.

Optimal Time for Engagement

Sometimes, struggling teachers fail to realize just how much time they waste in procedures that don't effectively engage learners and, therefore, don't maximize learning. If a failure to optimize time for engagement is the issue, the leader can observe the focus teacher and script the lesson detailing how much time it took to complete each instructional activity and transition. By recording the duration of each lesson component and transition, the teacher and leader then can reflect on what lesson elements stoked student engagement, as reflected, for example, through interactive participation in class discussions, collaborative group work, and self-directed independent projects. The leader can then work with the teacher to compare those blocks of time occupied by elements that resulted in silent compliance, disruptive behaviors, or other demonstrations of disengagement.

A time study forms a good foundation for this assessment, but it isn't a cudgel that leaders should use to drive instructional improvement. Instead, leaders can use the assessment to help struggling teachers focus on specific ways they can optimize class time by making sure lesson content is relevant to student interests, abilities, and personal goals for learning, and by engaging students in active learning experiences.

Transition of Responsibility for Learning

Many teachers need individualized help in improving their skills at transitioning the responsibility for learning to students, an important element in building student engagement. Often, this problem is connected to a failure to properly prepare students to take more ownership of their own learning. When the focus teacher and leader agree that this area needs improvement, they can work together to create a plan.

For example, organizing students into small groups before the students are familiar with relevant content can bring learning to a screeching halt. Some instructional tasks may fail to engage students because they aren't confident enough with the content to complete the task. Furthermore, if teachers release students to do independent work without offering a clear structure for supporting those students when they experience difficulty, the students are likely to become frustrated and insecure and then disengage from the learning process. If, on the other hand, teachers fail to structure group and independent learning activities that keep students engaged and learning throughout the time assigned for those activities, they also fail to optimize learning.

In each of these instances, we can help teachers plan to better present focus lesson content and guided instruction that adequately prepare students to take on subsequent learning challenges. Together with the teacher, we can determine what specific instructional weakness may have contributed to the difficulty by analyzing the teacher's individual instructional components and their effects on student engagement. Again, by reviewing an element-by-element analysis of the focus teacher's instructional process, we can work collaboratively with the teacher to identify the source of the problem and search for a remedy.

Meaningful Goals

Sometimes, students fail to engage in learning because their teacher has presented them with no meaningful goal for the lesson. In order for lesson goals to be meaningful, they must be relevant to students and their personal learning goals, align with student competencies, and offer students interesting challenges. Again, we can work with the teacher to create meaningful learning goals and make sure the teacher adequately outlines those goals in well-designed focus lessons.

To accomplish this work, we can accompany the focus teacher to observe other classrooms together to find effective means for introducing learning goals. By observing how other teachers interact with students around a learning goal, we can work with struggling teachers to set challenging and attainable goals for students and each instructional component. Presenting a relevant and meaningful goal for learning may seem like an essential teaching task, but we have to remember how easy it is for overwhelmed teachers to shortchange this area of their instruction. Excellent teachers set goals for learning with enthusiasm and hold students accountable for reaching the goal. By helping struggling teachers improve their abilities in defining and articulating these goals for every lesson, we can boost their instructional skills in student engagement *and* help their students achieve greater levels of learning excellence.

Problem Simplification Plan

In previous chapters, I offered problem simplification plans for assisting in developing individualized supports for improving teacher skills. Using the problem simplification plan shown in figure 5.6, we can help teachers analyze the areas of instruction that they need to develop to improve student engagement. The information in this tool can help focus teachers and leaders as they work together to create a focused plan for improving those skills. Using Google Sheets, teachers can design a template based on this plan and share it with leaders, teacher teams, coaches, or other staff members who can help support teachers in professional development. After we have observed lessons and conducted walkthroughs based on the lesson, leaders can use the plan to articulate their observations to the teacher.

Problem Simplification Plan: Student Engagement
1. The teacher is struggling with the following concepts regarding engagement (describe problems associated with each applicable item below). ☐ Relevance ☐ Beginning of class ☐ Middle of class ☐ End of class ☐ Transitions ☐ Bell ringer ☐ Focus lesson ☐ Guided learning ☐ Collaborative learning ☐ Independent learning ☐ Exit ticket Notes:
2. What are the expectations for engagement in this area?
3. How does the teacher's communication encourage students to engage?

Figure 5.6: Problem simplification plan—student engagement.   continued →

4. Identify the best intervention to help the teacher develop higher student engagement in learning.

☐ Learn more about creating relevant lessons through _____.

☐ Observe _____ at the beginning, middle, or end of class.

☐ Observe _____ in instructional delivery component, _____.

☐ Co-teach a lesson with _____.

☐ _____ will model engagement with the struggling teacher's class.

☐ Other: _____

Notes:

5. On what date can we expect the teacher to have established successful student engagement?

6. What metrics will we use to determine that student engagement is effective?

*Visit **go.SolutionTree.com/leadership** for a free reproducible version of this figure.*

Engaging students of varying aptitudes, abilities, and affinities is a challenging task for all teachers. For teachers who are struggling at this level in the Hierarchy of Instructional Excellence, personalized learning plans for engagement must leverage the teacher's strengths in connecting students with content. These plans must be targeted and specific to help struggling teachers make their lessons relevant to students to enhance their engagement. Part of this process includes the intentional transfer of responsibility for learning to students, finding ways to better optimize time, and connecting content to students' personal interests and motivations.

Conclusion

Anyone who has to present in front of a live audience knows that you have to hook your listeners early on, or you could lose them forever. Teachers face the same challenge in engaging their students in the learning process. If students fail to see the relevance of the lesson topic, or if they decide that it's too far beyond their capabilities to grasp or not challenging enough to be interesting, their minds will go elsewhere. Engaging students in the learning process is about igniting their minds and connecting what they already know to what they need to know. Teachers can have strong relationships with students, but students also must be connected with the content in order to maximize their learning experience. Effectively establishing that connection demands that teachers capture and hold students' attention, guide students to actively pursue lesson content, and deliver all that essential content and activity in the crowded confines of class time. Every minute counts.

Teachers maximize student engagement within those minutes by planning relevant content and by structuring learning activities that gradually transfer the responsibility for learning content from the teacher to the students. When students are actively engaged in group and individual learning processes that challenge and motivate them, rather than silently listening to lectures, they can develop a sense of ownership over their learning that can boost outcomes and build self-esteem.

Teaching to an engaged classroom enables teachers to focus on guiding student exploration and promoting learning excellence, rather than trying to force-feed content and deal with the disruptive behavior and limited learning success that can result when learners are disengaged. If we want to be excellent leaders, therefore, we need to master effective tools, practices, and systems for supporting our teachers in the ongoing work of developing their skills in student engagement.

We can't sit back and expect teachers to provide excellent learning from bell to bell if we don't articulate a specific vision for what that learning should involve and how it should be structured. While highly skilled teachers need the flexibility to continue to innovate and find new and better ways to engage students, we have a responsibility to ensure that teachers have access to schoolwide, teacher team, and individualized systems that can help them understand the skills necessary for building student engagement and to identify areas where they can improve. We also must provide concrete tools, practices, and advice to guide them in that improvement process. That's how we can help transform classes of content delivery into laboratories of learning where every instructional minute is rich with cognitive challenge and every learning process is fueled by the fire of student engagement.

To help in that process, leaders can use the following reflection tool (pages 114–115) to gauge their understanding of the challenges involved in engaging students in the classroom, the strength of current systems for supporting the skills necessary for building student engagement, and specific methods they might use to improve those support systems, based on the strategies and tools reviewed in this chapter.

Reflection Tool: Student Engagement

Definition of Excellence for Student Engagement

What is our school's definition of teacher excellence in the area of student engagement in learning, and how well does it address relevance, responsibility, and optimized time?

Schoolwide Supports

1. How well do we clearly articulate our philosophy of instructional delivery that leads to relevance, responsibility, and optimized time in student learning?

2. How well do we utilize instructional coaching to help teachers grow through the three-part model for feedback (feed up, feed back, feed forward)?

3. What is our system for ongoing professional development in the area of student engagement?

4. How effectively do we curate the engagement practices in place on our campus and use these excellent teachers to teach our faculty more about engagement?

5. How well does our schoolwide learning plan address our school's weaknesses in the area of student engagement?

A Leader's Guide to Excellence in Every Classroom © 2017 Solution Tree Press • SolutionTree.com
Visit **go.SolutionTree.com/leadership** to download this free reproducible.

Teacher Team Supports

1. What norms do our teachers have to ensure that they learn more from each other about student engagement?

2. How well do our teams plan instruction together to increase student engagement through the components of relevance, responsibility, and optimized time?

3. How can our teams conduct instructional rounds together to discover more ways to engage students or learn more about specific engagement activities or strategies?

4. When the team experiences difficulties with engagement, what steps does it take to have an experienced teacher model engagement strategies for the team?

Individualized Supports

1. Before we help a teacher with difficulty in student engagement, what steps should we take to evaluate the systemwide supports and teacher team supports and their effectiveness at helping the teacher? *(If schoolwide or teacher team supports are not in place, they are addressed as needed.)*

2. What data do we collect to confirm that the teacher has difficulty with engagement and ensure that the difficulty is not associated with lower levels in the Hierarchy of Instructional Excellence?

3. Before we help the teacher, what steps do we take to isolate the teacher's area of greatest difficulty in student engagement: communication, optimizing time, transferring responsibility for learning, or setting meaningful learning goals?

4. When we prescribe a personalized plan of supports, how well do we prescribe targeted interventions from a wide variety of options, including using Google Sheets for instructional planning, observing, coaching, collaborating with another teacher or the teacher team, and using outside resources?

5. Once we prescribe a plan of supports, what steps do we take to set a goal that defines the desired improvement needed, a date by which that improvement will be made, and a date by which we will follow up to ensure that improvement has been made?

CHAPTER 6

Leading for Excellence: Rigor and Mastery

If schools are to establish a truly guaranteed and viable curriculum, those who are called upon to deliver it must have both a common understanding of the curriculum and a commitment to teach it.

—Richard DuFour and Robert J. Marzano

When teachers have developed the fundamental skill sets of their profession—a command of learning resources and classroom routines and procedures and an ability to build strong learning relationships and high levels of student engagement—they can turn their focus to developing more complex and demanding skills. Among these is the ability to guide their students in rigorous learning and content mastery. In Maslow's (1943) Hierarchy of Needs, the need to know and understand represents the first level of a person's growth needs. At this parallel level in the Hierarchy of Instructional Excellence, teachers develop the skills necessary to fuel their students' desire to go beyond surface knowledge to develop a deep understanding of the content they are learning.

Rigorous learning has become a hot topic among educators, and with good reason. We live in an increasingly complex world in which few people can succeed without the ability to understand issues and ideas deeply, to analyze data from multiple perspectives and combine it in innovative solutions, to immerse themselves in team-driven efforts, and to leave the crowd to forge new paths forward. Willard Daggett and Susan Gendron (2015), of the International Center for Leadership in Education, describe rigor as involving *thoughtful work* that prepares students to engage in "high-quality learning intentions"; *high-level questioning*, in which students can ask and answer probing questions that can increase understanding and lead to higher levels of thinking; and *academic discussion*, that enables students to engage in "vocabulary-rich, academic conversation with adults and peers" (p. 5). While many definitions for rigorous learning are in circulation, I believe that developing this kind of deep, inquisitive, flexible, and self-motivated thinking and approach to problem solving is what rigorous learning and content mastery are all about.

Rigorous learning empowers students to direct their own learning experiences and to own their learning outcomes. Inspired by relevant content and their own interests and passion, students engaged in rigorous learning ask challenging questions and formulate solutions based on investigation, experimentation, and analytical thinking. When students master content, they aren't just absorbing information; they are developing an understanding of that content that enables them to move beyond rote memorization and repetition of data. As educator and author Grant Wiggins (2014) notes, content mastery marks a difference between *knowing* and *understanding* learning content. Students who *know* content can "recall, repeat, perform as practiced," and so on. Students who *understand* content, can "*justify* a claim; *connect* discrete facts on their own; *apply* their learning in new contexts; *adapt* to new circumstances, purposes or audiences; *criticize* arguments made by others; *explain* how and why something is the case" (Wiggins, 2014).

While strong learning relationships and high levels of student engagement are essential elements for that kind of deep understanding and the rigorous learning that drives it, student empowerment plays an equally (if not more) powerful role. Engagement in learning certainly motivates students to take responsibility for learning, but empowerment inspires students to take full ownership of the learning processes they use to master learning content.

This chapter outlines the techniques excellent teachers use to create inspiring environments where students master challenging content through rigorous learning. It then explores specific strategies we, as leaders, can use to create an effective system of schoolwide, teacher team, and individualized supports to help teachers as they work on the challenges of developing the professional skills and educational environments that empower every student to strive for mastery.

First, however, we begin with another story from the classroom. Here, one teacher uses her own powers of investigative thinking, comparative analysis, and deep reflection to gain an understanding of how she could transform her actively engaged students into empowered, rigorous learners capable of mastering content and succeeding at the highest levels of learning.

Promoting Students From Average to Excellent

Claire was a great teacher. Every time her principal, Mrs. Davis, conducted a walkthrough, Claire's classroom routines and procedures were flawless and students followed them with seeming effortlessness. Relationships for learning accelerated the students' thirst for knowledge, as even the most apprehensive students used the learning environment as though it were designed just for them. Mrs. Davis rarely observed even a minute of lost instruction time in Claire's classes, because every student was engaged in the learning tasks and pursued learning with evident excitement.

When the end of the year rolled around, both Claire and her principal were confident that the state assessment data would confirm what everyone saw and felt: Claire's students would not only succeed; they would exceed expectations. Then the results were released. Student performance in Claire's class was merely average. It was average when compared to the state results and average in comparison to her district counterparts. Claire was shocked to say the least.

"How can this be?" she asked herself. "I don't understand where I could be missing the mark. My lessons are engaging. The students work extremely hard, and they love what they are doing. I just don't get it."

As Claire left school that day, questioning not only her professional choices but her worth as a teacher, Mrs. Davis gave her a call. "Hey, Claire, I don't want you to get frustrated about your performance. Data are information, not condemnation, and we're going to use the data to figure out how we can get your students performing at higher levels of mastery. I know how hard you worked this year, and I don't want you to get down about it."

Claire visited with Mrs. Davis the next day to talk about her frustration and concern over her students' results. Mrs. Davis asked some questions that both challenged Claire to examine her lesson content and encouraged her to explore ways of enriching it. "Your students are obviously inspired by you and engaged in the content you're teaching," Mrs. Davis noted. "But is that content challenging enough to move them beyond a standard level of proficiency? And are you addressing all standards equally in your instruction, rather than giving extra weight to those that are essential?"

As she considered these questions, Claire felt her self-doubt slowly transform into resolve, and she recommitted to ensuring that her students would move beyond average to master rigorous learning content.

Following Mrs. Davis's suggestions, over the summer, Claire reflected on every lesson for her class. Meticulously analyzing her data and comparing assessment questions to the rigor of her lessons revealed one recurring theme: her engaging and exciting instruction was not challenging enough to help students develop and demonstrate content mastery. When Claire reflected on her instructional activities, she found that the relevance of her content hooked students, but it didn't lead them to the rigorous learning necessary to truly *use* the content. She picked apart every question that she posed through her instruction, assessments, and interventions and again found that she wasn't helping her students develop the depth of knowledge of essential content necessary to demonstrate true mastery.

Claire's focus for the next school year was simple. She was going to ensure that her students took on challenging lessons that had high levels of complexity and developed the deep understanding and critical thinking skills that matched even the most rigorous content standards. By helping her students meet those challenges, Claire could help them boost their command of essential content from average to excellent.

Of course, guiding students in rigorous learning demands that teachers have a deep level of content mastery as well. That mastery extends beyond the content they are teaching to the *way* they teach it. Promoting rigorous learning demands instructional processes and techniques capable of inspiring students to take on the challenges of a self-driven pursuit of content understanding. It also demands fostering in students the perseverance and motivation to maintain that pursuit as lifelong learners. As Wiggins (2014) writes:

> Content mastery is a means, in the same way that decoding fluency is a means toward the real goal of reading. . . . This logic requires teacher-designers to be clear, therefore, about which *uses* of content have course priority since understanding is about transfer and meaning-making via content.

The sections that follow examine the skills excellent teachers leverage in developing learning rigor and content mastery in their students.

Implementing Rigor and Mastery

Rigor is predicated on the teacher's ability to create an engaging learning environment in which high levels of expectation for learning, and the supports necessary to help students meet those expectations, are tightly interwoven into the structures that connect students to content. This is a difficult but essential task that stretches teachers' skills above the fundamentals and on to higher levels of professional development. As such, skills for developing rigor and mastery among students represent the first growth area of a teacher's professional development. As figure 6.1 illustrates, teachers build skills for developing rigor and mastery among their students upon the fundamental, or *deficit*, skill sets all educators must command in order to teach effectively.

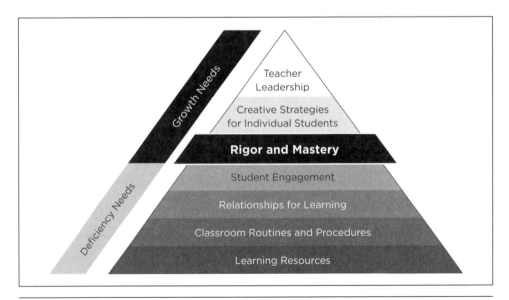

Figure 6.1: Hierarchy of Instructional Excellence—rigor and mastery.

While teaching for rigor and mastery demands professional growth above the fundamental skill sets for educators, it isn't merely a nice-to-have skill set. In an excellent school, all teachers need to cultivate and maintain their skills in boosting students' knowledge of essential content to the deep understanding that enables them to question, manipulate, and use that content in a variety of contexts. Students require a rigorous curriculum, innovative instruction, and challenging assessments to prepare them for the 21st century, a college-ready future, and a solid career path.

The definition of *rigorous learning* may vary slightly from school to school, but, as Daggett and Gendron (2015) explain, each school must clearly set forth its own definition, based on the DNA of that school and its district, because helping all teachers learn how to reach high levels of rigor requires a common definition and a well-defined plan. Administrators and teachers can work together to create that definition and then to agree on a plan that determines how teachers can plan and deliver lessons that promote rigorous learning and inspire students to master content and achieve learning success at the highest levels.

Figure 6.2 (page 122) shows a cycle flowchart that illustrates the instructional milestones teachers can incorporate into the process of moving students through rigorous learning and on to content mastery. I modeled this cycle after instructional components outlined in the Texas Teacher Evaluation and Support System (T-TESS; Texas Education Agency, 2014). As the rigor to mastery cycle indicates, excellent teachers bring to the instructional model their own mastery of content knowledge and expertise. Then, through planning and assessment, they create instructional activities to engage student interest in thoughtful work that encourages them to pursue content understanding. Teachers then employ strong questioning strategies to develop students' higher-level thinking, engage students in academic discussions related to content, and assess student understanding of lesson content. Finally, teachers continually monitor student participation and learning outcomes in order to adjust their instructional process to improve on those assessed results.

While these components apply to the teacher evaluation system in Texas, the components of teaching for rigorous learning are universal, as all five are found in the Danielson (2013) framework, the Four Marzano Teacher Evaluation Domains (Learning Sciences International, n.d.), and virtually every teacher evaluation system in North America.

The rigor to mastery instructional cycle continually supplies answers to two of the critical questions: (1) What do we expect all students to learn? and (2) How will we know if they learned it? Through each component of the cycle, excellent teachers pursue the answers to these questions before they teach, while they teach, and after they teach. If at any point in the cycle teachers lose track of these critical questions, they run the risk of leading students in inadequately rigorous instruction that fails to prepare them to demonstrate content mastery. The sections that follow outline the essential skills teachers must develop in order to effectively prepare and deliver

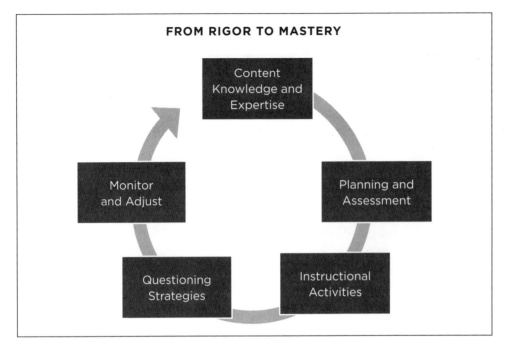

Source: Adapted from Texas Education Agency, 2014.

Figure 6.2: Rigor to mastery instructional cycle.

instruction that promotes students' learning rigor and content mastery, as well as the reflection skills excellent teachers use to continually monitor and adjust the strength of their instructional content and model.

Preparation

Before teachers can begin the arduous task of helping students master learning at high levels, they must determine how to meet the most rigorous demands of the most essential standards. As the rigor to mastery cycle illustrates, the pathway toward that goal begins with the teacher's learning and preparation, then proceeds through instructional planning for rigorous student learning and ongoing assessment to determine that students are succeeding.

The foundation of rigorous learning is the teacher's content knowledge and expertise. If the teacher doesn't possess a thorough knowledge of both the content and the best ways to help students learn that content, rigorous learning has little to no chance of becoming a reality. To develop a deep and flexible understanding of the content, teachers must spend time analyzing the standards that comprise the content and identify which standards are essential and which are not as essential. Buffum, Mattos, and Weber (2012) define this as *concentrated instruction*:

> A systematic process of identifying essential knowledge and
> skills that all students must master to learn at high levels, and

determining the specific learning needs for each child to get there. Thinking is guided by the question, Where do we need to go? (p. 10)

To avoid the trap of covering content that is "a mile wide and an inch deep," teachers should identify the eight to twelve skills or content standards that all students must master in order to learn the current year's content and be prepared for next year's content. Reeves (2002) writes that the essential standards should meet three criteria:

1. **Endurance:** Will this standard provide students with knowledge and skills that are valuable beyond a single test date?

2. **Leverage:** Will it provide knowledge and skills that are valuable in multiple disciplines?

3. **Readiness:** Will it provide students with knowledge and skills essential for success in the next grade level of instruction? (p. 51)

Teachers must *vertically align* the essential standards that they choose for the current year's content with prerequisite and future standards. In that process, teachers determine that their students have successfully met any prerequisite standards to ensure that they are prepared to undertake the rigorous study of the essential standards for this year's instruction. At the same time, teachers also have to be certain that the essential standards they choose for the current year's instruction adequately prepare students to undertake the rigorous learning of next year's standards. Figure 6.3 illustrates this vertical alignment of essential content standards.

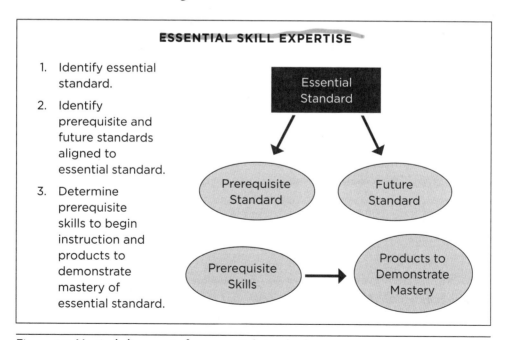

ESSENTIAL SKILL EXPERTISE

1. Identify essential standard.

2. Identify prerequisite and future standards aligned to essential standard.

3. Determine prerequisite skills to begin instruction and products to demonstrate mastery of essential standard.

Essential Standard

Prerequisite Standard

Future Standard

Prerequisite Skills

Products to Demonstrate Mastery

Figure 6.3: Vertical alignment of an essential standard.

After teachers identify and align essential standards for their content, they turn their attention to developing the pedagogy associated with those standards. Danielson (2013) writes, "Different disciplines have 'signature pedagogies' that have evolved over time and been found to be most effective in teaching" (p. 6). Excellent teachers not only know these pedagogies, but they also determine which pedagogies work best based on students' learning styles and profiles. Teachers committed to excellence, but who are uncertain of their command of these signature pedagogies, seek professional development, work with their collaborative teams, and engage in personal research to enrich their pedagogical skill sets.

Next, teachers must include plans for ongoing formative assessments. The purpose for formative assessments is critical to the rigor and mastery cycle. They help teachers determine if their lessons are effective and which students are doing well and which need improvement: "One of the main differences between effective and ineffective teachers is that effective teachers know 'the learning intentions and success criteria of their lessons'" (Hattie, 2009, as cited in DuFour & Marzano, 2011, p. 94). Great teachers know how to use formative assessments to drive rigorous learning and produce content mastery: "Formative assessments should shape instruction [just as] our formative experiences are those that have shaped our current selves" (Wiliam, 2011, p. 40).

Figure 6.4 illustrates the interwoven relationship between planning for rigorous learning and assessing for rigorous learning and content mastery. In this relationship, as students progress through instructional activities designed to help them develop a deep understanding of the essential standard, educators use three forms of assessments to ensure that students are achieving that learning goal.

Individual formative assessments include both formal and informal checks for understanding, such as student observations and anecdotal records, that individual teachers utilize throughout their lessons every day to determine which students are learning and which students are not learning. *Common formative assessments* are formal checks, such as weekly quizzes and curriculum-based assessments, that a team of teachers creates to assess for learning at the beginning, middle, and end of the unit of instruction. These assessments use the data to drive interventions and instruction simultaneously. *Summative assessments*, such as unit tests or semester exams, represent the final assessment of learning to determine which students learned the content and which students need further intervention.

Planning and assessment take much forethought and intentionality, but without high levels of content expertise, teachers can't truly plan for instructional rigor. Excellent teachers understand that their knowledge and expertise set the stage for the level of rigorous learning that students can successfully master. When teachers successfully plan for high levels of learning and assess for learning at those levels, their instructional delivery has a strong chance of being rigorous as well.

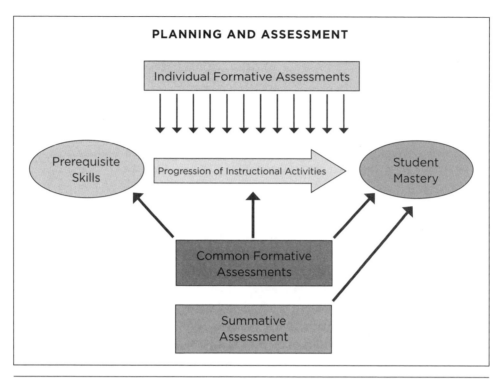

PLANNING AND ASSESSMENT

Figure 6.4: Planning and assessment.

Delivery

The delivery of instruction for rigorous learning isn't limited to asking harder questions or demanding more work. Instead, instruction for rigorous learning stretches student understanding so students can create meaningful products that serve as evidence of their work. It inspires students to evaluate the quality of their own work as well as that of their peers, and it challenges them to ask introspective questions that lead to a deeper understanding of themselves and their learning.

There are two basic components in the delivery of this type of instruction—instructional activities and questioning strategies. In order for teachers to reach excellence in both components, they must know how to apply their content expertise in planning and assessment through instructional activities driven by challenging questions.

When selecting instructional activities, many teachers choose those that are aesthetically pleasing first and connected to the standard second. Excellent teachers, however, consider many factors before choosing instructional activities, and they opt for those that best develop students' academic rigor and content mastery. Because they know that rigor can't be left to chance, excellent teachers consider the following four questions before deeming an activity rigorous enough for instruction.

1. Does the activity match the level of rigor in the standard?

    a. If not, is it aligned to the rigor of the prerequisite standard?

b.   If not, can it be used as an intervention for struggling students through guided learning?

2.   Does the activity challenge students with high-level questions and create opportunities for students to generate their own high-level questions?

3.   Does the activity inspire students to learn from one another, and does it motivate them to take ownership of their learning?

4.   Does the activity structure learning in such a way that students can set academic growth goals and monitor their growth toward the mastery of those goals?

Rigorous learning activities work best when teachers determine where the activity best matches the confidence and competence levels of their students. If the activity aligns with student competencies and meets the criteria for rigor in the questions previously listed, teachers then need to determine where the activity best fits in the gradual release of responsibility model (see chapter 5, pages 97–98). If the activity relies on the students' independent work, then teachers may determine that it works well as an independent learning activity. If the activity requires more teacher support, teachers may need to model the activity for students through a focus lesson. In some cases, activities may need a more hands-on approach, in which case, the teacher can use guided learning to lead students through the activity. Alternatively, the teacher can use the activity as a collaborative learning opportunity so students can work together and support each other through the learning experience.

Most teachers ask questions throughout instruction, but excellent teachers intentionally prompt learning and thinking through strategic questioning. Understanding that all students are at different places in their level of mastery, these teachers are prepared to ask three levels of questions throughout their lesson.

1.   **Scaffolding questions:** These lower-level questions guide below-level or struggling students to think through the process or concept in smaller, attainable chunks.

2.   **On-level questions:** The questions at the appropriate level of rigor and cognitive complexity in the standard lead students to generate answers or products that serve as evidence of their mastery of content.

3.   **Extension questions:** These high-level questions prompt students to apply or transfer their learning in unpredictable situations, synthesize their thinking about the concept in new or different ways, or create products that expand on their mastery of the standard.

Great teachers understand that questioning is a challenging skill in and of itself; therefore, they put as much effort into developing challenging questions as they do in creating rigorous instructional activities. Great teachers also believe in using student mistakes as teachable moments in the lesson, and they use questioning strategies to challenge students to reflect on their mistakes to determine how they can learn from them.

The hallmark of an excellent teacher's delivery is in his or her ability to stretch students and their thinking through selecting activities that intentionally and appropriately incorporate high levels of critical thinking. The ultimate goal of questioning strategies is to create a learning environment and activities that encourage students to ask these questions of themselves, their peers, and their teachers.

Reflection

Throughout the lesson and at the end of every lesson, excellent teachers reflect on the effectiveness of their instruction and their approach to teaching. During reflection, "the teacher makes an accurate assessment of a lesson's effectiveness and the extent to which it achieved its instructional outcomes" (Danielson, 2013, p. 62). Excellent teachers evaluate all aspects of their lesson to determine where students struggled, where activities were unable to connect students to the learning target, and where questioning strategies failed to transform rigorous learning into content mastery. When teachers have built great lessons aligned to the rigor of standards, therefore, they also need to develop an observation protocol for determining student success in learning. Additionally, teachers need to develop specific protocols for giving all students descriptive feedback to help deepen their knowledge.

Monitoring and adjusting instruction is one such protocol, one that takes much practice to perfect. To effectively monitor instruction, teachers must be able to continuously adjust the pace of the lesson to ensure high levels of learning. Monitoring and adjusting are not just about knowing when to speed up, slow down, or change the lesson altogether. The teacher should know if all students are learning, how to respond if they aren't, and how to extend the learning when they succeed.

Teachers gather formative data on individual students and on the class as a whole to determine which activities promote high levels of rigorous learning and which activities stifle it. To gather more precise data about individual students, teachers can employ explicit checks for understanding with probing questions and give students specific feedback to help them learn at high levels. Finally, excellent teachers establish both short-term and long-term goals for future learning and communicate those goals clearly to students.

Observation and *feedback* are two essential skills for monitoring and adjusting instruction to ensure rigorous learning and content mastery. When students succeed in learning rigorous content, excellent teachers go beyond offering an affirmative "good job" by giving those students specific feedback that acknowledges their progress and encourages them to take their learning to the next level. If students are not adequately learning the content, excellent teachers provide constructive feedback that helps students understand where they have advanced in their learning, where their learning has stopped, and what they need to do to improve. If observation reveals that the lesson is not succeeding with the entire class, excellent teachers apply the same feedback principle. They stop the lesson, show the class members what they have done successfully, where they are struggling, and what they need to do next.

When teachers effectively reflect on the rigor of their lessons, they help all students learn at high levels and complete the cycle of rigor and mastery. If teachers plan for rigorous learning by developing assessments, they are more prepared to deliver that learning throughout each component of instruction. They also are more capable of transferring the responsibility for rigorous learning to students. On the other hand, if teachers never or rarely reflect on their own performance and that of their students, they miss a huge opportunity to provide concentrated instruction that fully prepares students for the following year of instruction. An inability to reflect on instructional effectiveness can lead to deficits in student learning that will most likely fall on the shoulders of next year's teachers to remediate.

Building an Excellence Support System: Rigor and Mastery

An educator's lack of content knowledge and the expertise necessary to deliver it through instruction can form a serious barrier to promoting rigorous learning in the classroom. Given the wide array of content taught in most schools, and the fact that most school leaders typically possess expertise in a single content area, no leader has all the time, knowledge, and experience to help every teacher create and deliver rigorous learning for every standard. We can, however, create an environment where the expectation of rigorous learning and content mastery is the norm and then build and maintain a system of supports that can help teachers develop the knowledge and expertise necessary to meet that norm.

Step 1: Schoolwide Supports

The school's first priority in accomplishing the goal of *learning for all* is to create a guaranteed and viable curriculum. "The process of creating a guaranteed and viable curriculum begins with identification of content that is considered essential to a course or subject area within a grade level" (DuFour & Marzano, 2011, pp. 94–95). We should pay close attention to the term *essential* in that statement. Even the best teachers limit their ability to engage students in rigorous learning when they try to deliver it for every established learning standard. Districts owe it to teachers to relieve the pressure of giving every standard equal weight. We can move toward this goal by allowing teachers the time, tools, and professional learning opportunities that can help them identify the essential, or *power*, standards, for their content and align their expertise, common language, and instructional strategies around those standards. We also can offer teachers necessary support for developing their content knowledge and expertise so they are prepared to align their chosen standards within the vertical continuum described earlier in this chapter. Finally, our support systems must aid teachers in designing rigorous learning around those standards that help their students master the associated content.

Vertically Aligned Standards and Formative Assessments

As we have seen, vertically aligning standards with prerequisite standards and future standards requires that teachers determine their students' preparedness for the new standard *and* its effectiveness at preparing students for future standards. To support teachers in that process, we can offer them tools and practices for building knowledge and expertise around the standards' content. One powerful tool for this purpose is the *depth of knowledge* (DOK) framework that Norman L. Webb (2002) developed. Teachers can use the DOK framework to categorize standards into four levels of cognitive demand—(1) recall of information, (2) basic reasoning, (3) complex reasoning, and (4) extended reasoning—based on the complexity of the tasks necessary to learn the content. Using this framework, educators can evaluate and identify power standards that help develop students' rigorous thinking based on the level of thinking the standard demands, the complexity of the content, and the context necessary to master the standard. The DOK framework analysis helps to deepen teachers' familiarity with standards and ensure that the power standards they include in their instructional plan fit into the vertical curriculum alignment.

Systemwide supports for this area of professional growth also need to help teachers determine the appropriate assessments for demonstrating student content mastery at a level of rigor that either meets or exceeds the standard's DOK level. The schoolwide supports, therefore, also can include the template in figure 6.5.

Skill	Standard	Prerequisite Skills Required to Master the Standard	Depth of Knowledge Required to Master the Standard	Student Product Required to Demonstrate Mastery of the Standard
Aligned Skill From Grade Level Above				
Aligned Skill on Grade Level				
Aligned Skill From Grade Level Below				
Notes				

Source: Wink, 2014.

Figure 6.5: Vertical standard analysis.

Visit **go.SolutionTree.com/leadership** *for a free reproducible version of this figure.*

Teachers can use the template to guide their thinking as they deconstruct the selected power by listing their prerequisite skills and the depth of knowledge required to master them. To complete the template, teachers can assess all those elements by determining which student products will demonstrate mastery over the chosen standards' content. If teachers are unable to complete any element of this template, they can always turn to other professional development resources at the schoolwide or teacher team level to improve their content and process expertise.

Professional Development on Instructional Delivery

Beyond content knowledge and expertise, to develop students' rigorous learning and content mastery, teachers also must be skilled at transferring that knowledge to every student. Questioning strategies are an easy and effective method for increasing students' rigorous thinking through instruction. As a natural part of instruction, effective questioning is a skill that has been modeled for centuries. Asking questions that help students develop complex understanding and critical thinking, however, is essential to move students from mere comprehension to command of content. That kind of questioning can be difficult.

To address this difficulty, systemwide supports can offer teachers professional development focused on creating rigorous questions. Since questioning starts with content knowledge, teachers must learn how to identify the DOK level of thinking required to master content within each standard and then create questions that match that level. Teachers also can use Webb's (2002) DOK framework to scaffold questions in order to help systematically move students toward more rigorous thinking.

Schools can provide teachers quick and ready access to resources and tools that can help them deepen their instruction with the use of more rigorous questions and activities that require students to apply their learning through creation, analysis, synthesis, and evaluation. These supports can include a multitude of instructional activities and extensions accessible to teachers through the campus webpage or blog. Figure 6.6 illustrates just one such a resource. This template offers examples of DOK level 2 and level 3 question stems and instructional activities teachers can either use or adapt to their current instructional plans in order to promote more rigorous student learning.

Curriculum Guides

Teachers can use well-designed curriculum guides as tools for helping them develop and deliver content for rigorous learning. Aside from listing standards and examples of test questions, these documents include critical vocabulary, prerequisite skills, essential questions, and successful instructional strategies that teachers can find especially helpful when working with struggling students. Some curriculum documents also provide teachers with model lessons that experienced teachers have used successfully. These scripted lessons show teachers how to frame a lesson and how to leverage collaborative learning, guided learning, and independent learning to help students master the content.

DOK Descriptors	Analyze: To examine a thing to know its parts Compare: To examine for likenesses and differences Contrast: To show differences when compared Group: To cluster	Infer: To derive as a conclusion from facts or premises Sequence: To chronologically order events Synthesize: To combine parts or elements of a whole
DOK 2 Question Stems	Can you explain how _____ affected _____ ? How would you apply what you learned to develop _____ ? How would you compare _____ ? Contrast _____ ? How would you classify _____ ? How would you group by characteristics? What factors would you change? How are _____ alike? Different? How would you classify the type of _____ ? What can you say about _____ ? How would you summarize _____ ? What steps are needed to edit _____ ? When would you use an outline to _____ ? How would you estimate _____ ? How would you organize _____ ? What would you use to classify _____ ? What do you notice about _____ ? Do you know another instance where _____ ? Could this have happened in _____ ? What was the turning point of _____ ? What was the problem with _____ ?	Can you apply these methods in your own experiment? What questions would you ask of _____ ? Would this information be useful if you had a _____ ? Which events could have happened _____ ? If _____ happened, what might the ending have been? How was this similar to _____ ? What was the underlying theme of _____ ? What do you see as other possible outcomes? Why did these changes occur? Can you compare _____ with those presented in _____ ? How is _____ similar to _____ ? What are some problems associated with _____ ? Can you distinguish between _____ ? What were some of the motives behind _____ ?

continued ↓

Figure 6.6: DOK question stems and activities chart.

DOK Descriptors	**Analyze: To examine a thing to know its parts** **Compare: To examine for likenesses and differences** **Contrast: To show differences when compared** **Group: To cluster**	**Infer: To derive as a conclusion from facts or premises** **Sequence: To chronologically order events** **Synthesize: To combine parts or elements of a whole**
DOK 2 Activities	Construct a model showing how something works.	Identify and summarize the major events in a narrative.
	Make a diorama about an event.	Use context clues to identify the meaning of unfamiliar words.
	Make a scrapbook.	
	Create a collection of photographs to demonstrate a point.	Solve routine, multiple-step problems.
		Describe the cause and effect of a particular event.
	Make a clay model.	Identify patterns in events or behavior.
	Design a market strategy.	Formulate a routine problem given data and conditions.
	Dress a doll in a national costume.	Organize, represent, and interpret data.
	Paint a mural.	Make a jigsaw puzzle.
	Write a textbook for others.	Make a family tree showing relationships.
	Design a questionnaire to gather information.	Put on a play.
	Write a commercial to sell a product.	
	Conduct an investigation to support a view.	
	Make a flowchart to show critical stages of investigation.	
	Construct a graph to illustrate information.	

DOK Descriptors	Analyze: To examine a thing to know its parts Compare: To examine for likenesses and differences Contrast: To show differences when compared Group: To cluster	Infer: To derive as a conclusion from facts or premises Sequence: To chronologically order events Synthesize: To combine parts or elements of a whole
DOK 3 Question Stems	How is _____ related to _____?	Can you design a _____ to _____?
	What conclusions can you draw from _____?	Can you see a possible solution?
	How would you adapt _____ to create a different _____?	If you had access to all resources, how would you deal with _____?
	How would you test _____?	Can you devise your own way to deal with _____?
	Can you predict the outcome if _____?	How many ways can you _____?
	What is the best answer? Why?	Can you create new and unusual uses for _____?
	What conclusion can you draw from these three texts?	Can you predict the outcome if variables are changed?
	What is your interpretation of this text? Support your rationale.	Is there a better solution for _____?
	How would you describe the sequence of _____?	How can you judge the value of _____?
	What facts would you select to support _____?	Can you defend your position about _____?
	Can you elaborate on the reason for _____?	Do you think _____ is a good idea or a bad idea?
	How would you test _____?	How would you have handled _____?
	Are you a person who _____?	What changes to _____ would you recommend?
	How would you feel if _____?	Do you believe _____?
	How effective is _____?	
	What do you think about _____?	

continued ↓

DOK Descriptors	Analyze: To examine a thing to know its parts Compare: To examine for likenesses and differences Contrast: To show differences when compared Group: To cluster	Infer: To derive as a conclusion from facts or premises Sequence: To chronologically order events Synthesize: To combine parts or elements of a whole
DOK 3 Activities	Invent a machine. Design a building. Create, name, and market a new product. Write about your views on _____. Write a TV show, role play, song, or pantomime. Design a book or magazine cover or a Facebook or Instagram page. Make up a new language code and write material using it. Sell an idea. Devise a way to _____. Compose a rhythm or put new words to a known melody. Prepare a list of criteria to judge a _____ show. Indicate priority and ratings. Conduct a debate about an issue. Prepare a case and present it to an audience.	Support ideas with details and examples. Use voice appropriate to the purpose and audience. Identify research questions and design investigations for a scientific problem. Develop a scientific model for a complex situation. Determine the author's purpose and describe how it affects the interpretation of a reading selection. Convince others to agree with what you feel is important. Form a panel to discuss views about an issue. Write a letter to _____ proposing changes needed. Write a half yearly report.

Source: Adapted from Zelenak, 2014.

Instruction Monitoring and Adjustment

Most leaders understand that monitoring and adjusting instruction can make the difference between excellent teaching and average teaching that, in turn, can make the difference between excellent and average student learning outcomes. In the same way that we provide teachers with resources and tools to support instruction, we also can offer teachers strategies for monitoring and adjusting their instruction to better guide students in rigorous learning.

These strategies can include a variety of tools and practices, from protocols for giving feedback to multiple ways to gather observation data. As an example, Bellingham Public Schools (n.d.) in the state of Washington have created an online resource for teachers that includes such instruction monitoring and adjustment strategies as recording assessments, asking students to self-assess and evaluate, reteaching and revisiting, and posing open-ended questions.

We also can encourage teachers to employ anecdotal records as a simple but effective tool for gathering observational data. Using little more than paper on a clipboard, teachers create these records by circulating around the room and taking notes about individual students, their progress in learning, and the level of content understanding demonstrated in their work. They can use these notes to inform and drive the instructional needs of each student or the entire class. Teachers can apply what they've learned from these notes either immediately or during the next day's class. This is an especially useful strategy for helping teachers create a quick, focused assessment of every student's ability to keep pace with rigorous learning.

Step 2: Teacher Team Supports

There are multiple ways that collaborative teams can work together to create and implement tools and practices for supporting teachers' skills in developing rigorous instruction. Teacher teams can offer members various tools and strategies for promoting rigor and mastery at every stage of the instructional process, from planning for instruction to designing assessments to reflecting on data. Excellent leaders understand that the purpose of collaborative teams is not to ensure that members complete some "teaching for content mastery" checklist. Instead, these teacher team supports are most effective when they're designed to help members clarify rigorous learning goals for developing content mastery and the most effective instructional processes for delivering it: "Teachers are most effective in helping all students learn when they are clear regarding exactly what their students must know and be able to do as a result of the course, grade level, or unit of instruction" (DuFour et al., 2010, p. 70).

To build the most effective system of teacher team supports, we can work with teachers to create multiple types of teacher teams in order to address multiple opportunities and challenges for professional growth in teaching for rigor and mastery. The sections that follow outline five such team types, including (1) subject-level teams, (2) vertical teams, (3) interdisciplinary teams, (4) singleton teams, and (5) virtual teams.

Subject-Level Teams

Subject-level teams are organized around content, and therefore, members have a great deal in common. Members of these teams work with the same curriculum, the same standards, the same age group of students, and the same instructional outcomes. As a result of these commonalities, perhaps the most important product to come from these teams is an aligned understanding among members as to their instructional goals, processes, and assessments. Since content knowledge and expertise is the foundation for successfully teaching rigorous content, subject-level teacher teams can begin by focusing their collaborative efforts on clarifying power standards. Then, for each standard, they should answer this question: How would student work demonstrate mastery of the content within this standard? DuFour et al. (2010) state, "This strategy of clarifying standards through the lens of student work leads teams through a natural progression of questions" (p. 66).

Careful analysis of the essential skills at all levels can help teams collectively develop a deeper knowledge of their shared subject's content and what form rigorous learning of that content might take. The essential skill analysis and planning tool in figure 6.7 can help subject-level teacher teams improve their knowledge of the learning standards and the rigor associated with them while simultaneously designing instruction and crafting assessments to help students master the standards at the highest levels.

Team members can use columns two and three of the tool to collaboratively determine how they should deliver rigor in instruction by analyzing essential standards together. Teams can then identify the level of thinking, content, and context needed to pursue rigorous learning of the standard, and then clarify what mastery of that content looks like in the standards below, above, and on grade level. Subject-level teams can use columns four and five of the planning tool to identify the resources, questioning strategies, and instructional strategies that are most likely to lead all students to mastery. By collaboratively agreeing on the elements that fill this tool, teachers develop their collective expertise in guiding students through the rigorous learning processes necessary to master content.

Vertical Teams

Vertical teams have less in common than subject-level teams, but they offer huge potential for teacher collaboration around rigor and mastery. Like subject-level teams, vertical team members can discuss content using the questions in the essential skill analysis and planning tool (see figure 6.7). However, vertical teams tackle these questions through a lens of vertical alignment. Discussions about essential standards within vertical teams can encourage members to ensure that their instruction is aligned with prerequisite skills their students learned the previous year and that it also prepares students to master content included in next year's standards.

We should encourage vertical teams to pay special attention to alignment of the following items: vocabulary, language of instruction, instructional strategies, and

Skill	Standard: Content + Context + DOK Level	Prerequisite Skills Required to Master the Standard	Instructional Implications	What Demonstrates Mastery of the Standard?
Aligned Skill From Grade Level Above			Tech resources Textbook resources Other resources Critical vocabulary	How will we check for understanding daily? Sample test question
Aligned Skill on Grade Level			Critical strategies to help students Manipulatives and tools needed	
Aligned Skill From Grade Level Below			What review will be required prior to instruction?	How will we preassess prerequisite skills?
Critical Questions	What are the critical curricular components in this three-year strand?	How will we remediate students who are lacking the foundational skills?	How will we take students from the prerequisite skill to mastery of the essential standard?	How will we check for understanding in many ways?

Source: Wink, 2014.

Figure 6.7: Essential skill analysis and planning tool.

problem-solving models. When vertical teams collaborate with the mindset of providing students with three to four years of continuity in rigorous content instruction, they have the potential to accelerate student content mastery and, at the same time, strengthen each teacher's content knowledge and expertise.

Interdisciplinary Teams

We can build interdisciplinary teams with members who share students rather than subject content. Interdisciplinary teacher teams have the power to positively affect students *and* their ability to engage in rigorous learning. While members of these teams don't necessarily share content standards, they share expectations for learning and a collective responsibility to help students learn at high levels. Interdisciplinary teams can collaborate about positive approaches for improving the learning of specific students, and they can collaboratively develop shared strategies for promoting rigorous thinking and content mastery in all students. These shared strategies can help teachers:

- Deepen students' critical thinking and problem solving

- Utilize technology tools to strengthen instruction

- Set instructional expectations for students

- Establish the level of rigor expected within each component of the instructional delivery model

Leaders often relegate interdisciplinary teams to collaborative tasks, such as behavior management or intervention, but these teams also have the potential for raising the level of rigor learning for students. Because of the diversity of their members, who may represent a broad range of content knowledge and expertise, interdisciplinary teams bring a wide array of strategies to the table. As education administrator, author, and educator Ben Johnson (2014) writes, "We can promote deep learning by encouraging multiple teachers working together in helping students to understand math in the context of science, coordinating timelines of scientific discovery and literature, and demonstrating how a painter uses light to express meaning." Johnson (2014) goes on to describe the power of such interdisciplinary collaborations to drive rigorous learning: "When professional educators combine their energies and reinforce the same deep learning, the stream of information is clearer for the student, the learning activities are more fluid, and the student's reservoir of knowledge and skills fills faster."

Singleton Teams

Excellent teachers who don't share content or even students still share the same goal—student learning at high levels. Singletons, such as art teachers, music teachers, technology teachers, and so on, frequently are the only educators within their schools who teach their specific subject. Even in small schools, singletons can form teams that take the work of interdisciplinary teams one step further by focusing collaboration on shared instructional components. For example, an arts-focused singleton team could develop strategies to engage and inspire rigorous learning through collaborative experiments with music genres, dance, or graphic arts technologies. A singleton team of advanced placement (AP) teachers could focus their collaboration on the questioning strategies and interventions to help students earn a score of three or higher on the AP test. Career and technical education teachers could form a singleton team to align their instruction with a rigorous nationally recognized industry certification program or to create plans that help students master content in order to prepare to transition into a college or career path after graduation.

Singletons often work in isolation within their school systems, and so they may find it difficult to see the value in collaborating with others. To help overcome this reluctance, leaders must be particularly creative and adept at helping to form these teams and support them in implementing their strategies. Not only do we owe it to our singleton teachers to help build these teams, we stand to gain a great deal from their collaborative efforts to help deepen students' understanding of content, broaden their scope for using that content, and extend their learning in new and innovative directions.

Virtual Teams

When determining what types of teacher teams can best address the need for promoting rigorous learning and content mastery, we need to remember that these collaborations don't have to revolve around a common meeting time or place. Schools with dwindling resources and limited time overcome these limitations by providing teachers ample opportunity to collaborate through the use of virtual tools.

Virtual teams can create Google Docs and folders to share documents and simultaneously create planning documents and assessments for rigorous learning, such as those described earlier in this chapter. Virtual teams can use websites, such as Smore (www.smore.com), to create a library of digital creations or discoveries to share with one another to support their common purpose. Virtual teams also are using social media tools, such as Voxer (www.voxer.com), to communicate instantly through live or recorded voice and text messages and photos to one person or an entire group.

While small or remote school systems might offer challenges for forming the kind of diverse and highly functional teams necessary to most effectively collaborate, virtual teams can be a powerful way to meet those challenges. By providing the time and technologies necessary to support virtual teams, we can offer our teachers a strong and viable tool for collaborating with other teachers and teams at any time and from locations around the world. That's a powerful way to support excellent teaching that results in rigorous learning and content mastery for our students.

Step 3: Individualized Supports

If a teacher is struggling in the area of rigorous instruction, it's our responsibility to individually address that teacher's issues and help remediate them. Before we can create a plan for individualized supports, however, we first need to ensure that the cause for the teacher's difficulty doesn't rest in one of the four fundamental areas of the Hierarchy of Instructional Excellence. If that isn't where the problems lie, we can assume that we are working with a good teacher who is striving to become an excellent teacher.

Rigor can be a nebulous idea, as personal affinities and preferences shape our perceptions of what represents rigorous learning and mastery of content. Systemwide and teacher team supports address the school system's accepted definitions of rigor and mastery, so we needn't focus on those definitions in individualized supports. Instead, we can focus on helping teachers develop instruction that successfully leads to rigorous learning, observe the strategies involved in that instruction, and then learn to use those strategies. The following sections describe four strategies—(1) co-teaching, (2) observation and feedback, (3) instructional coaching, and (4) co-planning—that can aid in that process.

Co-Teaching

If a teacher has adequate levels of content knowledge and expertise but struggles to deliver rigorous instruction, we can partner that teacher with another teacher who succeeds in that delivery. Co-teachers plan a lesson together, deliver it together, share joint responsibility for the lesson, and reflect together after the lesson is complete. The expert teacher models for the struggling teacher, and the struggling teacher emulates the expert's approach, strategies, and instructional style. Both teachers are peers; there is no hierarchy or title differentiation to muddy the waters. The two teachers are colleagues with the twofold purpose of helping each other grow in the craft of teaching, while simultaneously improving the students' rigorous learning.

Co-teachers will need to overcome scheduling constraints. If both teachers have the same schedule, they can plan together during their conference and combine their classes to teach the lesson. If they don't have the same schedule, they can plan together before or after school and take turns teaching together when one of them has a conference period. They also can work with the principal to request a substitute teacher for one period or for the day so they can arrange a compatible co-teaching opportunity. Co-teaching is collaboration in action, so we need to go beyond supporting it to avidly promoting co-teaching and making it widely available to all teachers.

Observation and Feedback

Teacher observation is a common strategy for evaluation and feedback. In the typical form of this process, principals spend time in a classroom observing the teacher and leave feedback to help that teacher improve. This approach may be appropriate when we are working to help the teacher improve fundamental areas of professional performance or his or her general use of instructional strategies and methods. When we are using observation and feedback to help teachers improve their skills in delivering rigorous instruction for content mastery, however, it's important that we initially work with the teacher to agree on which areas of instruction our observation and feedback will focus. Next, we can determine whether the teacher has an adequate level of content knowledge and expertise. Then we can analyze planning and assessment, instructional activities, and questioning strategies. Finally, we can help the teacher review his or her processes for monitoring and adjusting. Using this structured process, we can be certain that our observation and feedback are more targeted toward specific areas of need and, therefore, more effective.

We can facilitate this process by examining the teacher's lesson plan rather than observing entire units and evaluating every instructional element that takes place within them. Based on our review, we can provide specific feedback about the rigor of the planned lesson and its instructional elements. Then we can offer ideas for improvement focused on the targeted areas for growth we have agreed on with the teacher. Again, this approach allows us to focus our work on helping the teacher grow in the skill sets for rigor and mastery rather than delivering a general and all-encompassing critique of the teacher's work.

Instructional Coaching

Instructional coaching incorporates elements of both co-teaching and observation and feedback, but it is more intense than either of those other individualized supports. A coaching relationship isn't supervisory; it's about working together to facilitate growth through conversation, reflective questioning, planning, and observation. Janice Dole (2004) observes:

> [Coaches] have the knowledge base to provide classroom teachers with the support they need to learn new content and research-based instruction and to assist teachers as they practice new strategies and programs in their classrooms until they become a part of teachers' daily work lives. (pp. 464-465)

Coaching offers many positive benefits to accelerate teacher growth. Using reflective questioning to guide a teacher's thinking about instruction is one example of an effective coaching technique. This strategy can help teachers solve instructional problems. Additionally, the coach can observe the class and then offer observations and guiding questions to help the teacher arrive at a self-assessment of his or her performance and identify steps for improvement. When a talented and committed coach helps a teacher gain more skill in the rigor to mastery cycle, that teacher's chance for successful improvement grows exponentially.

Co-Planning

Collaborative teams plan much of their instruction together, but sometimes that isn't enough to help a teacher struggling to develop more rigorous instruction. Co-planning is a great activity to help these struggling teachers in such areas as content knowledge and expertise or planning and assessment. By planning a lesson with a coach or a colleague, teachers can converse about their plan as they develop it. They can bounce ideas, questioning, activities, and assessments off their expert partner to get immediate feedback and further ideas. This kind of constructive collaboration not only strengthens the ability to plan for rigor, it refines the teacher's ability to deliver rigor in a more effective manner.

Problem Simplification Plan

Before incorporating specific strategies into an individualized plan for helping a teacher improve his or her skills for teaching rigorous content, it's critical that we meet with the teacher to identify his or her greatest area in need of improvement. Then we can work together to create an effective plan for achieving that improvement. For this process, we can use a problem simplification plan, such as that shown in figure 6.8.

To begin using this plan, we can meet with the struggling teacher to determine in which of the five components of the rigor to mastery instructional cycle (see figure 6.2, page 122) the teacher exhibits strength and which areas offer room for professional growth. Next, through observation, we can review the teacher's current instructional strategies within these necessary growth areas. We can then come to an agreement with the teacher regarding which component we will target in our individualized plan. When we have identified areas for improvement, we can build strategies into the problem simplification plan. As part of that plan, we also can specify a target date when we agree that the teacher will demonstrate that he or she has accomplished the agreed-on improvements.

Conclusion

An educator's pathway toward rigor begins in the familiar territory of fundamental skills for instructional excellence, including leveraging learning resources, creating and maintaining effective classroom routines and procedures, developing strong relationships for learning, and building student engagement. When teachers command those skills, they will be better prepared to create the conditions that challenge all students to learn at high levels.

As noted early in this chapter, people and institutions vary in their definition of *rigor*. If we want to give teachers a valuable map for their journey toward professional development in this area, we must be prepared to work with teachers and teacher teams to form *our* system's standard definition of rigor and arrive at a common set of standards and metrics for assessing both rigor and content mastery. When those definitions and the conditions for learning are set, the real work of teaching students to learn and master rigorous course content can begin.

As outlined in this chapter, teachers require high levels of content knowledge and expertise to help students develop their own deep understanding of that content. They also must be skilled at identifying which content standards they will address and how those standards align with prerequisite and future standards to continually develop students' learning rigor and content mastery. They also should be adept at choosing the most effective instructional strategies for developing rigorous learning and the most efficient assessment tools for gauging student content mastery. Finally, teachers must engage in ongoing reflection in order to identify methods for

Problem Simplification Plan: Rigor and Mastery

1. Identify the teacher's ability to deliver powerful instruction and rigorous assessments.

   S: Area of strength for the teacher   **G:** Areas of growth for teacher

   _____ Content knowledge and expertise

   _____ Planning and assessments

   _____ Instructional activities

   _____ Questioning strategies

   _____ Monitor and adjust

   Notes:

2. What are the current actions in place for this target area? How are students responding to current creative strategies? How well are strategies crafted to engage and empower students to own their learning?

3. Describe the best intervention to help the teacher develop a better understanding of the targeted area for growth.

   ☐ Observation of _____.

   ☐ Plan or develop instruction, questions, assessments, or activities with _____.

   ☐ Co-teach with _____.

   ☐ _____ models intervention or extension with the struggling teacher's class.

   ☐ Read or research _____.

   ☐ Other: _____

   Notes:

4. Set a date by when instruction and assessments should be successfully established.

5. What strategies will we implement to ensure rigorous instruction and assessments have improved?

Figure 6.8: Problem simplification plan—rigor and mastery.

Visit **go.SolutionTree.com/leadership** *for a free reproducible version of this figure.*

continually improving their skills in planning and delivering rigorous content in their classrooms. In other words, teaching for rigor and mastery is a complex process. Supporting teachers in that process is an equally complex task, but one that's essential if we want to ensure that our schools guarantee learning excellence for all students.

We must remember that we can't just set expectations for rigorous learning. We have to accompany those expectations with a plan to ensure that every teacher develops the skills necessary to move students from merely knowing the relevant content to understanding the content deeply enough to ask critical questions, form independent ideas about the content, and use the content in multiple contexts. If we want to prepare students to deeply understand the content they have learned, and to be able to *use* that content rather than just memorize and repeat it, we must be serious about building the structures and systems necessary to guide them through that work.

Rigor can be an elusive creature, but it's one that we must harness if we want to prepare students to succeed in whatever educational and career opportunities await them. That's why excellent leaders don't leave rigor and mastery to chance. By ensuring that all educators in our system have access to the plans, strategies, collaboration, coaching, modeling, assessments, and other systematic supports necessary to help them reach high levels of instructional rigor, we can be sure that we are putting our best effort into helping students master even the most rigorous content in preparation for meeting the many challenges that lie ahead.

The following reflection tool can help leaders assess how well they are doing in that effort and identify ways to improve going forward.

Reflection Tool: Rigor and Mastery

Definition of Excellence for Rigor and Mastery

What is our school's definition of teacher excellence in the area of rigor and mastery?

Schoolwide Supports

1. How well do we clearly define our school's definition of rigor and mastery?

2. How well do we leverage school and district leadership to improve our school's definition of rigor and mastery?

3. How effective is our system for helping teachers identify the essential standards for each content area and their associated prerequisite and future standards?

4. How effective is our system for making sure teachers know how to develop strong formal and informal formative assessments and helping teachers know if students are learning the content?

5. How effective is our schoolwide system for helping teachers select instructional activities and rigorous questions that lead students to mastery of the standards?

6. How effective is our schoolwide system for helping all teachers monitor the rigor of their lessons and make the necessary adjustments to help more students learn at high levels?

A Leader's Guide to Excellence in Every Classroom © 2017 Solution Tree Press • SolutionTree.com
Visit **go.SolutionTree.com/leadership** to download this free reproducible.

Teacher Team Supports

1. What percentage of our teachers participate in collaborative teacher teams that work and learn together to ensure rigor and mastery?

2. What work have our teacher teams done to identify the essential standards for their content area and engage in collective inquiry to understand those standards?

3. How well do our teams plan to create formative assessments, select instructional activities, and create questioning strategies that guide students to mastery of the essential standards?

4. How well do our teacher teams use formative assessment data to reflect on the effectiveness of their instruction at meeting the rigor of the essential standards?

5. When a teacher experiences difficulty with rigor and mastery, what steps do teams take to help him or her gain new strategies and ideas for improvement?

Individualized Supports

1. Before we help a teacher with difficulty in rigor and mastery, what steps do we take to evaluate the systemwide supports and teacher team supports and their effectiveness at helping the teacher? *(If schoolwide or teacher team supports are not in place, they are addressed as needed.)*

2. What data do we collect to confirms that the teacher has difficulty with rigor and mastery?

3. Before we help the teacher, what steps do we take to isolate the teacher's area of greatest difficulty in rigor and mastery?

4. When we prescribe a personalized plan of supports, how well do we prescribe targeted interventions from a wide variety of options, including co-teaching, observation, coaching, collaboration with another teacher or the teacher team, and using outside resources to help the teacher?

5. Once we prescribe a plan of supports, what steps do we take to set a goal that defines the desired improvement needed, a date by which that improvement will be made, and a date by which we will follow up to ensure that improvement has been made?

CHAPTER 7

Leading for Excellence: Creative Strategies for Individual Students

Modern classrooms are teeming with students of varying interests, backgrounds, abilities and learning needs. To engage these students, learning must be every bit as diverse as they are.

—Dale E. Basye

In the preceding chapter, we examined the critically important and challenging process of bringing rigorous learning to all students in order to move them beyond merely knowing lesson content and on toward deep content understanding and mastery. Now, we look at the next natural phase of development for excellent teachers, the development of skills necessary to keep every student, no matter what his or her level of academic achievement, engaged in ongoing learning growth. I call this area of a teacher's professional development *creative strategies for individual students.*

As the sixth area of professional growth in the Hierarchy of Instructional Excellence, the skills involved in identifying and implementing creative strategies for individual students rests on a firm foundation of knowledge about students, knowledge about content, and instructional expertise. Defined as *individualized instruction,* with this approach, "learning strategies are based on student readiness, learning styles, interests, and best practices" designed to "help each student master the skills they will need as defined by established academic standards" (Basye, 2014).

All teachers must be adept at monitoring and adjusting their teaching approach and strategies in order to effectively challenge and inspire all students. As students gradually assume responsibility for their learning experience, they are fueled for the pursuit of ongoing learning by their own passion, curiosity, and confidence. That passionate pursuit engages students in rigorous learning and advances their growth toward content mastery.

As students attain higher levels of rigorous and self-directed learning, however, the teacher's role in guaranteeing learning excellence doesn't diminish. Instead, it takes on a more multifaceted role. For students who are achieving at higher levels of learning, teachers should find creative strategies customized to inspire and challenge each student to continually extend and expand their learning. For students who struggle at higher levels of learning, teachers must devise equally creative and individualized strategies to support them in overcoming their learning difficulties and becoming more rigorous learners. This chapter outlines the skills involved in those processes, along with processes, systems, tools, and techniques leaders can use to support teachers as they develop these essential skills for learning excellence.

In Maslow's (1943) Hierarchy of Needs, the sixth level is aesthetic needs, which can be defined as a need for the expression of "symmetry, order, and beauty" (Huitt, 2007). Creative strategies customized specifically to motivate each student can be organized around a common desire for individual expression. Similar to the human desire for individual expression, students who have advanced into the higher levels of their learning process need to find new information and creative avenues of thought and study that can challenge and inspire them to *continue* learning and growing.

This chapter examines the creative approaches and strategies excellent teachers use to help every student continue to advance toward higher levels of learning. It also describes schoolwide, teacher team, and individualized supports excellent leaders can provide for teachers as they tackle this complex, yet essential, process.

As with previous chapters, this chapter describes systemwide interventions that offer all teachers throughout the system ongoing support in extending learning for individual students who have demonstrated content mastery. It also offers proven methods leaders can use to improve our RTI processes to help teachers better support struggling students. Through professional development, collaboration, and personalized plans of action, teachers have multiple avenues that they can use to become experts at finding ways to promote the most meaningful learning for every student.

In the following story, a teacher learns that creative strategies, individualized to students' interests and capacities, can inspire even the most engaged students to advance their understanding and grow in their learning.

Accepting It's All in the Details

Dian was a great teacher known for high levels of academic rigor and student engagement. Students loved her. Teachers admired her. Leaders respected her, and parents requested her to teach their children. In essence, everyone seemed to consider Dian to be the epitome of a great teacher—except Dian.

True, when Dian received her end-of-year assessment results, she was once again at the top of the school. Her scores were well above state and regional averages, and she had every reason to be pleased. But she wasn't. Her students grew from last year's performance, but in her opinion, they didn't grow enough. High performers stayed at roughly the same level or grew just slightly. Average performers and low performers didn't grow as much as she hoped, and some students who failed the previous year had improved somewhat but failed again this year. So Dian wasn't proud of her results as an educator. She gauged her own performance based on one standard—all students learning at high levels.

Excellent teachers always seek growth, and Dian wanted to know what she could do to improve, so she approached her principal for feedback. Her principal was excited about her desire for growth but couldn't give her tips about how to improve her performance. When she met with her collaborative team, her colleagues were puzzled (and a little annoyed) that she needed more help when she already achieved such great results. Why would she be seeking advice from them when so many students, parents, and other teachers considered her to be the epitome of educational excellence?

Dr. Perez, the district's assistant superintendent for curriculum, was making the rounds in May to congratulate everyone for their hard work during the school year. When she came to Dian, Dr. Perez expressed high praise. "Thank you, Dian, for being a model of great teaching and for going above and beyond for your students, your colleagues, and this school. We are so pleased with the great work that you do here."

Seeing this exchange as an opportunity to gain new ideas, Dian responded, "Thank you, Dr. Perez, but do you mind if I ask you a question?"

"Sure!" Dr. Perez replied.

Dian continued, "I appreciate your kinds words, but I would like to know where I can improve. I know my scores are great, and I'm happy about that, but many of my students didn't grow as much in their learning as I believe they are capable of doing."

Dr. Perez smiled in pleasant surprise. "Sure, I'll be glad to help. Tell me more about your students and their growth."

Excited to get help, Dian told her story. "My students work hard, and I work really hard to know my content, develop relationships with the kids, set high expectations for their learning, and create the very best lessons to make sure they all learn. I don't want my students to merely pass; I want them to grow by leaps and bounds. So this is my question. What can I do to make sure that *every* student makes great growth next year?"

Dr. Perez smiled and said, "It's all in the details."

Dian was confused.

Dr. Perez repeated, "Yep, it's all in the details. You're at a point where rigorous instruction has gotten you this far, but you want to go further in your ability to help students achieve more in their learning, right? The key to your next phase for growth is all about building on your impressive expertise by personalizing it for each student. High achievers can be bored by the demands of one-size-fits-all activities, and low achievers can be overwhelmed by the same demands. To keep all students motivated and advancing in their content understanding, teachers have to look beyond skills for differentiating instruction and begin developing differentiated assignments as well. My challenge for you is to push yourself to find personalized activities for each student that will not only engage but also empower and inspire him or her to remain curious and find new and fresh ways to develop a deep understanding of lesson content."

A lightbulb came on in Dian's head as she beamed from Dr. Perez's words. "Yes, that's true. I more or less have to create an individualized education plan for every student. That's how I'll make sure that I'm giving all students the kind of targeted attention and instruction necessary to help them grow at high levels next year. It won't be easy, but I know I can do it, and I *must* do it if I want all my students to achieve at the highest level."

Dr. Perez responded, "I absolutely agree. It's very hard work, but in order to help every student grow to that level, we have to remember that all students learn differently. That means we have to help every student find his or her own unique pathway toward excellence."

As figure 7.1 illustrates, when teachers reach the level of professional growth and development where they are implementing unique, creative solutions for each individual student, they are reaching the top levels of the Hierarchy of Instructional Excellence. It might seem that when educators successfully implement rigorous learning and content mastery, they have achieved mastery of their own craft as educators. However, just as excellent teachers want their students to become lifelong learners who never stop growing, they can never stop growing either. Designing and delivering creative strategies that motivate individual students to engage in ongoing learning is the next natural step for educators striving for excellence.

As Dian and Dr. Perez both articulated, advancing to this level of excellence in instruction is difficult work for teachers, but supporting that advancement can be equally challenging for leaders. There is no guide for developing more creative, individualized learning activities that will engage and inspire each student in the classroom. It is that individualization, however, that can move average student performance to extraordinary learning. As Sam Redding (2013), of the Center on Innovations in Learning, writes, "The teacher is more than a facilitator for a student's learning. . . . Through the teacher's example and her instruction, the student learns

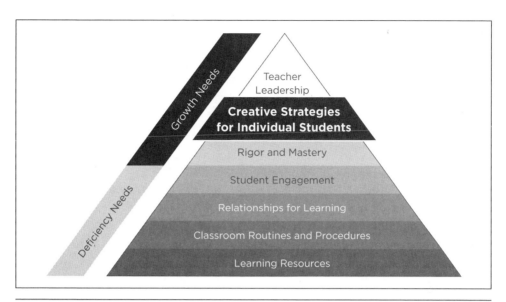

Figure 7.1: Hierarchy of Instructional Excellence—creative strategies for individual students.

to value mastery, to raise expectations, to manage learning, and to broaden interests" (pp. 6–7).

It is our responsibility to support teachers as they take on this complex work. We can help meet that responsibility by using our own creativity to build and offer carefully designed, stepped systems of support to help teachers transition from delivering rigorous learning to their classrooms to personalizing that rigorous learning process for each student.

Developing Creative Strategies for Individual Students

There is some gray area surrounding the term *individualized learning*. For the purposes of this book, I offer educational consultant Glen Heathers's (1977) definition: "Individualized instruction consists of any steps taken in planning and conducting programs of studies and lessons that suit them to the individual student's learning needs, learning readiness, and learning characteristics or 'learning style'" (p. 342). Additionally, "With individualized instruction, learning strategies are based on student readiness, learning styles, interests and best practices . . . to help each student master the skills they will need as defined by established academic standards" (Basye, 2014).

The essential task for teachers in employing creative strategies for individualized instruction is to apply their existing content knowledge in new and innovative ways designed to engage and inspire individual students. At this level, excellent teachers acquire many signature pedagogies and an arsenal of instructional skills to respond to both low-performing students and high-performing students. The following sections outline those skills in more detail.

Preparation

Teachers should offer all students the opportunity to extend their learning. Finding the most effective ways to accomplish that involves preparing a menu of instructional strategies and learning choices that can continually develop each student's rigorous learning and content mastery. As Heathers (1977) notes, "A chief justification for individualized instruction is that it can permit every student to achieve mastery of tasks undertaken" (p. 344).

Teachers can draw on skills from three essential areas of knowledge in order to prepare creative strategies for individual students.

1. They must know their students, their histories, aspirations, previous learning struggles and successes, and personal interests.

2. They must have a deep knowledge of the content they will be teaching and equally well-developed instructional expertise.

3. They must know how to differentiate their planning and delivery of content in order to engage and inspire individual students.

Teachers committed to this kind of rich learning know that they need to offer many relevant activities to extend student learning. They also must build time into their instructional plan for implementing creative individualized strategies for learning. Finally, they need to be sure these strategies are available to *all* students, including those who struggle.

Teachers should begin devising creative, individualized strategies for students who are not meeting learning targets as soon as those struggles come to light. To deal with students' struggles before they blossom into full-blown failure, excellent teachers anticipate and watch for warning signs, such as mistakes that point to common challenges within the content. Teachers can review student histories and transfer sheets to understand students' home lives and personal aspirations, along with the types of challenges and learning problems students have experienced in previous classes. This can help teachers identify instructional techniques that have been most successful in addressing those issues. That way, they can plan interventions that leverage modalities that work best for individual students.

By having a working knowledge of struggling students' personal and academic histories, strong content knowledge, and broad instructional expertise, excellent teachers can create plans for responding immediately to any student difficulty with content. That kind of quick and caring response can help motivate struggling students to keep working. Redding (2013) writes, "When teachers exhibit the right blend of caring and expectation, showing that the teacher knows the student and thinks there is something special about him or her, students respond positively" (p. 9).

Deciding who needs extension or intervention can be difficult and time-consuming; however, one of the most important instructional delivery components can be the teacher's best friend—the end-of-class wrap-up activity or *exit ticket*, which is a short formative assessment that students complete for the teacher before leaving the classroom at the end of the period. When great teachers routinely employ the exit ticket in their instructional plan, they create a specific mechanism for identifying students who have mastered the concept and those who are still struggling. Including this data-gathering tool in their instructional plan can help teachers devise prescriptive interventions student by student, while simultaneously selecting students who are ready to push themselves with more rigorous and personalized learning activities.

Delivery

Excellent teachers make a plan for teaching students, not content. Excellent teachers use questions and assessments to determine which students need remediation and which students need extension. Danielson (2013) comments, "The teacher's adjustments to the lesson, when they are needed, are designed to assist individual students" (p. 58). The reason for constantly adjusting to individual students is obvious, as Buffum and Mattos (2015) describe:

> Because all students do not learn the same way, develop at the same speed, enter school with the same prior knowledge, or have the same academic supports at home, students will be provided additional time and support to achieve these rigorous expectations. (p. 5)

Beyond strategies to guide students in learning content standards, excellent teachers must strategize to deliver content that can extend learning for high-achieving students as well as offer remediation for students who do not master the standard. "The teacher conveys to students that she won't consider a lesson 'finished' until every student understands" the essential learning objective or target (Danielson, 2013, p. 58).

The ongoing process of identifying students' learning progress and strategizing the best path forward for extended or remedial action involves continually assessing individual student learning. The flowchart in figure 7.2 (page 154) illustrates this ongoing assessment process, in which teachers persistently ask about each student, "Did he or she learn the standard?" And based on the answer to that question, teachers determine the appropriate strategies for either extension or remediation.

If teachers want to prepare students to thrive in the 21st century, their instruction must provide rigorous learners with the opportunity to extend their learning to prepare them for the rapidly developing skill sets necessary to succeed in 21st century careers. According to Hale and Fisher (2013), this includes teaching students to:

- Think critically about the information they access
- Discern credibility and intended meaning of the information they access
- Reason fluently, both inductively and deductively
- Make logical and thoughtful decisions based on collected, curated, and analyzed information (p. 22)

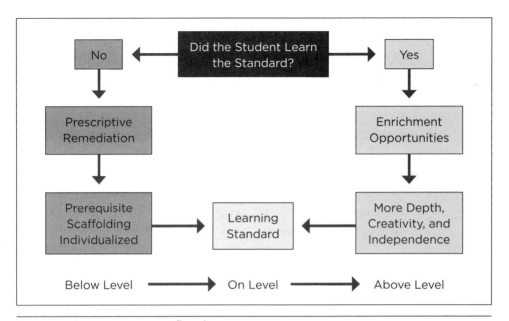

Figure 7.2: Learning progress flowchart.

The ultimate goal of any type of learning is to transform students from consumers of knowledge into game changers. Excellent teachers use meaningful extension learning activities as the platform for this transformation. Two examples of the kinds of creative strategies teachers can use for extending student learning include *choice boards* and *purpose-driven learning*.

1. **Choice boards** (see figure 7.3) are menus from which students can choose personalized activities to extend their learning. For example, if a student masters his or her multiplication learning for the day, he or she could choose a creativity task by making a flipped video about that learning for other students to review on their own schedule, or explore college degrees and careers that leverage math skills.

2. **Purpose-driven learning** is an instructional strategy that involves leading students in activities that encourage communication, collaboration, critical thinking, and creativity. As William M. Ferriter (2015) writes in *Creating Purpose-Driven Learning Experiences*, "Meaning drives motivation for any learner" (p. 3). Examples of purpose-driven learning strategies Ferriter has used in his class include project-based exercises, such as studying global poverty and then creating and participating in microlending activities (involving making small loans to organizations in foreign countries); and blogging to raise awareness about current issues such as obesity.

When students fail to meet standards, excellent teachers respond with well-designed interventions that can address each struggling student's individual learning challenges. Figure 7.4 and figure 7.5 (page 156) illustrate the right kind of thinking and

Creativity	Service projects	Project-based learning	Flipped videos
Evaluation	Peer tutoring	Write a review	Blog
Extension	Personalized learning activity	Instructional games	Academic websites
Research	College and career	Topic of interest	Compare and contrast content

Figure 7.3: Choice board.

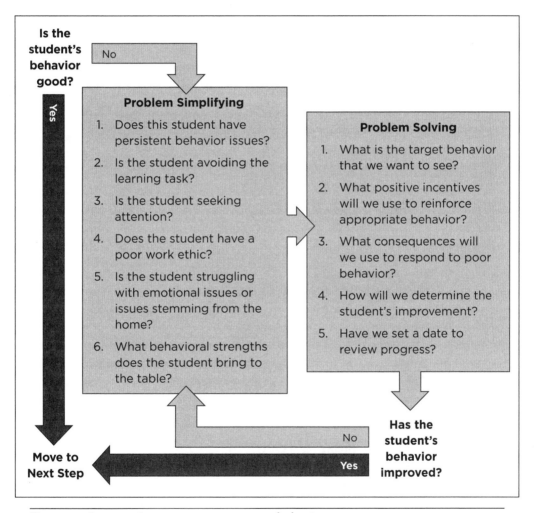

Figure 7.4: Intervention process—response to behavior.

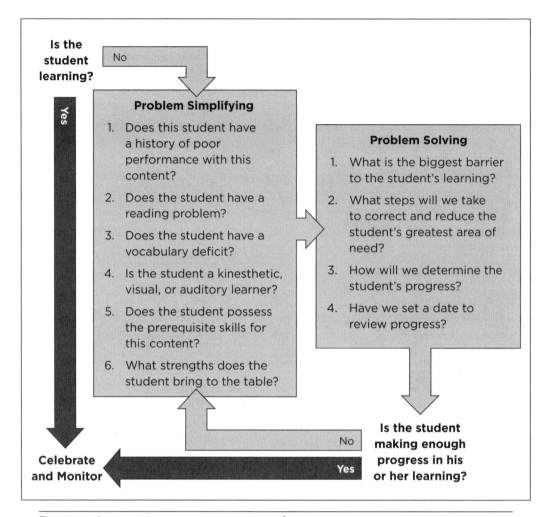

Figure 7.5: Intervention process—response to learning.

response that excellent teachers instinctively use to isolate each student's greatest area of need, solve the problem, and gauge the effectiveness of the intervention. The intervention in figure 7.4 addresses behavioral issues, while that in figure 7.5 addresses academic issues. Both processes follow these three steps for intervention.

1. **Simplify the problem:** Teachers can't solve a learning challenge until they simplify the problem by identifying its root cause. Teachers also must determine the student's existing strengths in relationship to the problem, as these will serve as the foundation for developing solutions. Teachers can determine solutions by observing student work and behavior, through conversations with the student, and by familiarizing themselves with student records, transfer sheets, and other historical data.

2. **Solve the problem:** Next, the teacher determines the best course of action for solving the problem. As the problem-solving section of figures

7.4 and 7.5 indicates, teachers can determine the most significant deficit to address first. From there, the teacher can outline the action steps for addressing it and set a date for determining if progress has been made.

3.   **Gauge improvement:** If the intervention helped the student improve in learning or behavior, the teacher decides whether to continue or stop the intervention. If the student can succeed without the teacher's help, then the teacher can discontinue the intervention. If the intervention failed to help the student, the teacher can return to the information in figures 7.4 and 7.5, simplify the problem again, modify his or her previous plan of action, or create a completely new plan.

In delivering content that extends learning for students at, below, and above standard, teachers need more than just a willingness and ability to inspire every student to stretch his or her learning capabilities. They also must maintain a willingness to extend their own capabilities and teaching processes into new and innovative territory. Essentially, teachers have to do their research and remain flexible in designing the most effective strategies for reaching each student. At this level of professional growth, even the most successful teachers can't rely on their existing toolkit of instructional strategies. As Ellen Moir (2008), executive director of the New Teacher Center at the University of California at Santa Cruz, writes, "The commitment to adapt instruction to individual needs comes from a belief that students learn better with the use of many styles and methods."

Reflection

Excellent teachers base their decisions about students on evidence, and so they collect data in a systematic way in order to fully reflect on the success of their strategies for individualizing student learning. Danielson (2013) states that a fully effective process for collecting this data involves "the teacher's system for maintaining information on student completion of assignments, student progress in learning, and noninstructional records" (p. 65).

Reflection on instruction at this level of a teacher's professional development is a two-part process. While collecting the aforementioned data is the first component for effective reflection on individualized instructional strategies, the second component involves providing targeted feedback. This process includes daily reflection to analyze student work and determine the most purposeful feedback to help students grow in their learning. And that feedback should emphasize specific areas for student growth. Rick Stiggins (2007) states:

> For communication to be effective in the context of formative assessment, it needs to inform the learner about how to do better the next time; that is, it must be descriptive rather than judgmental. Feedback is most helpful when it focuses on attributes of the student's work. (p. 68)

Connie M. Moss and Susan Brookhart (2009) emphasize that "teachers have various choices about the methods they use when they deliver feedback and about the content of that feedback" (p. 48). When giving feedback, teachers should consider the following questions.

- How often should I give feedback?
- How many points should I make in the feedback?
- Should I give feedback in oral form, written form, or demonstration form?
- Should I give feedback to groups or to individual students?

Excellent teachers understand that how they answer these questions for each student determines how quickly students will grow in learning. Teachers can achieve the most effective results by targeting their feedback toward one or two specific points rather than weighing down students with a long list of objectives for learning growth. "Too much feedback is also counterproductive," Wiggins (2012) writes. "Better to help the performer concentrate on only one or two key elements of performance than to create a buzz of information coming in from all sides."

Teachers also should reflect on the best format for delivering feedback. For struggling students, one form of feedback may not suffice; therefore, teachers might consider providing oral, written, and demonstrative feedback, depending on the student. Finally, if multiple students struggle with learning a concept for the same reason, teachers can efficiently provide feedback to students in groups. Timely feedback tied to the learning target is imperative to complete the cycle of learning, and that is what separates excellence from mediocrity.

Building an Excellence Support System: Creative Strategies for Individual Students

As noted earlier in this chapter, developing the skills for effectively individualizing instruction to meet the needs of every student is a difficult task for even the most experienced teacher. To keep students at, below, and above level continually striving to learn and grow requires a broad range of creative instructional strategies that apply directly to each student's interests, background, learning style, and capabilities. The role of the school in helping teachers achieve and maintain this level of instructional skill should not be limited to setting expectations. Instead, schools must transform themselves into support systems to help teachers learn how to create vibrant learning environments where personalized learning transitions from the goal into the norm.

The Excellence Support System can offer tools and best practices for supporting teachers in this area of their professional development at the schoolwide, teacher team, and individualized levels.

Step 1: Schoolwide Supports

Teachers are bombarded with so many different tasks and demands that, without effective and multitiered support systems, it can very difficult to meet the needs of individual students. To be truly effective, those systems must be well established, well defined, and well maintained. Even the very best teachers wonder, "How can I meet the needs of *every* student?" That's an understandable concern; however, we have a responsibility to ensure that teachers have the collaborative tools and supports necessary to succeed in this area of their professional development. Through schoolwide supports, we can provide teachers with two critical tools for developing and continually improving these skills: (1) a schoolwide tiered intervention model and (2) continuous professional development in the best practices for providing interventions and extensions simultaneously.

Tiered Intervention Model

Chapter 6 discussed the importance of developing informal formative assessments. In this section, I will connect the outcomes of those common formative assessments to a system of interventions. After all, the very best assessments mean nothing if the school is not prepared to respond to the data when students fail.

Before developing assessments, school leaders must have a living system of interventions in place that defines how the school responds when students fail to learn. I use the term *living* to describe this intervention system, because it only succeeds when leaders and teachers work together to continuously identify the barriers to learning and then address those barriers with precision and automaticity. Building such a system is no simple matter when you have many teachers, many students in need, and continuous scheduling constraints. "The real obstacles begin when a school *challenge!* considers the logistics of having potentially hundreds of students transitioning to specific interventions" (Buffum & Mattos, 2015, p. 7).

Figure 7.6 (page 160) illustrates a schoolwide tiered intervention model that can help guide educators as they craft and plan to respond to students who fail to learn. As previously mentioned in the introduction, the three-step Excellence Support System is modeled on three-tiered interventions for students. This model allows teachers some flexibility in choosing the most effective responses to individual students who struggle to continually extend their learning due to academic or behavioral issues.

As the model indicates, teachers make Tier 1 interventions available to all students within the class during classroom instruction. We can work with teachers to create a menu of Tier 1 intervention strategies that teachers throughout the school can use to respond when any student fails to learn.

Tier 2 interventions provide students with additional time and support. Leaders can help teachers make those interventions more targeted, specific, and effective by limiting them to approximately the 15–25 percent of students who are most at risk. "A successful Tier 1 program should meet the needs of at least 75% of the student

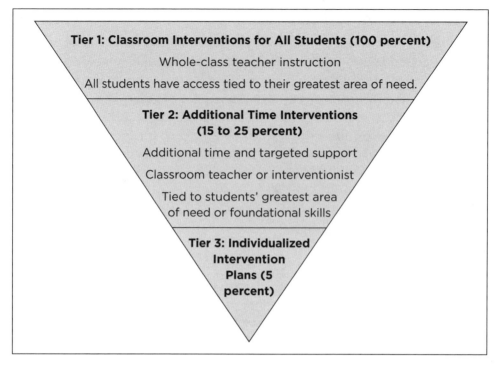

Source: Adapted from Buffum, Mattos, & Weber, 2012.

Figure 7.6: Schoolwide tiered intervention model.

body, and an effective Tier 2 supplemental level will meet the needs of at least 15% more" (Buffum, Mattos, & Weber, 2009, p. 89). If more than one-fourth of students in a class need additional time and assistance in order to succeed at learning, we should step back and help the teacher assess whether he or she should adjust the content or his or her instructional strategies, rather than merely provide intervention to struggling students.

Tier 2 interventions differ from Tier 1 in that they target not only the 15–25 percent of students most at risk in the class, but also focus on the most essential skills that struggling students must master. In Tier 2, students in small groups receive additional attention and opportunities to practice learning those essential skills throughout their day. Leaders can assist teachers in using Tier 2 interventions by helping them arrange a time for preteaching sessions and review for students scheduled to enter the Tier 2 process. To make Tier 2 interventions most effective, teachers gather specific data to gauge student progress. Teachers and leaders then use the data to determine whether to continue the Tier 2 interventions, release the student from Tier 2, or refer the student to individualized Tier 3 support. Leaders play an important role in coordinating with teachers to ensure that the interventions are organized and managed for maximum effectiveness.

The next level within the tiered intervention model involves targeting Tier 3 supports, which:

> generally last 12–18 weeks, and usually serve no more than 5–10% of the student population. Tier 3 interventions are designed for students who show low content-area skills and/or lack of progress over time when provided with Tier 1 and Tier 2 interventions. (Buffum et al., 2009, p. 100)

Tier 3 interventions, such as individualized reading instruction or individual counseling for students with significant behavioral issues, demand extra time and coordination to schedule during the school day. Again, the tiered intervention model is designed to help the teacher, with support from the student intervention team, identify individual students' greatest areas of need and create a personalized plan of supports aligned to those needs.

Beyond providing a framework for choosing and applying creative strategies for intervention, we also can provide schoolwide supports for ongoing professional development, with an emphasis on RTI practices. For a schoolwide intervention system to be successful, we need to build the system in collaboration with teachers. As we do so, we must bear in mind that if teachers balk at employing RTI or other schoolwide intervention strategies and practices, it may be because we've done a poor job of explaining those strategies and how the Excellence Support System works. We can't expect teachers to believe in strategies that we don't clearly explain and support.

Intervention and Extension in Professional Development

Excellent teachers believe in helping all students learn, so we rarely need to persuade them why using creative strategies to help students succeed is important. It can be more difficult, however, to support teachers with specific mechanisms for achieving that goal. A fundamental element of that support includes providing ongoing schoolwide processes for professional development in learning the most effective practices for implementing intervention and extension activities.

This professional development should offer teachers training and strategies for helping individual students at every level of academic success learn—and continue to learn. It also should help teachers determine *how* they can implement those strategies within their already crowded schedules. Professional development can address this latter issue by helping teachers learn how to structure their instructional time to provide intervention to some students, while other students work independently.

Professional development at this level of an educator's growth also needs to focus on helping teachers understand how to manage the simultaneous processes of extension and intervention. By outlining such strategies as the use of choice boards, project-based learning (described earlier in this chapter), and other self-guided activities for extending learning, we can offer teachers examples, models, templates, and continuous support in finding creative ways to give students choice and ownership in extending their learning.

As with all learning, extension activities work best when students see them as meaningful and relevant. Many extension activities fail and lead to disruption or even chaos because, to students, they're mere busywork. Knowing this, teachers should provide a variety of relevant and meaningful activities to engage students and empower them to take their learning to the next level. But excellent leaders never leave it up to teachers to develop this extremely difficult skill set in isolation. Instead, we need to create a system in which developing these skills is integral to and supported by our schoolwide processes for professional development.

Step 2: Teacher Team Supports

With respect to intervention and extension, if you don't plan for it, you won't be able to deliver it. DuFour et al. (2010) claim, "A school characterized by weak and ineffective teaching will not solve its problems by creating a system of timely intervention for students" (pp. 111–112). The primary purpose of teacher team supports in this area of a teacher's professional development lies in strengthening Tier 1 instruction as a first step in meeting the individual needs of all students.

An intervention created in isolation has as much chance of remediating student failure as instruction and assessment created in isolation. In fact, RTI processes are collaborative by design. Teacher teams design effective interventions based on two shared assumptions: (1) teams must anticipate student failure and plan to minimize and prevent it wherever possible and (2) when students are failing, teachers must respond collectively. To address teacher team supports, this section outlines both preventive and responsive team interventions. First, however, let's address teacher team supports for learning extension.

Collaborative Extension Activity Menus

Teacher teams can be a primary source for meaningful and relevant activities collaboratively designed to extend student learning in the classroom while the teacher engages in intervention with individual students. Effective teacher teams invest time in creating and planning extension activities that students can access independent of the teacher. The broader the variety of these activities, the more support they provide to individual students. Team members collaborate to craft extension activities that can serve the twofold purpose of deepening understanding for proficient students and fostering independent learning. When teacher teams collaborate to create a broad and diverse menu of those activities, teachers can choose from them based on their understanding of individual student struggles, capabilities, and needs.

Choice boards, described earlier in this chapter, offer collaborative teams an effective medium for making these activities available. Teacher teams can save time by using Google Docs to create and distribute a menu of choice-board activities. Team members can continue to identify and create extension activities throughout the school year and add them to the choice board. Team members can use the comment feature to discuss strengths and weaknesses in the activity or ask questions about implementing the choice board in instruction. By using such collaborative tools for circulating extension activities, teams can preserve their face-to-face collaborative time together to focus on individual students who are not learning.

Aside from using virtual tools to collaboratively create and refine extension activities, teacher teams can work together to learn about using extension activities to accelerate learning. Collaboration about extension activities can take many forms, as teachers work together to learn new ways to empower students to own their learning. The team can, for example, have a teacher or instructional coach model how to incorporate choice boards into instruction. Alternatively, the team can visit the classroom of a teacher who is successfully using extension activities to empower students in order to observe that teacher's approach.

Preventive Interventions

Teacher teams can design preventive interventions before students begin studying a new concept. During this stage of the intervention process, teacher teams, with the support of curriculum coaches and administrators, can discuss the challenges they predict students will have during initial learning. By familiarizing themselves with student histories, transfer sheets, and other academic and behavioral background information about individual students, team members can take student learning styles and previously learned content into consideration. Additionally, they can prepare for students who do not have the prerequisite skills necessary to learn the new content and discuss how they will remediate those skills from the start. Responding to these students with instructional strategies and language from the previous year's instruction is a great starting point for remediating foundational skills. Finally, teacher teams can discuss common misconceptions that students form when learning a new concept and create effective responses for students who demonstrate these misconceptions during initial instruction.

We can offer teacher teams templates and tools for planning preventive interventions, such as that shown in figure 7.7 (page 164). Teacher teams can use this template to gather insights and strategies from vertical team members for preventing student failure with a given skill. I have had great success in using this template to encourage deep conversations among teachers about their practices. The first row of the table lists the individual skill the team will address. In the second row, team members (either independently on separate templates or collaboratively on a single template) list three common mistakes students make when initially learning the skill. The team then seeks collaborative input—from team members teaching at the skill's grade level, above it, and below it—on strategies for preventing or responding to these common mistakes. Teachers can use the Notes section to record supplemental information and suggestions to help team members hone their methods for teaching the skill.

Skill	
Three Common Mistakes Students Make When Initially Learning the Skill	
Interventions	
Grade Below Suggestions	
Grade Above Suggestions	
Notes	

Figure 7.7: Preventive intervention—preparing for failure.

Visit **go.SolutionTree.com/leadership** *for a free reproducible version of this figure.*

Responsive Interventions

If teacher team supports focus on preparing and continually updating and improving effective tools for preventive responses in advance of learning, fewer students will need responsive interventions. Responsive interventions become necessary when students continue to fail to demonstrate learning after teachers have delivered initial instruction *and* preventive intervention responses. In designing responsive interventions, teacher teams, coaches, and administrator discussions center on students, not content. In these situations, teams can employ the 1-2-3 process (Buffum & Mattos, 2015). This three-step process helps collaborative teams respond to an individual student's repeated failure.

1. **Identify the student's greatest area of need:** The referring teacher's responsibilities in this step are to: (1) identify a student struggling in academics or behavior; (2) name the biggest issue that prevents the student from learning; and (3) share samples of student work or data. "Without greater clarity regarding what is causing the failure, [teachers] will be unable to intervene effectively" (DuFour & Marzano, 2011,

p. 178). In this step, the teacher provides samples of student work or behavior logs to support his or her prognosis of the student's difficulties, barriers to learning, and potential. The team can then determine if the teacher needs to change core instructional practices or classroom management procedures to further support the student.

2. **Define the results of current interventions:** In this step, the referring teacher: (1) names two classroom interventions that the teacher has tried; (2) describes the frequency of those interventions; and (3) describes the student's response to the interventions. DuFour et al. (2010) write, "Intervention will offer a setting and strategies that are different from those that have already proven to be ineffective for the student" (p. 111). By listening to the referring teacher's detailed descriptions of interventions that have failed, the team has more information to assess the fidelity of those intervention efforts and to create more targeted and specific interventions.

3. **Generate ideas for more prescriptive interventions:** In this step, it is the teacher team's responsibility to: (1) ask questions about student behavior or learning; and (2) recommend interventions that may help the student. Ferriter et al. (2013) write, "While it is important to create an initial list of approved interventions, it is also important to provide PLTs [primary lead teachers] with some flexibility to innovate" (p. 71). Here, the team can revise current interventions to make them more effective, or it can recommend new interventions to better address the student's needs. For example, if a student with reading difficulties is not responding to small-group instruction due to peer distractions, a logical response would be to pull the student individually at a time without distractions to see if he or she responds positively.

The 1-2-3 process offers teacher teams a viable method for finding creative strategies to help individual students who struggle with academic or behavioral issues. There are times, however, when even the most effective and committed teacher team fails to produce effective solutions. That's why we must ensure that it also includes procedures for encouraging teachers to seek assistance from an instructional coach, a counselor, or an administrator.

Step 3: Individualized Supports

No matter how experienced a teacher is, we can be certain that he or she eventually will struggle with trying to meet the needs of individual students:

> The idea that a single teacher, working alone, can know and do everything to meet the diverse learning needs of 30 students every day throughout the school year has rarely worked, and

it certainly won't meet the needs of learners in years to come.
(Carroll, 2009, as cited in DuFour et al., 2010, p. 105)

Since all students are different, any student can present a new challenge that individual teachers may not be prepared to address. That's the primary reason why excellent teachers continuously develop creative strategies for individual students. We, as leaders, might need to do a better job in helping those teachers understand how to make the system work in their favor. We know, for example, that students who excel need extension opportunities that are meaningful and relevant. Individual supports for teachers in this area of professional growth can offer strategies for teachers to periodically update their extension activities to match a broad variety of student capabilities and interests.

Interventions With Intervention Staff

Many schools have personnel whose sole responsibility is to work with at-risk or struggling students by providing them Tier 2 and Tier 3 interventions through independent intervention labs. There are multiple ways this arrangement can suffer from disconnects. Sometimes, for example, the regular classroom teacher doesn't reinforce the interventions provided by intervention staff. Other times, student struggles that occur in the classroom are never communicated to the interventionist. To avoid these situations, we should incorporate specific strategies for aligning the work of intervention staff with teachers who continue to struggle to find creative strategies to promote student learning.

Individualized supports, for example, must include specifically allocated time in which struggling teachers can collaborate either virtually or face to face with intervention staff in aligning intervention supports. For example, we can outline a process by which interventionists relay and demonstrate to the classroom teacher interventions that have proved effective in working with a struggling student in the intervention lab. That way, the teacher is prepared to continue those interventions during the student's classroom experience. This kind of collaborative approach to applying individualized interventions is essential, because even the most well-designed intervention is ineffective if it doesn't help the student perform better in the classroom.

Problem Simplification Plan

Problem simplification, as outlined in previous chapters, offers a powerful tool for helping teachers who continue to struggle. Leaders can use the chart in figure 7.8 to work with these teachers to develop creative strategies for individual students. The first step to improvement is isolating whether the teacher is having difficulty with extension or intervention activities. It is best to check for the teacher's effectiveness in extension first.

If the teacher hasn't established effective extension activities, it is likely that proficient students in the classroom won't be engaged in meaningful work while the teacher attempts to deliver interventions to struggling students. In that case, the

Problem Simplification Plan: Creative Strategies for Individual Students

1. The teacher is struggling with the following concepts regarding creative strategies for individual students. Check all that apply.
 	
  ☐ Extension
  ☐ Intervention
  ☐ Proficient students
  ☐ Average students
  ☐ Struggling students
 	
Notes:

2. What are the current actions in place for this target area? How are students responding to current creative strategies? How well are strategies crafted to engage and empower students to own their learning?

3. List the best intervention to help the teacher develop a better understanding of the targeted students and how to build strategies that best address their individual needs.
 	
  ☐ Observation of _____ class during intervention or extension.
 	
  ☐ Plan intervention or extension with _____.
 	
  ☐ Co-teach with _____.
 	
  ☐ Have _____ model intervention or extension with the struggling teacher's class.
 	
  ☐ Read or research _____.
 	
Notes:

4. Set a date that creative strategies should be successfully established.
5. How will we know if creative strategies for individual students are effectively implemented?

Figure 7.8: Problem simplification plan—creative strategies for individual students.

Visit **go.SolutionTree.com/leadership** *for a free reproducible version of this figure.*

teacher's intervention activities won't be particularly effective, because students are not authentically engaged in collaborative or independent learning tasks. Again, when using problem simplification, we succeed best by first targeting the teacher's greatest area of need and then creating further plans to deal with needs in their decreasing order of urgency.

Working with the problem simplification process, we can collaboratively decide with the teacher on the best plan of action for improvement by listing professional development activities and setting a date to check for growth. Finally, we can work together with the teacher to establish a goal of what improvement should look like in the targeted area.

Conclusion

No matter how hard we work to create an excellent school staffed by excellent teachers, we can never sit back and assume that we have succeeded. The reality is that not all students have excellent teachers all the time. If we want all students to grow by leaps and bounds, we mustn't rely solely on teacher experience and initiative to guarantee student growth. Instead, we need to shoulder the critical responsibility of growing students by growing teachers first.

1. The first step to helping all teachers grow in developing creative strategies for individual students is defining what excellence looks like. Excellent teachers don't *find* time for intervention and extension—they *make* time for it. During that time, they empower their students to learn by offering the personalized learning experiences and activities that build students' self-esteem and pride. Teachers succeed at this task by knowing their students' backgrounds, interests, previous struggles and successes, and personal goals and interests. They also know their content thoroughly, and they are adept at mastering a broad range of creative strategies and then choosing among them to most effectively target the needs of individual students. These skills need constant updating and expansion, which means that leaders must have systems in place to help teachers learn and master these demanding areas of professional growth and development.

2. The second step is to provide teachers with a schoolwide system of supports, including a pyramid of interventions. We can accompany this pyramid with a plan that outlines for teachers how they can most effectively use those supports and what role they play in making the system work. Whether in face-to-face or virtual collaboration, we can use the collaborative tools and practices outlined in this chapter to help our teachers learn and expand their skills in creating strategies for targeting interventions and extensions to help individual students become successful, lifelong learners.

3. The third step in supporting teacher growth in this area involves forming and supporting collaborative teams in which teachers can learn and develop these strategies together. That means teacher teams have collaborative time to develop extension

activities that engage every student so they can focus on responding to students who fail to learn. Teams can use collaborative time to thoughtfully design instruction and employ the 1-2-3 process and other structured programs that can both respond to student needs and make the most efficient use of each team's collaborative time and resources.

4. The fourth step focuses on individual teachers. If teacher teams don't provide the support needed for a struggling teacher, we must develop individualized plans based on that teacher's specific needs. These plans should include supporting this teacher in providing individualized instruction for struggling students, average students, and high-performing students, addressing extension opportunities and remediation geared to their interests and learning styles.

Leaders can use the questions and ideas in the following reflection tool (pages 170–171) to help assess our current approach to supporting teachers in designing creative strategies to extend learning for individual students and to help identify ways we can improve that approach as we advance our own skills in guaranteeing learning excellence.

aha moment!
Without having authentic and relevant extension activities teachers will not be able to focus on responding to S who fail to learn.

Reflection Tool:
Creative Strategies for Individual Students

Definition of Excellence for Creative Strategies for Individual Students

What is our school's definition of teacher excellence in the area of creative strategies for individual students, which includes providing students with extension and intervention opportunities?

Schoolwide Supports

1. How well do we clearly articulate our philosophy of learning that ensures all students have access to extension opportunities as a critical part of their learning?

2. How well do we clearly articulate our philosophy of learning that ensures all students have Tier 1 intervention as a part of their instruction?

3. How effectively does our RTI system define interventions at Tier 1, Tier 2, and Tier 3, systematically identifying students in need of additional time and support, and prescribing interventions that are aligned to students' greatest areas of need?

4. How effective is our professional development for all staff at providing ongoing training on extension and intervention strategies?

A Leader's Guide to Excellence in Every Classroom © 2017 Solution Tree Press • SolutionTree.com
Visit **go.SolutionTree.com/leadership** to download this free reproducible.

Teacher Team Supports

1. What norms do our teachers have to ensure that they learn more from each other about extensions and interventions?

2. How well do our teams plan extension activities, including the use of virtual tools such as Google Docs, to develop extension activities and choice boards?

3. How well do our teams plan for interventions with a preventive mindset that anticipates student failure with proactive interventions?

4. How well do our teams collaborate when students fail to learn using a system such as the 1-2-3 process?

5. When a team experiences difficulty with extension or intervention, what steps do they take to learn together, observe interventions and extensions, model these strategies for one another, or seek assistance from an instructional leader?

Individualized Supports

1. Before we help a teacher with difficulty with creative activities for individual students, what steps do we take to evaluate the systemwide supports and teacher team supports and their effectiveness at helping the teacher? *(If schoolwide or teacher team supports are not in place, they are addressed as needed.)*

2. What data do we collect to confirm that the teacher has difficulty with extensions or interventions, and how do we ensure that the difficulty is not associated with lower levels in the Hierarchy of Instructional Excellence?

3. Before we help the teacher, what steps do we take to isolate the teacher's area of greatest difficulty and determine if the difficulty is in helping low-, average-, or high-performing students?

4. When we prescribe a personalized plan of supports, how well do we prescribe targeted interventions from a wide variety of options as listed in the problem simplification plan?

5. Once we prescribe a plan of supports, what steps do we take to set a goal that defines the desired improvement needed, a date by which that improvement will be made, and a date by which we will follow up to ensure that improvement has been made?

A Leader's Guide to Excellence in Every Classroom © 2017 Solution Tree Press • SolutionTree.com

Visit **go.SolutionTree.com/leadership** to download this free reproducible.

CHAPTER 8

Leading for Excellence: Teacher Leadership

The need for truly effective educational leadership is great. The time for improving our schools is short. The opportunity to lead is ours.

—Robert J. Marzano

At the pinnacle of his Hierarchy of Needs, Maslow (1943) placed the human need for self-actualization. Maslow (1943) describes this need as "the desire for self-fulfillment . . . the desire to become more and more what one is, to become everything that one is capable of becoming" (p. 383). Fulfilling that need involves an ongoing process of discovery, creativity, and reflection on our roles in life and our effects on others.

In the Hierarchy of Instructional Excellence, teacher leadership is the area of professional growth parallel to Maslow's pinnacle of self-actualization. In my experience and observation, when teachers have advanced to the highest levels of their professional skills and expertise, they don't suddenly lose their desire (or capability) for professional growth. Instead, they seek out ways to share their knowledge with colleagues, work to improve processes and systems beyond their classrooms, and find new avenues and understandings to explore. This chapter examines how we, as leaders, can support teachers in that form of self-actualization as they work and grow to assume a leadership role.

A primary challenge for all of us is to transform our schools into organizations that guarantee student learning by ensuring that *all* teachers possess the skills necessary to make good on that guarantee. Realizing this goal of organizational transformation, however, demands transformational leadership. In his research, Marzano discovered that the most successful leaders become transformational when they create followers and transform them into leaders and, eventually, into moral agents (Marzano, Waters,

& McNulty, 2005). After all, "a principal cannot be the only leader in a complex organization like a school" (Lezotte, 1999, p. 3). As researchers from the University of Minnesota and the University of Toronto write, "Successful leaders develop and count on contributions from many others in their organizations. Principals typically count on key teachers for such leadership" (Leithwood, Louis, Anderson, & Wahlstrom, 2004, p. 5). If we want to count on those kinds of contributions within our schools, we have to do better than merely wishing for good teacher leaders. *We have to create them.*

Unfortunately, traditional leadership structures and mindsets can actually suppress teacher voices and the potential solutions they could offer for positively shaping student learning. That's a tremendous waste of talent. While none of us can understand and solve every problem in our schools alone, by working collectively and collaboratively with excellent educators throughout our system, we can find those solutions. Our job, therefore, must be to develop the leadership potential within every teacher and, in turn, empower him or her to develop leadership in one another. That's how we build an organization where excellent teachers are leading and great leaders are teaching (DuFour, as cited in Dollar, 2013).

Becoming a teacher leader requires a completely introspective and interpersonal mindset, and no two leaders are alike in the way they develop that mindset—or in the way their leadership shapes their world. For that reason, the structure of this chapter is quite different from that of the other chapters in this book. For example, this chapter doesn't outline the elements we can use to build an effective system of professional development or supports to help teachers excel at developing their leadership skills. That's because *we*, as leaders, must *be* the Excellence Support System for teachers at this level of their professional development. In fact, we are the *only* resource that can directly facilitate or support that growth for teachers. That support is another critical responsibility we bear for guaranteeing educational excellence throughout our schools and districts. When leaders directly develop leadership capacity in their teachers, they position their schools for more rapid growth toward excellence.

This chapter examines how we can best approach the critical and complex task of supporting teachers as they embark on this most challenging and fulfilling area of their professional growth and development. Before we begin that examination, however, I want to offer a short profile of one educator who mastered the role of teacher leadership. The following isn't a story formed from a hypothetical example, such as those in previous chapters. Instead, this story describes the teacher who first taught me the true nature of teacher leadership and how essential it can be for any leader committed to building a school of excellence.

Introducing Shirley Copeland, the Queen of Mathematics

Many teachers have played a formative role in my professional development, but Shirley Copeland is one of the most influential teachers I ever had the pleasure of working with. Shirley was an exceptional mathematics teacher, but in reality, that was only one of the many reasons she was exceptional. She was one of the longest-tenured teachers at our school, and she had a passion for helping all teachers and leaders grow. She understood the importance of teacher leadership, and that understanding shaped the way she exercised her power as an informal leader. She was a master at using her down-to-earth personality, charismatic charm, and sense of humor to help everyone get better at his or her job. Her colleagues lovingly referred to her as the *Queen of Mathematics*, but her command of leadership skills far outweighed her command of mathematics in winning their admiration.

As great as Shirley was at teaching mathematics, she also taught me some important lessons in the nature of transformational leadership. Among those lessons was the importance of developing teacher leaders. Shirley was open and trustworthy, but she was also brutally honest. If some process or practice I had put in place was not working, Shirley often would solve the immediate problem but also report her observations and offer her insights.

If I made a decision that the campus had a difficult time accepting, she didn't hesitate to share their concerns with me and listen to my rationale. She helped support new initiatives, advise other teachers, and advance student learning throughout the school system. If I wanted to discuss tough decisions or gather informed input before putting new policies in place, Shirley was a strong and savvy partner in those conversations. Her leadership was invaluable to me, to her colleagues, and to our students.

I came to trust Shirley's feedback, because it was always grounded in her experience, knowledge, and understanding of the challenges we were undertaking in building excellence throughout our school. That trust also was founded in her confidence —the confidence she had both in herself and in me. Through working with Shirley, I developed a deep appreciation for the ideas, information, insights, and leadership teachers can offer to school leaders. I also developed a commitment to support educators in developing the skills of leadership as an essential part of my role as a leader committed to building a school of excellence. I continue in that work today.

Fostering Teacher Leadership

When teachers are as influential as Shirley, they haven't reached the end of their journey toward professional growth. In fact, they have undertaken the ongoing work of continually extending that journey through the development of their skills of teacher leadership. Those skills rest at the pinnacle of the Hierarchy of Instructional Excellence, as illustrated in figure 8.1 (page 176). At this stage in their development, teachers are empowered by their deep levels of experience, skill, and understanding to lead within their own areas of expertise and to create an environment that empowers their colleagues to lead within their areas of expertise as well. In other words, they leverage the full power of their talents to help develop the talents of others.

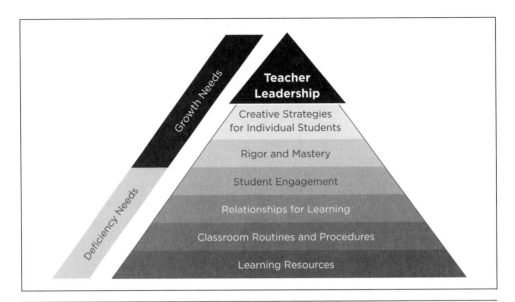

Figure 8.1: Hierarchy of Instructional Excellence—teacher leadership.

Teacher leaders never stop learning, and they embrace the obligation to share that learning with others. Learning grounded in that purpose epitomizes excellent leadership. A truly excellent teacher leader embraces that leadership purpose at four different levels: (1) self-leadership, (2) team leadership, (3) school and district leadership, and (4) global leadership.

The sections that follow outline the tasks teachers undertake in the process of developing their skills in each of these levels of leadership. They also offer strategies we can employ to support teachers in that development and offer our best advice and guidance as they work to transcend their roles as experts and embrace leadership.

We have a responsibility to establish the vision for our schools and to build the systems and supports necessary to achieve that vision. But no principal or administrator has all the time, knowledge, or expertise necessary to exhaust the possibilities for improving the entire instructional program of a school. If we want to do all we can to create schools of excellence, we must develop leadership capacity in our teachers. That way, we not only contribute to greater leadership to help our schools succeed now but we build the succession leadership that will bring our schools even greater excellence tomorrow. Building teacher leaders is our most effective way of bringing excellence to our teachers, our students, our schools, and our world.

Self-Leadership

Danielson (2013) writes that "the complexity of teaching requires continued growth and development in order for teachers to remain current" (p. 72). In other words, growth can never be the goal; it must be the constant. In developing skills in teacher leadership, therefore, one of the primary tasks teachers must engage in is reflection. Growth depends on strong roots, and the roots of teacher leadership lie in a deep and honest understanding of one's instructional effectiveness. As emphasized in previous chapters of this book, excellent teachers continually reflect on their instructional effectiveness, its strengths, and its weaknesses. Without honest reflection and a deep commitment to personal improvement, efforts to help lead others in achieving excellence can prove futile.

Of course, most people want to improve in some capacity. Fixed-minded people seek improvement when they're in a struggling relationship, they're behind at work, or their job is on the line. Growth-minded people seek improvement all the time. Excellent teachers inhabit this growth mindset and, therefore, are constantly assessing their performance to identify deficiencies and leverage strengths. Never leaning on last year's performance or yesterday's accolades, excellent teachers continually analyze their knowledge of learning resources. They seek out better and more efficient routines and procedures, and they determine how to make their learning environment more engaging for students. As the needs of students change over the years, these teachers are constantly re-evaluating their approach to developing strong learning relationships with their students. They look for new avenues and ideas for active learning experiences that can challenge their students and inspire them to pursue independent projects that can help them build a bridge toward future academic and career success. In exercising these skills and building these qualities, excellent teachers become teacher leaders.

Teacher leaders seek ideas from a multitude of sources. While excellent schools have a well-established system of professional development opportunities for educators, teacher leaders don't rely on those sources to provide every option for professional growth. They seek out and engage in learning experiences wherever they can find them. Most importantly, teacher leaders never assume that they've "been there and done that." Rather than relying solely on their own experience to solve problems, they avidly look for people who know more than they do, and then they learn from them. Ideas are welcome, not threatening, to teachers at the pinnacle of their profession. Like all self-actualized people, teacher leaders possess a deep desire to know more about the world, about themselves, and about the work that they do. Teacher leaders' insatiable appetite for knowledge and passion for their work separates them from the crowd.

Leaders at the district, school, and teacher level must model and promote self-leadership if we want more teachers to adopt a philosophy of continuous improvement. In essence, we must "strive to become a learner among learners" (Stronge, Richard, & Catano, 2008). Further, if we want teachers to consistently acknowledge and work to improve their own performance deficits, we should set a standard for that behavior by being confident enough to acknowledge and remediate our own performance weaknesses. We also can promote the concept of continuous improvement by spotlighting examples of self-leadership in our teachers through both public and private platforms: "Today's principals must become role models for learning while continually (or at least regularly) seeking tools and ideas that foster school improvement" (Lashway, 2003, as cited in Stronge et al., 2008).

In their report on research into the role of leadership on student learning, Kenneth Leithwood and his colleagues (2004) write that while leaders bear a clear responsibility to establish the school's guiding vision, that alone won't motivate members of the organization to move in that direction, nor will it make them better able to do so. Instead, "such capacities and motivations are influenced by the direct experiences organizational members have with those in leadership roles" (Leithwood et al., 2004, p. 6). The authors go on to cite examples of leadership practices that can positively influence those experiences as "offering intellectual stimulation, providing individualized support, and providing appropriate models of best practice and beliefs considered fundamental to the organization" (p. 7).

If our goal is to convert followers into leaders, we must demonstrate our interest in the professional development of teacher leaders in our organization as well as our own desire to be led toward continuous improvement by their support and informed feedback. The belief in ongoing learning for everyone within the organization can be our most powerful demonstration of the ideal of self-leadership in achieving educational excellence.

Team Leadership

Team leadership is another critical skill for teacher leaders. Teacher leaders put their expertise to effective use by leading their peers as well as by learning from them. Teacher leaders not only engage in ongoing reflection on their own performance but offer colleagues seasoned guidance and advice as they "conduct interactions with colleagues in a manner notable for honesty and integrity" (Danielson, 2013, p. 75). Teacher leaders embrace the role of leading their peers because they know that by helping their colleagues improve their performance, they also are helping more students learn at higher levels. Student improvement can't occur without teacher improvement, and teacher improvement can't occur without teacher leadership.

Collaborative teams engage in collaborative learning, and teacher leaders lead that learning by asking guiding questions that not only spur discussion but keep the focus on students. When the team gets frustrated with students, administration, or ambiguous mandates, teacher leaders help the team identify the problems and then shift its focus toward finding solutions. They provide guidance when the team ventures into uncharted waters with new initiatives or instructional experiments. When team members experience difficulties helping students learn, teacher leaders coach them through a problem simplification plan that enables teachers to isolate the problem and identify possible solutions. Teacher leaders are always finding creative ways to help their team use collaboration as a tool for continuous improvement.

When it comes to team leadership, teacher leaders assume roles very similar to our own roles as school leaders. Teacher leaders identify and develop leadership within each team member, and they encourage their peers to share their expertise with others. Just as we consult with teacher leaders to discuss emerging problems or opportunities, teacher leaders develop leadership in peers by asking colleagues to lead them or the team through similar discussions and problem-solving exercises.

We can support and guide teacher leaders in team leadership skills by observing, coaching, and reflecting with them on their leadership experiences and opportunities. Leading a team of peers can initially be a challenge for teacher leaders, so we should remember that teacher leaders must allocate time to make building leadership among their colleagues a priority. Our task, then, becomes making sure teacher leaders have time to work individually with campus or instructional leaders to plan for and lead meetings and to reflect on their own effectiveness as leaders.

To help teacher leaders plan for meetings, we can provide them with sample agendas or meeting structures. We also can help them hone the communication skills necessary for leading meetings and learn how to ask guiding questions that will help other teachers engage and contribute in meetings. For teams that struggle with adherence to norms, we can offer suggestions to proactively improve the deficit area or even become a participating team member in order to help confront those who intentionally deviate from team norms.

[handwritten margin note: PLC leader training]

To make the most effective contributions to our teacher leaders' skills in leading collaborative meetings, we need to be present in those meetings. That way, we can observe teachers exercising their leadership skills just as we would observe their approach to classroom instruction. We can model leadership in the meeting by co-leading, or we can provide feedback after the meeting based on our observations and shared experiences.

When teacher leaders struggle with specific skills in team leadership, we once again can help them achieve targeted improvements through collaboratively working through a problem simplification plan. By coaching teacher leaders in how to grow in targeted areas of leadership, we also help promote their professional development. In its 2004 report on instructional coaching, the Annenberg Institute for School Reform states that "coaching supports collective, interconnected leadership across a school system" (King et al., 2004, p. 4). The report goes on to note that "research findings indicate that effective coaching structures promote a collaborative culture where large numbers of school personnel feel ownership and responsibility for leading improvement efforts in teaching and learning" (King et al., 2004, p. 4).

Finally, teacher leaders improve tremendously through reflection, and we can offer teachers assistance with this process through reflective coaching. By using coaching strategies that probe the teacher leader's mind to identify areas of strength and areas for growth, we can guide the teacher leader to discover where he or she can grow next in his or her abilities as a leader. We also can offer our support in addressing areas of growth and change that might be uncomfortable. As with every form of effective instruction, we can't help teacher leaders truly maximize their learning by simply telling them what they need to do. We can, however, draw on our own expertise and understanding to help them discover those answers for themselves.

School and District Leadership

For many, teacher leadership at the school or district level can have either of two negative connotations: either it is reserved for pillars of the institution who have been at the school forever and do a great job providing superficial input, or it is relegated to whomever the school can scrounge up to serve on the team for the number of meetings required by state law. School and district leaders who misuse teacher leadership at the school or district level miss a huge opportunity to gain powerful information and insight into school improvement. If we want to be transformational leaders, we must realize that our goal is not to attract followers. Our purpose is to "form a relationship of mutual stimulation and elevation that converts followers into leaders and may convert leaders into moral agents" (Burns, 1978, p. 4). Building school and district leadership among teachers is our strongest mechanism for accomplishing that goal.

Many state laws require site-based teams to have decision-making authority over staff development. Staff development is the primary tool for developing teacher excellence, and teacher leaders can help us determine where our schools or districts are struggling as a whole to succeed in the skill sets for instructional excellence. Since teacher leaders are likely to have more current knowledge and expertise in teacher effectiveness than principals and superintendents, we should turn to teacher leaders for their valuable insights and advice in determining specific professional development practices that can help schools improve student performance. Teacher leaders, for example, can select professional development that actually matches the deficits identified through a comprehensive needs assessment. By having skilled practitioners influence school leadership in a constructive manner, our comprehensive needs assessments, school improvement plans, and staff development plans can evolve from meaningless bureaucratic checklists into purposeful plans for powerful improvement.

Teacher leaders also contribute to school leadership through their willingness and abilities to teach and learn from others throughout the district. To support this work, we can empower our teacher leaders to share their expertise and learning with others. Whether it is providing professional development to the campus or serving teams of teachers they don't normally work with, we should encourage teacher leaders to fulfill this role and afford them the time in which to do so. As teacher leaders help others improve in their craft, they in turn refine their own thinking about the work they are sharing with colleagues. Teacher leaders model learning for peers not out of obligation but out of a desire to promote their own professional growth, as well as that of their peers and students throughout the district. As transformative leaders, we can't just expect this kind of districtwide support from our teacher leaders; ~~we have to give them the time, encouragement, and tools they need to provide it.~~

(4) *Global Leadership*

The best teacher leaders commit to learning far beyond the confines of their schools' four walls or their districts' geographic borders. Because of advances in technology, most of us are influenced on a daily basis by people we have never met. The Internet has provided a forum in which skilled teacher leaders can contribute their knowledge, experience, and ideas to helping other teachers and students around the world learn and grow. One of the most encouraging aspects of this kind of global teacher leadership is that its processes and content are developed and driven by teachers, not companies.

Whether it's through Twitter, Teachers Pay Teachers, Pinterest, or Flickr, teachers all over the world are sharing their expertise and modeling what teacher leadership should be. These teacher leaders don't have to be the longest-tenured educators in their system or have the loftiest titles in their district to share their expertise with a worldwide audience. They just need a deep passion for leading others in the ongoing pursuit of learning. Similarly, we don't have to be leaders of the largest or most well-financed school districts in our area to support global teacher leaders. We just need to appreciate, identify, and encourage this kind of leadership in teachers throughout our schools.

Bill Ferriter is one example of a global leader. As a sixth-grade science teacher in North Carolina, Ferriter posts his thoughts and ideas on his blog *The Tempered Radical* (http://blog.williamferriter.com). There, Ferriter addresses a wide variety of topics that can aid the understanding and growth of both teachers and school leaders. Ferriter also maintains a visible presence on social media through Twitter (www.twitter.com/plugusin).

He has written several books and also leads presentations around the country on the topics of PLCs and educational technology. Ferriter is pushing the boundaries of traditional schooling and challenging educators to stop seeing themselves as "just teachers" or cogs in the system. His message is simple—embrace your true role as a powerful advocate for students and teachers. In all these ways, Ferriter offers a striking example of the potential all teachers have to make a difference in the world.

Vicki Davis offers another strong example of global teacher leadership in action. Her niche is a little different from Ferriter's, but the global influence of her leadership is similar. Davis uses Twitter (www.twitter.com/coolcatteacher) and her blog (www.coolcatteacher.com) to provide teachers with practical strategies to become more efficient and effective in their work. Her thoughts are not just practical, they're challenging. They inspire teachers and principals to continuously improve at the complex craft of leading students and schools to excellence.

These examples describe just a few of the thousands of teachers who are making a difference as global leaders. Becoming a global leader can radically transform teachers, their work, and even the culture of their own schools. Global teacher leaders learn more about the world, and they bring that learning and the insights it sparks to their schools and their classrooms. Becoming a global leader means that teachers take a huge leap in their professional development, and that can be quite scary. Sending out that first tweet, sharing that first blog post, and connecting with complete strangers can be an uncomfortable experience for even the strongest teacher. Making the process even more intimidating, many schools inadvertently frighten teachers away from using social media as a learning tool by issuing directives that vilify the use of social media altogether. Reviewing these policies and crafting them to offer necessary protections for teachers and students, while also encouraging the sensible use of these powerful tools for communication, is one way that we can make a big difference in a teacher leader's progress toward a global stage.

One way we can combat this fear is to be actively connected on social media ourselves. Then we are in a position to share our thoughts, experiences, and ideas in creating a culture that values global leadership. As part of that culture, we should encourage teachers to use their online presence to discover cutting-edge ideas and strategies that would otherwise take years to find their way into our schools.

We need to actively and publicly recognize the benefits of global teacher leadership and the ways that it can contribute to the teacher leader's own professional growth as well as the growth of other teachers and students throughout the district and around the world. To support a culture that values learning through the use of global tools, we can host weekly or biweekly Twitter chats with a school hashtag (for example, #pisdedchat), or we can tag tweets that we discover to teacher leaders in our schools.

Beyond using technology to build global leadership among teachers, we can work to engage teacher leaders in global education leadership classes, seminars, and experiences, such as those offered by the Institute of International Education (www.iie .org). As leaders of our education communities, we should use all our initiative and enterprise to help provide our teacher leaders with the time, tools, and organizational support they need to identify and pursue avenues for developing this kind of global understanding and leadership capability.

Furthermore, we can model our own global leadership by participating in global learning opportunities whenever possible, as well as by sharing our thoughts on educational instruction and leadership through personal blogs or by connecting our teacher leaders to people and ideas we discover through global learning. By being an active and productive model of global leadership, we can create a culture that celebrates connected educators and entices teachers to pursue leadership on a global level. As Harriett Stubbs (2009) writes:

> The world in which today's students live is rapidly changing, growing significantly smaller in scope as a new global society emerges.

As educators, it is essential we become active, participating members in this developing global network, maximizing our own knowledge so that we are better able to communicate with students. We must be collaborative members of the world community, cooperating with other teachers to educate the leaders for today, tomorrow, and the future.

Conclusion

Teacher leadership is the pinnacle of instructional excellence. Without it, we will never be able to move our schools and districts to the highest levels of educational excellence. And without a strong cadre of talented teacher leaders, we can't maintain a keen focus on our schools' current instructional excellence while simultaneously building and maintaining an effective and inspiring vision for their future evolution. Nor can we lead most effectively by surrounding ourselves with followers. Instead, we need to dedicate our time and efforts to developing teacher leaders who can help share and expand our vision for a continually evolving and improving school organization that can meet tomorrow's challenges by guaranteeing learning excellence for today's students. When more teachers are leading, more teachers are learning; that's a formula for helping more students achieve excellence.

A teacher's first step toward a leadership role lies in self-leadership—the practice of reflecting on and improving the effectiveness of his or her own practices. While this is by nature a self-directed experience, we should support teacher leaders in this stage of their development by meeting and consulting with them individually and providing our own coaching expertise as well as that of others within the system. We have a responsibility to be "learners among learners" by modeling a high standard for ongoing learning and professional development. We won't develop teacher leaders by waiting for them to step forward. Instead, we must actively seek out and develop the leadership skills of talented teachers around us and then model those leadership skills consistently within our own roles.

We also have multiple options for supporting teachers as they learn and assume the role of team leadership. A primary role for teacher leaders is in helping to advance the learning of their peers and colleagues throughout the system. By attending and observing team meetings, we position ourselves to actively participate in teachers' growth in team leadership by offering observations, co-leading experiences, and targeted feedback. By engaging in the collaborative experience of developing collaborative leadership, we can help teacher leaders become both more comfortable and more effective in their roles as peer leaders.

Finally, we have a responsibility to help talented teacher leaders assume their roles as global educators and leaders. Through the use of social media and blogs, teacher leaders can inspire people around the world by sharing their learning and their passion for education. By engaging teacher leaders in global teaching initiatives and learning opportunities, we can help them develop the international understanding and experiences necessary to help raise the global awareness, understanding, and skills of all instructors and students throughout our district and around the world. If we are truly committed to ongoing learning and instructional improvement, we can find no more relevant or meaningful arena for that growth than in the development of global teacher leaders within our own schools.

My experiences as a school and district leader have had a tremendous influence on my leadership skills. I have worked with amazing superintendents, assistant superintendents, and principals who have shaped my ability to positively impact student achievement. I was expected to follow these leaders, of course, but I *learned* from them because I wanted to and because I saw the limitless opportunities for my own professional growth in the lessons of leadership they offered. So I am grateful to all those leaders I worked with in the past, but they weren't the only sources of the essential lessons in leadership I learned over the years. In fact, I owe a great deal to all the tremendous teachers who helped guide my learning in ways that no superintendent could.

I had the benefit of training with countless teacher leaders who were confident in themselves and trusted in me. They taught me some of the most valuable lessons I learned about the rapidly changing world of education, the many responsibilities of instructional leadership, and the limitless challenges and opportunities inherent in the privilege of guiding teachers in a shared vision of excellence. These teacher leaders taught me that my true purpose as a school leader was to empower teachers to lead themselves and one another. They revealed to me that the pathway to excellence would always be guided by every teacher within the school. Through these teachers, I learned that leaders don't change organizations; they create the conditions for people to change themselves, which in turn, changes the organization.

Excellence in every classroom will always depend on an excellent *teacher* in every classroom. Our job as leaders is to do everything it takes to empower every teacher to discover the knowledge and skills within him- or herself to help every student reach excellence. When we accept this challenge as our ultimate goal and moral imperative, we truly begin the arduous task of creating schools that guarantee excellence for every student.

Leaders can use the following reflection tool to help guide teachers in becoming effective leaders through self-leadership, team leadership, school and district leadership, and global leadership.

Reflection Tool: Teacher Leadership

Definition of Excellence for Teacher Leadership

What is our school's definition of teacher excellence in the area of teacher leadership, and do our teachers know and believe that leadership is part of their role?

Self-Leadership

1. How well do we model self-leadership for our teachers?

2. Do teachers see leadership as their job or as every educator's job?

3. How well do we reinforce in all teachers the need for self-leadership in order to reach excellence?

4. What are some steps we can take right now to promote self-leadership with our teachers?

Team Leadership

1. How well do we promote to our teachers the need for teacher leadership as a tool for school improvement?

2. How effectively do we identify and then support teacher leaders in their efforts to lead their peers?

3. What steps can we take to further develop teacher leadership at the team level?

4. What are some steps we can take right now to promote teacher team leadership with our teachers?

page 1 of 2

School and District Leadership

1. How successfully do we encourage our school and district improvement teams to include teacher leaders and the ideas that they offer to help our school improve?

2. How well do we empower teachers to lead authentically at the school or district level?

3. How can we structure our school or district improvement team so that teachers truly feel that they are empowered to provide input and meaningful ideas to help all teachers within the organization grow?

4. What steps can we take right now to promote school and district leadership with our teachers?

Global Leadership

1. How well do we visibly embrace the idea of teachers leading on a global scale?

2. How well do we model global leadership through the use of social media and technology?

3. How comfortable do our teachers feel using social media as a tool for learning?

4. How well do we support teachers in their efforts to become leaders?

5. What steps can we take right now to promote global leadership with our teachers?

References and Resources

Barkley, E. F. (2010). *Student engagement techniques: A handbook for college faculty*. San Francisco: Jossey-Bass.

Barth, R. (2001). *Learning by heart*. San Francisco: Jossey-Bass.

Basye, D. (2014, August 5). *Personalized vs. differentiated vs. individualized learning*. Accessed at www.iste.org/explore/articledetail?articleid=124 on March 22, 2016.

Behrstock-Sherratt, E., & Rizzolo, A. (2014). Everyone at the table. *Educational Leadership, 71*(5), 64–69.

Bellingham Public Schools. (n.d.). *What's essential?: Seven essential instructional strategies for powerful teaching and learning*. Accessed at http://bellinghamschools.org/sites/default /files/learning/SevenEssentialStrategies.htm on March 17, 2016.

Berliner, D. C. (1988, February 17–20). *The development of expertise in pedagogy*. Charles W. Hunt Memorial Lecture presented at the Annual Meeting of the American Association of Colleges for Teacher Education, New Orleans, LA.

Blackburn, B. R. (2008). *Rigor is NOT a four-letter word*. Larchmont, NY: Eye on Education.

Boynton, M., & Boynton, C. (2005). *The educator's guide to preventing and solving discipline problems*. Alexandria, VA: Association for Supervision and Curriculum Development.

BrainyQuote. (n.d.). *Solomon Ortiz quotes*. Accessed at www.brainyquote.com/quotes /authors/s/solomon_ortiz.html on December 31, 2015.

Buffum, A., & Mattos, M. (Eds.). (2015). *It's about time: Planning interventions and extensions in elementary school*. Bloomington, IN: Solution Tree Press.

Buffum, A., Mattos, M., & Weber, C. (2009). *Pyramid response to intervention: RTI, professional learning communities, and how to respond when kids don't learn*. Bloomington, IN: Solution Tree Press.

Buffum, A., Mattos, M., & Weber, C. (2012). *Simplifying response to intervention: Four essential guiding principles*. Bloomington, IN: Solution Tree Press.

Burns, J. M. (1978). *Leadership*. New York: Harper & Row.

Carroll, T. (2009). The next generation of learning teams. *Phi Delta Kappan, 91*(2), 8–13.

Casas, J. [casas_jimmy]. (2015, June 23). *Too often we focus on what S's need 2 do differently when they don't learn rather than what we adults need to differently -DuFour #atplc* [Tweet]. Accessed at https://twitter.com/casas_jimmy/status/613416216770691073 on December 5, 2015.

Christenson, S. L., Reschly, A. L., & Wylie, C. (Eds.). (2012). *Handbook of research on student engagement.* New York: Springer.

Colvin, R. L., & Jacobs, J. (2010, April 7). Rigor: It's all the rage, but what does it mean? *The Hechinger Report.* Accessed at http://hechingerreport.org/rigor-its-all-the-rage-but -what-does-it-mean on December 31, 2015.

Council for Exceptional Children. (1998). *What every special educator must know: The international standards for the preparation and licensure of special educators* (3rd ed.). Reston, VA: Author.

Daggett, W. R., & Gendron, S. A. (2015, June). *Rigorous learning: Bridging students from our classrooms to successful lives.* Rexford, NY: International Center for Leadership in Education. Accessed at www.leadered.com/pdf/2015MSC_BridgingStudentsFrom OurClassroomstoSuccessfulLives.pdf on March 16, 2016.

Danielson, C. (1996). *Enhancing professional practice: A framework for teaching.* Alexandria, VA: Association for Supervision and Curriculum Development.

Danielson, C. (2007). *Danielson's framework for teaching.* Alexandria, VA: Association for Supervision and Curriculum Development. Accessed at http://sde.ok.gov/sde/sites /ok.gov.sde/files/SB-Feb12-7eDanielson.pdf on May 5, 2014.

Danielson, C. (2009). *Implementing the framework for teaching in enhancing professional practice: An ASCD action tool.* Alexandria, VA: Association for Supervision and Curriculum Development.

Danielson, C. (2013). *The framework for teaching evaluation instrument, 2013 edition.* Princeton, NJ: Danielson Group. Accessed at www.teachscape.com/binaries/content /assets/teachscape-marketing-website/products/ffteval/2013-framework-for-teaching -evaluation-instrument.pdf on January 5, 2016.

Darling-Hammond, L., & Sykes, G. (Eds.). (1999). *Teaching as the learning profession: Handbook of policy and practice.* San Francisco: Jossey-Bass.

Deci, E. L., Vallerand, R. J., Pelletier, L. G., & Ryan, R. M. (1991). Motivation and education: The self-determination perspective. *Educational Psychologist, 26*(3–4), 325–346.

Dole, J. A. (2004). The changing role of the reading specialist in school reform. *The Reading Teacher, 57*(5), 462–471.

Dollar, T. (2013, October). *Great leaders teach . . . great teachers lead! #edchat #colchat #21stedchat #leadership* [Tweet]. Accessed at https://twitter.com/TamraDollar /status/390088527070777345 on August 1, 2015.

Doppelt, Y., & Barak, M. (2002). Pupils identify key aspects and outcomes of a technological learning environment. *Journal of Technology Studies, 28*(1), 22–28.

DuFour, R., DuFour, R., & Eaker, R. (2008) *Revisiting professional learning communities at work: New insights for improving schools*. Bloomington, IN: Solution Tree Press.

DuFour, R., DuFour, R., Eaker, R., & Many, T. (2006). *Learning by doing: A handbook for professional learning communities at work*. Bloomington, IN: Solution Tree Press.

DuFour, R., DuFour, R., Eaker, R., & Many, T. (2010). *Learning by doing: A handbook for professional learning communities at work* (2nd ed.). Bloomington, IN: Solution Tree Press.

DuFour, R., DuFour, R., Eaker, R., Many, T., & Mattos, M. (2016). *Learning by doing: A handbook for professional learning communities at work* (3rd ed.). Bloomington, IN: Solution Tree Press.

DuFour, R., & Eaker, R. (1998). *Professional learning communities at work: Best practices for enhancing student achievement*. Bloomington, IN: Solution Tree Press.

DuFour, R., & Marzano, R. J. (2011). *Leaders of learning: How district, school, and classroom leaders improve student achievement*. Bloomington, IN: Solution Tree Press.

Eisenbach, B. B. (2014). Words that encourage. *Educational Leadership, 71*(5), 70–72.

Emmer, E. T., & Stough, L. M. (2001). Classroom management: A critical part of educational psychology, with implications for teacher education. *Educational Psychologist, 36*(2), 103–112.

Farmer, D. (1994). *Meeting the needs of gifted students in the regular classroom*. Sydney, Australia: Commonwealth of Australia.

Feistritzer, C. E. (2011). *Profile of teachers in the U.S. 2011*. Washington, DC: National Center for Education Information. Accessed at www.edweek.org/media/pot2011final -blog.pdf on December 23, 2014.

Ferriter, W. M. (2015). *Creating purpose-driven learning experiences*. Bloomington, IN: Solution Tree Press.

Ferriter, W. M., Graham, P., & Wight, M. (2013). *Making teamwork meaningful: Leading progress-driven collaboration in a PLC*. Bloomington, IN: Solution Tree Press.

Fisher, D. (2008). *Effective use of the gradual release of responsibility model*. Accessed at https://www.mheonline.com/_treasures/pdf/douglas_fisher.pdf on April 12, 2016.

Fisher, D., & Frey, N. (2008). *Better learning through structured teaching: A framework for the gradual release of responsibility*. Alexandria, VA: Association for Supervision and Curriculum Development.

Fleming, L. (n.d.). *Worlds of learning @ NMHS*. Accessed at http://worlds-of-learning .com/worlds-of-learning-nmhs on December 4, 2015.

Frey, N., & Fisher, D. (2009). The release of learning. *Principal Leadership, 9*(6), 18–22.

Fullan, M. G. (1991). *The new meaning of educational change* (2nd ed.). New York: Teachers College Press.

Fullan, M. G., & Hargreaves, A. (Eds.). (1992). *Teacher development and educational change*. Washington, DC: Falmer Press.

Geocaris, C. (1996). Increasing student engagement: A mystery solved. *Educational Leadership*, *54*(4), 72–75. Accessed at www.ascd.org/publications/educational -leadership/dec96/vol54/num04/Increasing-Student-Engagement@-A-Mystery -Solved.aspx on March 10, 2016.

Gill, E. (2015, March 31). *Harry Wong: Why teachers need classroom management.* Accessed at www.hotchalkeducationnetwork.com/harry-wong-interview on December 31, 2015.

Hale, J. A., & Fisher, M. (2013). *Upgrade your curriculum: Practical ways to transform units and engage students.* Alexandria, VA: Association for Supervision and Curriculum Development.

Hattie, J. (2009). *Visible learning: A synthesis of over 800 meta-analyses relating to achievement.* New York: Routledge.

Hattie, J. (2012). *Visible learning for teachers: Maximizing impact on learning.* New York: Routledge.

Hattie, J., & Timperley, H. (2007). The power of feedback. *Review of Educational Research*, *77*(1), 81–112.

Heathers, G. (1977). A working definition of individualized instruction. *Educational Leadership*, *34*(5), 342–345. Accessed at www.ascd.org/ASCD/pdf/journals/ed_lead /el_197702_heathers.pdf on March 22, 2016.

Himmele, P., & Himmele, W. (2011). *Total participation techniques: Making every student an active learner.* Alexandria, VA: Association for Supervision and Curriculum Development.

Huitt, W. (2007). Maslow's hierarchy of needs. *Educational Psychology Interactive.* Valdosta, GA: Valdosta State University. Accessed at www.edpsycinteractive.org/topics/conation /maslow.html on March 21, 2016.

Johnson, B. (2014, August 14). *Deeper learning: Why cross-curricular teaching is essential* [Blog post]. Accessed at www.edutopia.org/blog/cross-curricular-teaching-deeper -learning-ben-johnson on March 17, 2016.

Johnson, B. [dr_ben_johnson]. (2015, September 9). *A6 in the end it is going to be the basis of the relationship that allows the student to be vulnerable enough 2 engage in learning #SBLchat* [Tweet]. Accessed at https://twitter.com/dr_ben_johnson/status /641790048069771264 on December 31, 2015.

Katzenbach, J. R., & Smith, D. K. (1993). *The wisdom of teams: Creating the high-performance organization.* Boston: Harvard Business School Press.

King, D., Neuman, M., Pelchat, J., Potochnik, T., Rao, S., & Thompson, J. (2004). *Instructional coaching: Professional development strategies that improve instruction.* Providence, RI: Annenberg Institute for School Reform. Accessed at http:// annenberginstitute.org/sites/default/files/product/270/files/InstructionalCoaching.pdf on March 31, 2016.

Klem, A. M., & Connell, J. P. (2004a, September). Engaging youth in school. In L. R. Sherrord, C. Flanagan, & R. Kassimir (Eds.), *Youth activism: An international encyclopedia.* Westport, CT: Greenwood. Accessed at www.irre.org/publications /engaging-youth-school on March 9, 2016.

Klem, A. M., & Connell, J. P. (2004b). Relationships matter: Linking teacher support to student engagement and achievement. *Journal of School Health, 74*(7), 262–273. Accessed at www.irre.org/sites/default/files/publication_pdfs/Klem_and_Connell _2004_JOSH_article.pdf on April 11, 2016.

Lashway, L. (2003, July). *Role of the school leader: Trends and issues.* Eugene, OR: ERIC Clearinghouse on Educational Management. Accessed at http://files.eric.ed.gov /fulltext/ED479933.pdf on April 11, 2016.

Learning Forward. (n.d.). *Standards for professional learning.* Accessed at http://learningforward.org/standards/learning-designs# on October 21, 2015.

Learning Sciences International. (n.d.). *Four Marzano teacher evaluation domains.* Accessed at www.marzanoevaluation.com/evaluation/four_domains on June 1, 2015.

Leithwood, K., Louis, K. S., Anderson, S., & Wahlstrom, K. (2004). *How leadership influences student learning* [Executive summary]. New York: Wallace Foundation. Accessed at http://www.wallacefoundation.org/knowledge-center/Documents/How -Leadership-Influences-Student-Learning-Executive-Summary.pdf on April 11, 2016.

Levy, S., & Campbell, H. (2008). Student motivation: Premise, effective practice and policy. *Australian Journal of Teacher Education, 33*(5), 14–28.

Lezotte, L. W. (1999). *Correlates of effective schools: The first and second generation.* Okemos, MI: Effective Schools Products.

Mager, R. F. (1969). *Preparing instructional objectives: A critical tool in the development of effective instruction.* Atlanta, GA: Center for Effective Performance.

Martin, D. J., & Loomis, K. S. (2007). *Building teachers: A constructivist approach to introducing education.* Belmont, CA: Wadsworth. Accessed at www.cengage.com /resource_uploads/downloads/0495570540_162121.pdf on May 10, 2015.

Marzano, R. J. (2003). *Classroom management that works: Research-based strategies for every teacher.* Alexandria, VA: Association for Supervision and Curriculum Development.

Marzano, R. J. (2007). *The art and science of teaching: A comprehensive framework for effective instruction.* Alexandria, VA: Association for Supervision and Curriculum Development.

Marzano, R. J. (2012). *Becoming a reflective teacher.* Bloomington, IN: Marzano Research.

Marzano, R. J. (2013). *Becoming a high reliability school: The next step in school reform.* Bloomington, IN: Marzano Research.

Marzano, R. J., Pickering, D. J., & Pollock, J. E. (2001). *Classroom instruction that works: Research-based strategies for increasing student achievement.* Alexandria, VA: Association for Supervision and Curriculum Development.

Marzano, R. J., & Simms, J. A. (2013). *Coaching classroom instruction.* Bloomington, IN: Marzano Research.

Marzano, R. J., Waters, T., & McNulty, B. A. (2005). *School leadership that works: From research to results.* Alexandria, VA: Association for Supervision and Curriculum Development.

Maslow, A. H. (1943). A theory of human motivation. *Psychological Review, 50*(4), 370–396.

Maslow, A. H. (1954). *Motivation and personality.* New York: Harper.

McLeod, S. (2014). *Maslow's hierarchy of needs.* Accessed at www.simplypsychology.org /maslow.html on October 22, 2015.

Moir, E. (2008, October 8). *Ask Ellen: Individualize your instruction.* Accessed at www .edutopia.org/ask-ellen-differentiated-individualized-instruction on April 11, 2016.

Moss, C. M., & Brookhart, S. M. (2009). *Advancing formative assessment in every classroom: A guide for instructional leaders.* Alexandria, VA: Association for Supervision and Curriculum Development.

MotivationalUi. (2015, December 5). *When solving problems, dig at the roots instead of just hacking the leaves. -Anthony J. D'Angelo #quote* [Tweet]. Accessed at https://twitter .com/MotivationalUi/status/673224905471619073 on December 31, 2015.

Muhammad, A. (2009). *Transforming school culture.* Bloomington, IN: Solution Tree Press.

National Education Association. (2011, November 15). *NEA shares strategies for developing family-school-community partnerships.* Accessed at www.nea.org/home/49666.htm on April 13, 2016.

National Research Council Institute of Medicine of the National Academies. (2003). *Engaging schools: Fostering high school students' motivation to learn.* Washington, DC: National Academies Press.

Partnership for 21st Century Skills. (2009, December). *P21 framework definitions.* Accessed at www.p21.org/storage/documents/P21_Framework_Definitions.pdf on December 31, 2015.

Pearson, P. D., & Gallagher, G. (1983). The gradual release of responsibility model of instruction. *Contemporary Educational Psychology, 8*, 112–123.

Phillips, M. (2014, August 5). *A place for learning: The physical environment of classrooms* [Blog post]. Accessed at www.edutopia.org/blog/the-physical-environment-of -classrooms-mark-phillips on March 2, 2016.

Redding, S. (2013). *Through the student's eyes: A perspective on personalized learning and practice guide for teachers.* Philadelphia: Center on Innovations in Learning, Temple University. Accessed at www.centeril.org/publications/2013_09_through_the_eyes.pdf on March 23, 2016.

Reeves, D. (2002). *The leader's guide to standards: A blueprint for educational equity and excellence.* San Francisco: Jossey-Bass.

Robinson, K. (2013, May). *How to escape education's death valley* [Subtitles and transcript]. Accessed at www.ted.com/talks/ken_robinson_how_to_escape_education_s_death _valley/transcript?language=en on December 31, 2015.

Round Rock Independent School District. (n.d.). *Overview of the 5 E model of instruction.* Accessed at https://drive.google.com/file/d/0B1ZO8j6rlliSVkJ0cENmQ1E3VmM /edit?pref=2&pli=1 on April 11, 2016.

Schlechty, P. (1994, January). *Increasing student engagement*. Columbia: Missouri Leadership Academy.

Schlechty Center on Engagement. (n.d.). *Schlechty Center on Engagement*. Louisville, KY: Author. Accessed at www.schlechtycenter.org/system/tool_attachment/4046/original /sc_pdf_engagement.pdf?1272415798 on March 9, 2016.

Sears, N. (n.d.). *Building relationships with students*. Accessed at www.nea.org/tools/29469 .htm on March 7, 2016.

Sergiovanni, T. J. (1996). *Leadership for the schoolhouse: How is it different? Why is it important?* San Francisco: Jossey-Bass.

Sprick, R. (2009). *CHAMPS: A proactive and positive approach to classroom management* (2nd ed.). Eugene, OR: Pacific Northwest.

Stiggins, R. (2007). Assessment *for* learning: An essential foundation of productive instruction. In D. Reeves (Ed.), *Ahead of the curve: The power of assessment to transform teaching and learning* (pp. 59–76). Bloomington, IN: Solution Tree Press.

Strong, R., Silver, H. F., & Robinson, A. (1995). Strengthening student engagement: What do students want (and what really motivates them)? *Educational Leadership*, *53*(1), 8–12.

Stronge, J. H., Richard, H. B., & Catano, N. (2008). Chapter 1. Instructional leadership: Supporting best practice. In *Qualities of effective principals* (pp. 3–15). Alexandria, VA: Association for Supervision and Curriculum Development. Accessed at www.ascd.org /publications/books/108003/chapters/Instructional-Leadership@-Supporting-Best -Practice.aspx on March 28, 2016.

Stubbs, H. S. (2009). Using technology to develop global teachers: An innovative model. *Meridian: A Middle School Computer Technologies Journal*, *12*(1). Accessed at www .ncsu.edu/meridian/winter2009/stubbs/index.htm on March 28, 2016.

Svitak, A. (2012, February 8). *5 ways to empower students* [Blog post]. Accessed at www .edutopia.org/blog/empower-students-adora-svitak on March 3, 2016.

Taylor, L., & Parsons, J. (2011). Improving student engagement. *Current Issues in Education*, *14*(1). Accessed at http://cie.asu.edu/ojs/index.php/cieatasu/article /viewFile/745/162 on April 11, 2016.

Texas Education Agency. (2014). *Texas Teacher Evaluation and Support System (T-TESS) appraiser training handbook*. Austin, TX: Author. Accessed at www.pngisd.org /modules/groups/homepagefiles/cms/446867/File/Skyward%20EAPLUS/Ruberic %20only.pdf on December 31, 2015.

Voxer. (n.d.). *Home page*. Accessed at www.voxer.com on December 31, 2015.

Webb, N. L. (2002, March 28). *Depth-of-knowledge levels for four content areas*. Accessed at http://facstaff.wcer.wisc.edu/normw/All%20content%20areas%20%20DOK %20levels%2032802.pdf on December 31, 2015.

Wiggins, G. (2012). Seven keys to effective feedback. *Educational Leadership*, *70*(1), 10–16. Accessed at www.ascd.org/publications/educational-leadership/sept12/vol70 /num01/Seven-Keys-to-Effective-Feedback.aspx on December 31, 2015.

Wiggins, G. (2014, January 1). *Final exams vs. projects: Nope, false dichotomy—A practical start to the blog year* [Blog post]. Accessed at https://grantwiggins.wordpress.com/2014/01/01/final-exams-vs-projects-nope-false-dichotomy-a-practical-start-to-the-blog-year on March 15, 2016.

Wiliam, D. (2011). *Embedded formative assessment.* Bloomington, IN: Solution Tree Press.

Williamson, R., & Blackburn, B. (2010, February). *Recognizing rigor in classrooms: Four tools for school leaders.* Reston, VA: National Association of Secondary School Principals.

Wilson, L. O. (n.d.). *Madeline Hunter lesson plan model.* Accessed at http://thesecondprinciple.com/teaching-essentials/models-teaching/madeline-hunter-lesson-plan-model on March 31, 2016.

Wink, J. (2014). *Readiness standard analysis worksheet.* Accessed at www.dropbox.com/s/yievv34nu0o6rnt/Vertical%20Standard%20Deconstruct%202014.docx?dl=0 on December 31, 2015.

Wolpert-Gawron, H. (2015, February 24). *Kids speak out on student engagement* [Blog post]. Accessed at www.edutopia.org/blog/student-engagement-stories-heather-wolpert-gawron on March 9, 2016.

Wolpow, R., Johnson, M. M., Hertel, R., & Kincaid, S. O. (2009). *The heart of learning and teaching: Compassion, resiliency, and academic success.* Olympia: Washington State Office of Superintendent of Public Instruction.

Wubbels, T., Brekelmans, M., van Tartwijk, J., & Admiraal, W. (1999). Interpersonal relationships between teachers and students in the classroom. In H. C. Waxman & H. J. Walberg (Eds.), *New directions for teaching practice and research* (pp. 151–170). Berkeley, CA: McCutchan.

Wubbels, T., & Levy, J. (Eds.). (1993). *Do you know what you look like?: Interpersonal relationships in education.* London: RoutledgeFalmer.

Zehm, S. J., & Kottler, J. A. (1993). *On being a teacher: The human dimension.* Thousand Oaks, CA: Corwin Press.

Zelenak, S. (2014, August). *Using Depth of Knowledge (DOK) to support instructional rigor.* Presented at Tatum ISD Staff Development in Tatum, Texas.

Index

A

academic performance, impact of teachers, 4, 10–11, 129

Admiral, W., 72

assessments, rigor and mastery, 124–125

Association for Supervision and Curriculum Development (ASCD), 53–54

B

Barkley, E. F., 89

Barth, R., xv

Basye, D. E., 147

behavior. *See* classroom routines and procedures

Bellingham Public Schools (Washington), 135

Berliner, D., 51

Better Learning Through Structured Teaching (Fisher and Frey), 98

Boynton, C., 69

Boynton, M., 69

Brekelmans, M., 72

Brookhart, S., 158

Buffum, A., xiii, 2, 122–123, 153

C

CHAMPS, 34, 52–53, 77

choice boards, 154, 155, 162–163

Classroom Management That Works (Marzano), 10

classroom routines and procedures

behavior, team norms for student, 59

behavior, team responses to student, 58–60

collaborative framework, 56–57

delivery, 53–54

description and role of, 17–18, 47

excellence plan for improvement, 61, 63–64

Excellence Support System, 55–64

individualized supports, 61–64

management, importance of competency in, 51

preparation, 52–53

problem simplification plan, 61, 62

questions on expectations for appropriate behavior, 56–57, 60

reflection, 54–55, 66–67

schoolwide supports, 55–58

struggling alone without routines example, 48–50

teacher team supports, 58–61

universal, list of, 60

well-managed classroom, defined, 47

classrooms, physical design, 31

coaching, 15, 40, 106–107, 141, 179

collaboration. *See* teacher team supports

collaborative learning, 97

collective responsibility, 2

Common Core State Standards (CSS), 4

common formative assessments, 124, 125

communication

 elements of, 74

 for engagement, 109

 with families, 80–82

compassion, 75

concentrated instruction, 122–123

Connell, J. P., 94, 95, 96

Conscious Discipline, 77

consistency, 74–75

content mastery

 See also rigor and mastery

Copeland, S., 174–175

co-planning, 141

co-teaching, 140

counselors, role of, 77

Creating Purpose-Driven Learning Experiences (Ferriter), 154

curriculum guides, 130

D

Daggett, W., 117, 121

Danielson, C., xiv, 4, 30, 31–32, 42, 47, 51, 54, 71, 72–73, 121, 124, 153, 157, 176

Davis, V., 181

Depth of Knowledge (DOK), 129, 130, 131–134

digital badging, 36

digital tools, 36–37

Dole, J., 141

DuFour, R., xiii–xiv, 2–3, 22, 23, 136, 162, 165

E

Eaker, R., xiii–xiv, 22, 23

Educator's Guide to Preventing and Solving Discipline Problems, The (Boynton and Boynton), 69

effectiveness

 impact of school, 12

 impact of teacher, 10–12

 use of term, 10

engagement

 coaching for teachers, 106–107

 communication, 109

 defined, 93–94

 delivery, 99, 102

 description and role of, 18–19

 example, 90–92

 Excellence Support System, 103–112

 goals, 110

 impact of, 89, 94–96

 individualized supports, 108–112

 instructional delivery model, 104–105

 instructional planning, 107

 instructional rounds, 107–108

 lesson-planning template, 99, 100–101

 modeling, 108

 optimal time for, 109

 preparation, 96–99

 problem simplification plan, 111–112

 professional development programs, 105–106

promoting, 93–96

reflection, 102–103, 105, 114–115

schoolwide supports, 103–107

teacher team supports, 107–108

transition responsibility for learning, 110

Enhancing Professional Practice: A Framework for Teaching (Danielson), 4

excellence, use of term, 10

Excellence Support System

    See also individualized supports; schoolwide supports; teacher team supports

    classroom routines and procedures, 55–64

    critical questions, 23–24

    description of, 6–7, 21–24

    engagement, 103–112

    individual students, strategies for, 158–168

    learning resources and, 32, 34–42

    relationships for learning, 76–83

    rigor and mastery, 128–146

exit ticket, 152–153

experience levels, teacher

    views on, 13–14

Explain Everything Interactive Whiteboard, 35

F

families, communicating with, 80–82

feedback, 106, 108, 127, 140–141, 157–158

Feistritzer, C. E., 13–14

Ferriter, W. M., 38, 154, 165, 181

Fisher, D., 93, 97–98, 104, 106

Fisher, M., 153

5E Model of Instruction, 104

Fleming, L., 36

flipped videos, 34–36, 81

focus lesson, 97

formative assessments, 124, 125, 129

Four Marzano Teacher Evaluation Domains, 121

Framework for Teaching Evaluation Instrument, The (Danielson), 54

Frey, N., 93, 97–98, 104, 106

G

Gendron, S., 117, 121

Gilmer Elementary School (Texas), 34, 35

global leadership, 181–183

goals, engagement, 110

Google Sheets, 34, 99

gradual release of responsibility model, 97–98, 104

Graham, P., 38

guided learning, 97

H

Hale, J. A., 153

Hattie, J., xiv, 3, 4, 106

Heathers, G., 151, 152

Hierarchy of Instructional Excellence, xiv

    See also individual level

    description of, 6, 7, 15–21

Hierarchy of Needs, xiv, 6, 15–16, 42, 51, 69, 89, 117, 148, 173

I

iMovie, 35

independent learning, 98

individual formative assessments, 124, 125

individualized instruction/learning, defined, 147, 151

individualized supports
    classroom routines and procedures, 61–64
    description and role of, 22–23
    engagement, 108–112
    individual students, strategies for, 165–168
    learning resources, 40–42
    relationships for learning, 82–83
    rigor and mastery, 139–142

individual students, strategies for
    choice boards, 154, 155, 163–163
    delivery, 153–157
    description and role of, 20, 147–148
    example, 148–150
    Excellence Support System, 158–168
    individualized supports, 165–168
    intervention model, tiered, 159–161
    interventions, 154–157, 163–165, 166
    learning progress flowchart, 153, 154
    preparation, 152–153
    problem simplification plan, 166–168
    professional development, 161–162
    purpose-driven learning, 154
    reflection, 157–158, 170–171
    schoolwide supports, 159–162
    teacher team supports, 162–165

Institute of International Education, 182

instructional delivery model, 104–105

instructional planning, 107

instructional rounds, 107–108

interventions
    preventive, 163–164
    responsive, 164–165
    staff, 166
    tiered model, 159–161

It's About Time (Mattos and Buffum), xiii

J

Johnson, B., 69, 138

K

Klem, A. M., 94, 95, 96

Kottler, J. A., 69

L

leadership. *See*   teacher leadership

learning for all. *See* individual students, strategies for

learning progress flowchart, 153, 154

learning resources
    delivery, 31–32
    description and role of, 17
    Excellence Support System, 32, 34–42
    first day on the job experiences, 28–29
    flipped videos, 34–36
    individualized supports, 40–42
    mentoring, use of, 40
    preparation, 30–31
    problem simplification plan, 41–42

professional development, ongoing, 37

reflection, 32, 33, 44–45

schoolwide supports, 34–37

teacher team supports, 38–40

technology training on the fly, 36–37

wikis, 34, 35

Leithwood, K., 178

lesson-planning template, 99, 100–101

Levy, J., 72

Love and Logic, 77

M

Madeline Hunter's Elements of Lesson Design, 104

Making Teamwork Meaningful (Ferriter, Graham, and Wight), 38

Many, T., xiii–xiv, 22

Marzano, R. J., xiv, 3, 6, 10–12, 40, 52, 53, 72, 73, 121, 173

Maslow, A., xiv, 6, 15–16, 17, 18, 19, 20–21, 42, 51, 64, 69, 89, 117, 148, 173

mastery. *See* rigor and mastery

Mattos, M., xiii–xiv, 2, 122–123, 153

mentoring, 15, 40

mindset for teacher improvement, need for, 14–15

mission
    defined and role of, 2–3
    role of teachers, 3–4

modeling, 108

Moir, E., 157

monitoring instruction, 127, 135

Moss, C. M., 158

Muhammad, A., xiii

N

National Center for Education Information, 13

National Education Association, 81–82

National Research Council Institute of Medicine of the National Academies, 94

New Milford High School (New Jersey), 36

O

observation, 127, 140–141

Ortiz, S., 9

P

Parsons, J., 19

Phillips, M., 31

problem simplification plan
    classroom routines and procedures, 61, 62
    engagement, 111–112
    individual students, strategies for, 166–168
    learning resources, 41–42
    relationships for learning, 83, 84
    rigor and mastery, 142, 143

professional development
    on intervention, 161–162
    ongoing, 37
    programs, 105–106, 130

professional learning communities (PLCs)
    critical questions, xiii–xiv, 23–24, 56
    role of, 22

Professional Learning Community at Work™ model, xiv

Profile of Teachers in the U.S. 2011, 13

purpose-driven learning, 154

Q

questions, strategic, 126, 130

R

Redding, S., 150–151, 152

Reeves, D., 123

reflection

    classroom routines and procedures, 54–55, 66–67

    engagement, 102–103, 105, 114–115

    individual students, strategies for, 157–158, 170–171

    learning resources, 32, 33, 44–45

    relationships for learning, 76, 86–87

    rigor and mastery, 127–128, 145–146

    teacher leadership, 185–186

relationships for learning

    counselors, role of, 77

    delivery, 74–76

    description and role of, 18

    example, 70–71

    Excellence Support System, 76–83

    importance of, 71

    individualized supports, 82–83

    optimal, 72–73

    plan for building, 78–79

    preparation, 72–74

    problem simplification plan, 83, 84

    reflection, 76, 86–87

    schoolwide supports, 77–79

    student history files, 77–78

    teacher team supports, 79–82

    transition sheets, 78

resources. *See* learning resources

response to intervention (RTI), 6

    intervention model, tiered, 159–161

responsibility for learning, transitioning, 110

rigor and mastery

    assessments, 124–125, 129

    curriculum guides, 130

    definitions, 117–118, 121

    delivery, 125–127

    description and role of, 19–20

    essential standards, 123–124

    example, 118–119

    Excellence Support System, 128–146

    individualized supports, 139–142

    instructional cycle, 121, 122

    monitoring instruction, 127, 135

    preparation, 122–125

    problem simplification plan, 142, 143

    professional development, 130

    promoting, 120–122

    reflection, 127–128, 145–146

    schoolwide supports, 128–135

    teacher team supports, 135–139

    vertical standard analysis, 129–130

Robinson, K., 1

routines and procedures. *See* classroom routines and procedures

S

safe learning environment. *See* classroom routines and procedures

Schlechty, P., 93

school and district leadership, 180–181

schoolwide supports

    classroom routines and procedures, 55–58

    description and role of, 22

    engagement, 103–107

    individual students, strategies for, 159–162

    learning resources, 34–37

    relationships for learning, 77–79

    rigor and mastery, 128–135

Screencast-O-Matic, 35

Sears, N., 74

self-actualization, 20–21

self-leadership, 176–178

Simms, J. A., 40

Simplifying Response to Intervention (Buffum, Mattos, and Weber), 2

Smore, 139

Sprick, R., 52

Stiggins, R., 157

Stubbs, H., 182–183

student engagement. *See* engagement

student history files, 77–78

summative assessments, 124, 125

support. *See* Excellence Support System; individualized supports; schoolwide supports; teacher team supports

Svitak, A., 65

T

Taylor, L., 19

teacher leadership

    description and role of, 20–21, 173–174

    example, 174–175

    global leadership, 181–183

    levels of, 176

    reflection, 185–186

    school and district leadership, 180–181

    self-leadership, 176–178

    team leadership, 178–180

teachers

    experience levels, views of, 13–14

    influence of, 10–12

    mindset for improvement, need for, 14–15

    mission and role of, 3–4

    professional support for, 4–6

teacher-student relationships. *See* relationships for learning

teacher team supports

    classroom routines and procedures, 58–61

    description and role of, 22

    engagement, 107–108

    experts, role of, 38

    individual students, strategies for, 162–165

    interdisciplinary teams, 137–138

    learning resources, 38–40

    relationships for learning, 79–82

    rigor and mastery, 135–139

    singleton teams, 138–139

specifics, need for, 38–40

subject-level teams, 136

vertical teams, 136–137

virtual teams, 139

team leadership, 178–180

technology training on the fly, 36–37

Texas Teacher Evaluation and Support
System (T-TESS), 121

Timperley, H., 106

Transforming School Culture
(Muhammad), xiii

transition sheets, 78

V

van Tartwijk, J., 72

videos, flipped, 34–36, 81

Voxer, 139

W

Webb, N. L., 129, 130

Weber, C., 2, 122–123

Wiggins, G., 118, 120, 158

Wight, M., 38

wikis, resources, 34, 35

Wolpert-Gawron, H., 94, 98, 102

Wong, H., 47

Worlds of Learning, 36

Wubbels, T., 72

Y

YouTube, 35

Z

Zehm, S. J., 69

Solutions for Digital Learner–Centered Classrooms series

Gain practical, high-impact strategies to enhance instruction and heighten student achievement in 21st century classrooms. Using tech-based tools and techniques, your staff will discover how to motivate students to develop curiosity, become actively engaged, and have a sense of purpose in their education.

BKF691, BKF680, BKF636, BKF679, BKF681, BKF664, BKF666

Creating a Digital-Rich Classroom
Meg Ormiston

Design and deliver standards-based lessons in which technology plays an integral role. This book provides a research base and practical strategies for using web 2.0 tools to create engaging lessons that transform and enrich content.

BKF385

Teaching the iGeneration
William M. Ferriter and Adam Garry

Find the natural overlap between the work you already believe in and the digital tools that define today's learning. Each chapter introduces an enduring life skill and a digital solution to enhance traditional skill-based instructional practices. A collection of handouts and supporting materials ends each chapter.

BKF671

Deeper Learning
Edited by James A. Bellanca

Education authorities from around the globe draw on research as well as their own experience to explore deeper learning, a process that promotes higher-order thinking, reasoning, and problem solving to better educate students and prepare them for college and careers.

BKF622

Instructional norms in a school
Hierarchy of Instr Excellence
        21 I for teachers   teach teachers to save their own lives
Do you know what to do when you dont know what to do?
"mining" for resources
~~classroom mgmt~~ → classroom routines & procedures (slide 48)
What is your student: teacher workload ratio?

Align routines & procedures   slide 49
relationships keep the routines & procedures going

slide 61
ENGAGEMENT
Gradual Release Model fixes the "lost time" issue   slide 75
        teacher lead vs teacher feed

Lesson Plan pg 100 book

If the hard part is the How do I do it? then engagement is the issue

        # LeadExcel for teachers
          password - allteachers
Rigor in the next step.
essential skills
Q #1 slide 91   assess (Latin) = sit beside
Q #2   93
        student feedback
Levels of instruction
Levels of questioning
effective feedback
"ily Café" book Essential standards ... prepare to teach 4 times 4 diff ways
        "engagement gap"
        best intervention is prevention
        Our job is to create the system(s) to get the job done.
            Build the system thru building leadership.